Advance Praise

"This is an outstanding book. It provides essential information about newcomers, their backgrounds, their needs, and their strengths; and it includes a step-by-step guide for supporting these youngsters in the classroom in today's uncertain world. Examples of how to teach both language and content are detailed, time-tested, accessible, and anchored in the wisdom of practice. It is a must-read for teacher educators, practicing teachers, and all future teachers."
— Guadalupe Valdés, Ph.D., Bonnie Katz Tenenbaum Professor of Education, Stanford University

"In *Supporting Newcomer Students* the authors provide readers with a wealth of important and practical information using specific examples to show how to work successfully, meaningfully, and equitably with students of different language and cultural backgrounds in a variety of classroom settings. Chapters contrast common myths and realities about teaching newcomers and include multiple resources for teachers as they identify, assess, welcome, and teach language and content to their students and, at the same time, implement strategies to effectively advocate for them."
— David and Yvonne Freeman, authors and Professors Emeriti, The University of Texas Río Grande Valley

"This book offers a wealth of instructional practices designed to support newcomer students, but it does so much more than that. As readers, we gain a deeper understanding of who these children are, the social, emotional, and economic supports they and their families need, and the rich diversity they bring to our classrooms. The authors cultivate within us the moral obligation to be these children's advocates as well as their teachers."
— Dr. Elizabeth Jaeger, Department of Teaching, Learning, and Sociocultural Studies, University of Arizona

"This book is a much-needed resource that speaks holistically to the needs of newcomer students. Grounded in the most current research, the authors write for both the teacher practitioner, providing concrete and actionable guidance on responsive instructional practice, and for the teacher advocate, with useful information and tools to promote the educational and immigration rights of students and families. *Supporting Newcomer Students* will undoubtedly become one of OUSD's core professional texts."
— Nicole Knight, Executive Director of the Office for English Language Learner and Multilingual Achievement, Oakland Unified School District

SUPPORTING NEWCOMER STUDENTS

SUPPORTING NEWCOMER STUDENTS

ADVOCACY AND INSTRUCTION FOR ENGLISH LEARNERS

Katharine Davies Samway,
Lucinda Pease-Alvarez,
and Laura Alvarez

W. W. NORTON & COMPANY
Independent Publishers Since 1923

Note to Readers: This work is intended as a general information resource for teachers and school administrators who work with students who are newcomers to the United States and their caregivers. Although the authors have extensive experience in the subject matter, neither they nor the publisher can guarantee that any educational approach, strategy or technique that this book describes or proposes will work with every individual student, parent or caregiver. None of the authors is a lawyer, and nothing contained in this book should be construed as legal advice. For advice about how to handle particular problems and situations that involve or implicate education, immigration or healthcare law, or for any other legal advice or legal questions, please consult an attorney with relevant expertise.

Names and potentially identifying characteristics of individual students and educators other than the authors have been changed. Any URLs displayed in this book link or refer to websites that existed as of press time. The publisher is not responsible for, and should not be deemed to endorse or recommend, any website other than its own or any content, including any app, that it did not create. The authors, also, are not responsible for any third-party material.

*To immigrant children
and their families*

CONTENTS

ACKNOWLEDGMENTS

We would like to thank the many K–8 newcomer students and families in New York and California with whom we have worked. We have been inspired by and learned from their experiences, thoughtfulness, and resilience.

We are very grateful for the multiple opportunities we have had to work with many teachers, teacher educators, and researchers who so thoughtfully support newcomer and English learner students, in particular Beatriz Alvarez, Pilar Alvarez, Angela Barra, Jill Berg-Peterson, Hilda Bucio, George Bunch, Blanca Campillo, Sarah Capitelli, Kathy Davis, Concha Delgado-Gaitán, Carole Edelsky, Megan Hatschek, Rosemary Henze, Sarah Hudelson, Libby James-Pasby, Linda Kateeb, Jennifer Klem-Myers, Nora Lang, Teri Marchese, Andrea Maoki, Sydney Morgan, Betty Olson-Jones, Farima Pour-Khorshid, Pam Randall, Rachel Rothman, Luz Salazar-Jed, Sandra Schecter, Barbara Schmidt, Choji Schroeder, Judy Scott, Kyle Smith, Lydia Stack, Annie Swan-law, Dorothy Taylor, Carole Urzúa, Guadalupe Valdés, Lucia Villareal, Aída Walqui, Gail Whang, and Carrie Wilson. Thank you!

Many thanks to Antonio Alvarez, Jennifer Theakstone, and Joaquín Pellegrin-Alvarez for their help with photos and other images for the book.

In addition, we appreciate the support of the Norton staff, in particular Carol Collins, Mariah Eppes, and Jamie Vincent.

Finally, many thanks to our family members, Antonio, Brian-Martin, Joaquín, Marisol, Nathan, Patrick, Pilar, Tom, and Tomás, who have supported us in our work over many years with immigrant children and their families.

INTRODUCTION

OVER THE COURSE OF our combined careers, we have spent several decades as teachers, teacher educators, and researchers working to understand and enhance the educational opportunities of immigrant children and their families. We consider ourselves very fortunate to have engaged in this work as it has enabled us to gain important insights into the lives of a population that has made many important contributions to U.S. society. Immigrants have fueled our economy through their employment, spending, and tax contributions, and enriched our society as they have shared their cultures, values, and experiences. As people who have immigrated to the U.S. and/or are embedded in networks of friendships and family relations that include immigrants, we are grateful for the contributions immigrants have made to our personal wellbeing, understandings of the world, and decisions about what matters in our lives.

In recent years, an important segment of this population, youngsters who are both newcomers to the U.S. and new to English, have been particularly vulnerable. Along with their families, many have experienced poverty, violence, and/or political oppression in their home countries. Their journeys to and experiences in the U.S. have often left them traumatized and anxious, particularly in the case of those who have come without their parents or who have been separated from their parents upon their arrival. Further, the current administration, supported by some politicians and members of the public, have maligned them and called for and instituted inhumane policies that have harmed them, thereby conveying a very clear message—they do not belong in the U.S. and the U.S. must maintain its sovereignty at the expense of their wellbeing. Fortunately, schools in this country are obligated to educate newcomers, regardless of their immigration status, and many are responding well to this situation, with compassion and understanding.

Despite efforts to meet the needs of newcomers, our education system in the U.S. is struggling to meet the needs of these students. We know English language development (ELD), bilingual, mainstream, and content-area teachers who know how to work with and address the needs of newcomer students. However, even in states where there are large numbers of newcomer English learners (ELs), there are relatively few quality bilingual or ELD programs, and teachers often feel overwhelmed when working with newcomer students. Also, there is a shortage of experienced specialist bilingual and ELD teachers. Unfortunately, the learning experiences often provided to newcomer students are typically inferior to and less challenging than those provided to other students. Further, from our own experiences as teachers in four well-regarded teacher preparation programs, we know only too well how ill prepared teachers often are to work with newcomer ELs. With the increasing demand from politicians and government entities to limit the length of teacher preparation programs, this reality is further exacerbated. In fact, when teachers are surveyed, one of the most pressing issues they say they need help with is how to work with ELs (e.g., Gándara, Maxwell-Jolly, & Driscoll, 2006; Pease-Alvarez & Samway, 2014).

The central premise of this book is that newcomer students who are also new to English are best served by teachers who assume an advocacy role both in and outside their classrooms. Consequently, we do not subscribe to the all-too-common view that teachers are technicians responsible for implementing a mandated curriculum. Instead, we argue for a form of teacher advocacy that conceives of a) teachers as active agents in promoting educational equity and b) newcomer students and families as legitimate, valuable, and active contributors to the future of a democratic and equitable society. Building on this perspective, we make recommendations in this book about how teachers can act as advocates for newcomers through:

- Their curricular choices and classroom practices.
- Their actions beyond the classroom, paying special attention to collaboration with families and colleagues.

While our focus is on newcomers' development of English and subject matter knowledge in English, we see that goal as inextricably linked to the languages, cultures, and experiences that newcomers bring to school. These resources are the basis of their future learning, wellbeing, and civic participation. We focus on K–8 newcomer students because there is a dearth of professional literature on this topic.

Throughout the book, we include scenarios and examples based on what we have experienced and/or observed as teachers, researchers, and staff developers; some of our examples are composites of these experiences and observations. Names of teachers and students are pseudonyms. Chapters address the following issues.

Chapter 1: Who Are Our Newcomer Students? This chapter sets the stage for the rest of the book by describing the political, social, and economic contexts that have resulted in the recent flow of immigrants to the U.S.; the range of newcomer students' experiences in their home countries; the nature of their journeys to the U.S., including challenges they may have faced in making their journeys; and their experiences once they arrive in the U.S., including how they are schooled.

Chapter 2: Welcoming Newcomer Students. We describe what teachers need to know and what they can do to make schools and classrooms safe, nurturing, and welcoming environments for newcomer students and their families.

Chapter 3: Foundational Understandings about Second Language Learning and Teaching. This chapter focuses on foundational concepts underlying the meaning- and activity-based perspectives on learning and teaching English and content that we describe in subsequent chapters.

Chapter 4: Assessing Newcomer Students. This chapter addresses a range of assessment-related issues that impact the schooling of K–8 newcomers, including the role and limitations of standardized testing, the use of ongoing formative assessment, and linking assessment to instruction.

Chapter 5: Developing Newcomers' Listening and Speaking. In this chapter, we put a spotlight on instructional practices designed to support newcomers' listening and speaking development in English.

Chapter 6: Developing Newcomers' Reading. This chapter focuses on how to support newcomers' development as readers of English. We emphasize the importance of using ongoing assessment to guide instruction, as well as ways to modify frequently encountered reading experiences in U.S. classrooms to meet the needs of newcomers.

Chapter 7: Developing Newcomers' Writing. In this chapter, we focus on how to support newcomers' writing development in English, with an emphasis on using an inquiry, learner-centered approach to teaching writing that draws on and extends newcomers' knowledge and expertise.

Chapter 8: Engaging Newcomers in Content Learning. This chapter focuses on how to engage newcomers in learning content, including science, social studies, and math, as they develop English. We highlight inquiry approaches to teaching and learning and the integration of language and literacy with content.

Chapter 9: Teachers Advocating for Newcomers Beyond the Classroom. In this chapter, we focus on what teachers can and have done beyond classroom settings as advocates for their newcomer students and their families. We focus on teachers' relationships with students' families, ways teachers can support families' efforts to enhance the learning of their children, and teacher activism.

We are lucky to have experienced and observed the impact of teachers of K–8 newcomer students taking on an advocacy role. In fact, we have been impressed with how many mainstream, bilingual, and ELD teachers have been very active and successful advocates for their students and their students' families and strive to provide meaningful and challenging learning experiences. We hope that through this book many more mainstream, bilingual, and ELD teachers will become strong advocates for ELs, particularly newcomer students and their families. We also hope that our book will be supportive of preservice teachers as they learn to become teachers and that this will lead them to becoming strong advocates for their own students.

SUPPORTING NEWCOMER STUDENTS

CHAPTER 1

Who Are Our Newcomer Students?

DO YOU REMEMBER SEEING images in 2015 of three-year-old Alan Kurdi, who washed up on a Turkish beach, his tiny, lifeless body floating face down in the gentle surf? He and his father and other family members had fled war-torn Syria; they were in a flimsy, inflatable boat that capsized on its way to the Greek island of Kos. Do you remember reading or hearing about two children from Guatemala, seven-year-old Jakelin Caal and eight-year-old Felipe Gomez Alonzo, who died within weeks of each other in December 2018 while in U.S. custody? Do you remember reading about Jorge Aguilar, an unaccompanied minor from Honduras who died in Mexico while waiting to be reunited with his mother?

Although none of us will have the opportunity to teach Alan, Jakelin, Felipe, and Jorge, there are thousands more children who have survived the ordeals that many immigrants encounter as they attempt to make it to North America in search of safety and a way to feed their families. Each of these children has had a profound impact on how many people think about immigrants and U.S. immigration policies and practices. The circumstances and ordeals that they face have led to conversations about immigration. According to Jynnah Radford (2019) of the Pew Research Center, approximately 62% of Americans believe that immigrants "strengthen the country because of their hard work and talents." In many cases, news about immigrants has led to individuals, communities, and states speaking up for and helping immigrants, regardless of whether they are documented. It has also led to an enormous amount of disinformation and heightened hostility directed at immigrants. For example, some members of the public and U.S. politicians have maligned immigrants and called for and instituted policies that have harmed them. President Trump's contempt for immigrants from developing countries was notable when he announced his presidency. During a speech made in 2015, he said the following: "When Mexico sends its people, they're not sending their best. They're bringing drugs. They're bringing crime. They're rapists." In fact, the crime rate among immigrants is lower than that of native-born citizens (e.g., Ewing, Martinez, & Rambaut, 2015; Nadler, 2008).

According to the office of the United Nations High Commissioner for Refugees (UNHCR) (2019), the world is witnessing the greatest number of displaced people ever recorded. By the end of 2018, 70.8 million people were reported as forcibly displaced from their homes, including 25.9 million refugees, half of whom were not yet 18 years of age. UNHCR reports that one person is forcibly displaced every two seconds due to conflict or persecution.

- 70.8 million people have been displaced worldwide
- 25.9 million refugees worldwide
- 12.5+ million refugees are under 18 years of age

Different Categories/Classifications of Immigrants

There is often considerable confusion about the labels that are attached to immigrants. For example, there are several terms that are used to refer to immigrants who live in the United States without authorization. These include *illegal alien, illegal immigrant, unauthorized immigrant*, and *undocumented immigrant*. The term *illegal alien* is used by the U.S. government but is considered very offensive by many immigrants (regardless of their immigration status) and their advocates as the use of *alien* carries a very negative, inhuman connotation. We use the term *undocumented immigrant* in this book.

Who is documented and who isn't? Many **documented immigrants** enter the U.S. with temporary work or student visas. Others come to join family members, such as spouses or parents, and are lawful permanent residents, also known as Green Card holders; there is no limit on how long they can stay in the U.S., and many become citizens/are naturalized after three to five years of residence in the U.S.

Other documented immigrants have entered the U.S. with **refugee status.** According to Amnesty International (2019), a refugee is "a person who has fled their country of origin and is unable or unwilling to return because of a well-founded fear of being persecuted because of their race, religion, nationality, membership of a particular social group or political opinion." A refugee has requested protection while still outside the U.S. and is given permission to enter the U.S. For example, many Vietnamese immigrants came to the U.S.

as refugees after the Vietnam War. Many newcomer students have entered the U.S. with refugee status.

An *asylum seeker* is a person who, like a refugee, is seeking protection but applies for refugee status at the border or once they are in the U.S. Not every asylum seeker will ultimately be recognized as a refugee. Asylum seekers must make their request for asylum within one year of living in the U.S. While awaiting their asylum-request petition, children may attend school.

According to a report by the Pew Research Center (Ikielnik & Krogstad, 2017), the U.S. resettled 84,995 refugees in fiscal year 2016; however, this number dropped to about 31,143 refugees in fiscal year 2017. According to the Center for Immigration Studies (2018), this number dropped further in Fiscal Year 2018, to 22,491; the top five countries of origin for refugees admitted to the U.S. in 2018 were the Democratic Republic of the Congo, Burma (Myanmar), Ukraine, Bhutan, and Eritrea.

Undocumented immigrants include immigrants who entered the U.S. on a tourist, student, or work visa and overstayed their visas. For example, a study published by The Center for Migration Studies (CMS) showed that, between 2010 and 2017, more than half of all undocumented immigrants had overstayed a visa, and a majority had entered by air (Warren, 2019). Others are asylum seekers who were not granted asylum and remain in the United States. Still others entered the country without documentation and have often had to pay large amounts of money to *coyotes*, who guide them across the border; they have often encountered violence, robbery, and other hardships as they make their way to the U.S. Since 2012, more than 200,000 undocumented children, mostly from El Salvador, Honduras, and Guatemala, have come to the U.S. (Wu, 2018). While the majority of these children have sought asylum, the number who have been given asylum has fallen from a high of 85.1% during the third quarter of 2014 to 28.1% in the fourth quarter of 2018 (Wu, 2018).

Who Are Our Newcomer Students?

This book focuses on how to enhance the educational experiences of recently arrived immigrant K–8 students who are English learners, both documented and undocumented. Many of them come from low-income homes. They are also in the early stages of learning English. While these students are diverse in terms of their countries of origin, their native languages, and their documentation status in the U.S., the majority of them have faced challenges in their home countries and/or in the U.S. Many come from families that have experienced poverty, war, violence, and/or political oppression and persecution. Their journeys to the United States have often been very difficult, particularly in the case of those who have come without parents or who have been separated from their parents upon their arrival in the U.S.

Although a surge of immigrants from Central and South America has contributed to the number of Latinx students in the U.S., newcomers include youngsters from a variety of countries and are both documented and undocumented immigrants. (Latinx is a gender-neutral term to refer to a person of Latin American origin or descent). Although it is difficult to know how many newcomers enroll in U.S. schools each year, data from the U.S. Census Bureau's American Community Survey suggests that between 2010 and 2014, an average of 154,100 youth ages 12 to 21 who were deemed to be limited-English proficient immigrated to the U.S. annually (Sugarman, 2017). Many of the youngsters entering the U.S. have experienced the trauma of living in poverty, in war-torn nations, in refugee camps, and/or in detention centers.

In the U.S., several terms are used when referring to students who are learning English as a non-native language, as well as specialized programs for them. In this book, we use EL (English learner) when referring to students and ELD (English language development) when referring to English-medium instructional programs for them. We also often use the term *caregiver/parent* instead of *parent* in situations when it is unclear whether a parent was present or involved. In many immigrant families, particularly when a parent has been detained or deported or the newcomer is an unaccompanied minor, newcomer children are living with other family members or friends of the family, hence the use of the term *caregiver*.

The following data for ELs reported in 2015 by the U.S. Department of Education (USDOE) shows the percentage of public school students who were classified as ELs and where they live:

- Percentage of all students who were ELs was 9.5% (4.8 million ELs).
- The percentage who were ELs ranged from a low of 1% in West Virginia to a high of 21% in California.
- Eight states had EL student populations comprising 10% or more, most of them in the West (Alaska, California, Colorado, Kansas, Nevada, New Mexico, Texas, and Washington).
- Urban school districts accounted for the largest percentage of EL students—ELs constituted 14% of students in cities, 9.1% in suburban areas, 6.5% in towns, and 3.6% in rural areas.

- A greater percentage of ELs were in the lower grades than in the upper grades (e.g., 16.3% of kindergarteners, 8.2% of sixth graders, and 6.6% of eighth graders were ELs).

The following table shows the frequency of the 12 languages most commonly spoken by ELs in grades K–12 in the U.S. in 2016 (National Center for Education Statistics, 2019).

Many school districts, particularly urban districts, have students who speak many different languages. For example, in the 2014–2015 school year, public school students in New Jersey spoke more than 165 different languages at home (O'Dea, 2016). However, in some states, certain languages predominate, such as Spanish in California. According to the California Department of Education (2019), in the 2018–2019 school year, there were approximately 1.2 million ELs in California public schools, about 19% of the total student enrollment. About 42% spoke a language other than English and data were collected for 67 language groups. However, Spanish was by far the language most frequently spoken at home in California—it accounted for 81.56% of the

TABLE 1.1: Twelve Languages Most Commonly Spoken in 2016 by ELs in Grades K–12

Home Language	Number of EL Students	Percentage Distribution of EL Students[*]
Spanish	3,790,949	76.6
Arabic	129,386	2.6
Chinese	104,147	2.1
Vietnamese	78,732	1.6
Somali	38,440	.8
Russian	34,843	.7
Hmong	33,059	.7
Haitian, Haitian Creole	31,608	.6
Portuguese	28,214	.6
Korean	26,136	.5
Tagalog	26,074	.5
Urdu	24,668	.5

Source: Compiled from https://nces.ed.gov/programs/digest/d18/tables/dt18_204.27.asp

* *Does not add up to 100 percent because not all categories are reported.*

ten most frequently spoken languages. The remaining nine languages most frequently spoken at home in California were Vietnamese (2.21%), Mandarin (1.87%), Arabic (1.53%), Filipino (1.25), Cantonese (1.21%), Korean (.81%), Punjabi (.77%), Russian (.76%), and Hmong (.69%).

Newcomer Students' Previous and Current School Experiences

Newcomer K–8 students come having had a wide range of previous educational experiences, including the following, which we present in the chart below.

The 1974 Supreme Court decision *Lau vs. Nichols* held that schools that receive federal funding must provide English learners with instructional programming designed to develop their English. In the opinion, the court stated, "[T] here is no equality of treatment merely by providing students with the same facilities, textbooks, teachers, and curriculum; for students who do not understand English are effectively foreclosed from any meaningful education." In 1982, in Plyler v. Doe, the Supreme Court held that immigrant

FIGURE 1.1: Contrasts in the Educational Experiences of Newcomer K–8 Students

• They understand and speak a little English.	• They do not understand or speak any English.
• They have been well educated in their home countries.	• They have had little or no formal education in their home countries if they lived in remote rural areas and/or were from a war-torn country
	• They have had interrupted formal schooling due to war and displacement.
• They are literate in their home language.	• They are partially literate in a non-native language (e.g., English) if they attended school in a refugee camp or were educated in a non-native language in their home country (e.g., Spanish when they speak an indigenous language).
• They read and write their native language, which has a Latin-based script (e.g., Spanish).	• They read and write their native language, but it does not have a Latin-based script (e.g., Chinese).
• They read and write their native language, which has an alphabetic system, even though it isn't Latin based (e.g., Arabic).	• They read and write their native language, but it does not have an alphabetic system (e.g., Japanese).

students, including those who are undocumented, cannot be denied a free public education.

Despite these rulings, schooling tailored to the needs and experiences of newcomer students has varied enormously, from extensive to nonexistent. Accountability reports indicate that there is reason to be concerned about the academic development of ELs. Although data on foreign-born children is difficult to obtain, researchers and policymakers who use the EL subgroup as a proxy for newcomers report troubling gaps in the standardized test score averages of all learners and ELs in English language arts, math, and science. Further, the high school graduation rates of ELs has consistently been lower than that of other students; Sugarman (2017) reports that, in 2014–2015, the average nationwide high school graduation rate was 83%, whereas the rate for ELs was 65%.

Over the course of the last two centuries, assimilationist and deficit perspectives have shaped the way young newcomer students living in the U.S. are educated. These approaches assume that newcomers' success is entirely dependent on the degree to which they are able to assimilate into U.S. society. During the Americanization movement of the early 20th century, public schools were considered to be places where immigrant children could be molded into American citizens by instructing them in English, American history, and the democratic process. English was a focus of instruction and a number of policy initiatives mandated its exclusive use in schools. As part of character education programs instituted in the 1920s, immigrant students were required to memorize lists of morals and values thought to be absent in immigrant communities (e.g., honesty, hard work, punctuality, cleanliness, and respect for authority).

A single-minded focus on the acquisition of English, presented as a set of discrete skills, structures, and vocabulary items that must be mastered in a prescribed order, persists as a dominant pedagogical approach used to teach English language learners, including many newcomers. This approach can result in students being tracked into a never-ending cycle of remedial classes that focus on the mastery of these skills and structures and very little else. This is particularly unfortunate when it prevents English learners from a) gaining opportunities to learn content and build on and further develop their linguistic and cultural resources and b) segregates them from their English-speaking peers.

Types of Programs for Newcomer Students in U.S. Schools

Many school districts did not anticipate or plan for the arrival of newcomer students. As a consequence, schools have often struggled to figure out what to do with them. As a temporary measure, some schools have placed newcomers in classrooms with much younger students, which is not advisable as the needs of newcomers are not the same as those of younger, non-newcomer students. Other schools have immersed them in English-medium, mainstream classes where they have no or only a limited understanding of what is going on around them. Newcomer students have told us they had little or no idea what was going on in these classrooms, and many talk about spending weeks filling out worksheets or coloring while their classmates engaged in a variety of other instructional activities that were not available to them.

Although some newcomer students never receive specialized instruction geared to their needs, others do, and the following are some of the most common programs for ELs:

FIGURE 1.2: Common Types of Programs for ELs

Type of Program	Language(s) of Instruction
English as a second language (ESL) English language development (ELD)	English
Bilingual Education: • Transitional or early exit • Dual language • Two-way immersion	English and another language (e.g., Spanish or Chinese)
Newcomer centers or programs	English and sometimes another language

English as a Second Language (ESL) or English Language Development (ELD)

These programs are typically pullout programs that meet for one or two periods a day and in which there is focused instruction on English. Sometimes, an EL specialist may push in and work with the newcomer student(s) alongside the classroom teacher. The content of ESL/ELD programs varies considerably, from a focus on communication in the real world to a focus on isolated grammar and vocabulary skills and drills. Some programs focus on oral language, whereas others integrate all language modalities (listening, speaking, reading, and writing). Some programs focus on content-area learning that is aligned with Common Core content standards and is designed specifically for ELs. A wide range of people, including specially trained teachers, nonspecialist teachers or aides, speech and language teachers, and volunteers, teach ESL/ELD classes.

Bilingual Education

This is a less common option in the U.S. than ESL/ELD classes and has several variations. The most common version of this approach is ***Transitional Bilingual Education*** or ***Early Exit Bilingual Education***. Students who are deemed to be English language learners are taught in their native language and also receive instruction in English; typically, there is more instruction in the native language in the early grades and, over the years, the amount of instruction in the native language is reduced while the amount of time in English is increased. The goal is to transition students into English-only classrooms as soon as possible. Even in its heyday, very small numbers of students were enrolled in bilingual programs. According to Ulloa (2016), fewer than 5% of public schools in California offered bilingual and multilingual programs.

A second bilingual program option is ***Dual Language Instruction***. Students in these programs are taught language and literacy in two languages—English and an additional language—with the goal of developing bilingualism and biliteracy. In most elementary dual language programs, the additional language (e.g., Spanish or Chinese) is used for at least half of the instructional day. These programs usually start in kindergarten and last for at least five years. The goal is to maintain and develop the two languages, not transition students into English-only programs. In some districts, they may extend into middle school and high school. Many of these programs are in neighborhood schools.

A fourth bilingual program option is ***Two-Way Immersion***, in which native speakers of English are placed in the same classroom as students who speak the additional language (e.g., Spanish or Chinese). Instruction is in both English and the additional language, and the goal is that both student populations become bilingual and biliterate. Many of the native English-speaking students come from middle-class homes and their parents have been very vocal advocates for these programs.

Newcomer Centers or Programs

In these programs, newcomer students are placed in a half-day or full-day program designed to help them acclimate to U.S. schools, learn English, and develop their academic skills in English and, often, their native language(s). ELs typically spend no more than one year in newcomer centers or programs and are then mainstreamed into regular classes. Newcomer centers or programs are most often found at the secondary level, but there are a few that serve elementary and middle school students.

How Appropriate Are Programs for Newcomer Students?

We have observed classes where newcomers receive very focused, appropriately challenging instruction that fosters students' English language development (listening, speaking, reading, and writing), their academic and sociocultural development and curiosity, and sometimes native language development. In these cases, the teachers have been well prepared to work with ELs, either in their basic teaching credential program or in a specialized MA or ongoing professional development program. In contrast, we have observed classes where there is limited attention to the specific needs of EL students and instruction is often rather mindlessly focused on drilling discrete grammar points and vocabulary items that are present in a textbook. A focus on teaching decontextualized skills was exacerbated from 2002 to 2015 by the passage of No Child Left Behind (NCLB).

Impact on Newcomers of U.S. Immigration Policies

It is important to acknowledge the fear that newcomer students often face in the U.S. as a consequence of how their communities have been targeted by politicians and administrations. For example, a 2016 survey of K–12 educators conducted by Teaching Tolerance and reported by Costello (2016) of the Southern Poverty Law Center concluded that the 2016 presidential campaign, with its anti-immigrant and racist rhetoric, particularly that of Trump, "is having a profoundly negative impact on schoolchildren across the country, producing an alarming level of fear and anxiety among children of color and inflaming racial and ethnic tensions in the classroom. Many students worry about being deported."

In a post-2016 election survey of educators, the Southern Poverty Law Center found that 90% reported the election had a negative effect on school climate, and 80% reported "heightened anxiety and concern on the part of students worried about the impact of the election on themselves and their families." A number of reports cite the need for schools and school districts to provide non-academic as well as academic support to newcomers. Of particular concern is ensuring that resources are available for socio-emotional support (Sugarman, 2017).

Why Do Immigrants Leave Their Homes to Come to the U.S.?

In the remainder of this chapter, we delve a little into what causes people to leave their homelands, to often embark on very dangerous journeys, particularly for children. We are doing this so that readers can more fully understand the impact of U.S. foreign policy on the movement of people around the world and, consequently, better understand the realities of many newcomer students. In particular, we will focus on the following:

a. A brief history of U.S. immigration policies and practices;
b. Circumstances that lead immigrants to leave their home countries;
c. The impact of U.S. economic and foreign policy on immigration;
d. Immigrants' journeys; and
e. Some common myths about immigrants.

A Brief History of U.S. Immigration Policy and Practices

Although the U.S. has long been a destination for immigrants, for the first 200 years of its existence, most immigrants were white Europeans, first from the U.K. and Ireland (most of them Protestants) and then, later, from Germany and Scandinavian countries (History.com, 2019). The Naturalization Act of 1790 clearly laid out the prejudices of the leaders of the country. In order to apply for citizenship, one had to be a free white person of "good character" who had been living in the U.S. for two or more years. This meant that anyone without citizenship would not be allowed to vote, own property, or testify in court.

It must be remembered that the early leaders of the U.S. did not take into consideration people from Africa who were brought to North America as slaves. Nor did they consider the original occupants of what became the U.S., the native peoples (Indians or Native Americans), who were forced off their land and often internally displaced onto reservations in order to make room for western expansion by primarily white people. The predominantly white and Protestant people in power did not regard people from these communities as equals and they did not have voting rights. Also, the U.S. government broke many of the treaties it made with Indian tribes.

According to the Library of Congress (n.d.), in 1841, the population of Ireland was about 8.2 million. By 1891, it had fallen to about 4.7 million people; the 1845 potato famine led to the exodus of hundreds of thousands of Irish people. Between 1820 and 1860, Irish immigrants made up more than one third of all immigrants to the U.S. and many of them were destitute. In the early 1800s, many Irish people came to work in construction, canal building (e.g., the Erie Canal), and lumbering in the northeastern U.S.

In the mid-1800s, Chinese workers were brought to the U.S. to work in mines and factories and to help build the transcontinental railroad. Most of them were men who came to work and send back money to their families in China, and many of them returned to China. They were not allowed to bring in their families and they were not allowed to become citizens. The Chinese Exclusion Act of 1882 prohibited Chinese immigration, which also prevented the reunification of families for men who were already living and working in the U.S. This was the first law that restricted immigration according to race/ethnicity/country of origin. In 1943, when the U.S. and China became allies in World War II, the U.S. once again allowed Chinese immigration to the United States, ending 61 years of racial discrimination directed at Chinese people. Also in the mid-1860s to the 1930s, many Chinese were brought in to work on farms, as were Japanese and Filipinos.

The history of Mexican immigrants to the U.S. is complex. Many people of Mexican descent point out that their ancestors were the original occupants of much of what is now California, New Mexico, and Texas. At the conclusion of the Mexican-American war (known in Mexico as the *American Intervention in Mexico*), which lasted from 1846 to 1848, Mexico was forced to cede parts of what we know now as New Mexico and California; Texas had already been declared a U.S. state in 1945. After this war ended, tens of thousands of Mexican workers came to the U.S. for temporary work; in many cases, they moved freely back and forth across the border. During the Great Depression of the 1930s, many Mexicans, Mexican Americans, and people suspected of being Mexican, were deported. In many cases, these workers had been recruited to come to the U.S. a decade earlier. Due to labor shortages during World War II, the U.S. and Mexico established the *Bracero Program,* which allowed Mexicans to enter the U.S. to work on a temporary basis in agriculture. This program lasted until 1964.

By the end of the 19th century, large numbers of immigrants were also coming from Southern and Eastern Europe (from Italy, Greece, and Poland). About one million people arrived, which alarmed many white Protestants. As a consequence, a commission was established to investigate and propose immigration policy. In 1911, the Immigration Commission of the U.S. published the *Dictionary of Races or Peoples*, which defined which ethnicities were desirable and which were not; this led to national origin quotas. In the first quota system in 1921, immigrants from northern and western Europe received preferential treatment. For example, northern and western Europe were allocated about 200,000 visas; southern and eastern Europe were allocated about 156,000 visas; Asia was allocated 492 visas; and Africa was allocated 359 visas.

TABLE 1.2: 1921 Visa Slots Allocated by Regions

Northern and western Europe	200,000 visas
Southern and eastern Europe	156,000 visas
Asia	492 visas
Africa	359 visas

Source: Gjelten, 2019

Tom Gjelten (2019) captured the racist underpinnings of this policy when he commented, ". . . the notion of national origin quotas really suggested that there were . . . second-class people, that there were second-class nationalities, that there were less desirable nationalities." It wasn't until the mid-1960s, when civil rights legislation was at a highpoint, that the U.S. changed its immigration policies by passing the 1965 Immigration Act, which welcomed immigrants from non-European countries. This was also the same year in which the Voting Rights Act was passed (see box on next page).

President Johnson had proposed eliminating the quota system and replacing it with a system grounded in what immigrants could offer the country through their education, skills, and training. However, conservatives in Congress rejected this idea because they thought it would open the door to too many people from non-European countries. Instead, they proposed that the new policy give preference to family members of immigrants who were already in the country—that is, a family reunification program. Interestingly, the 1965 Immigration Act did not produce the results that conservatives had expected because the greatest demand to immigrate to the U.S. did not come from Europe; instead it came from developing countries in regions such as South Asia and Africa. Consequently, people from these regions who had obtained student or work visas were able to bring in family members. Many immigrants at this time also came from Latin American countries as a consequence of civil wars.

In contrast to the earlier wave of immigrants coming to the U.S. at the turn of the 20th century, when they came primarily from European countries, significant numbers of immigrants have come from Asia, Latin Amer-

THE VOTING RIGHTS ACT OF 1965

In 1870, the 15th Amendment to the U.S. Constitution was ratified, which prohibited states from denying male citizens the right to vote based on "race, color or previous condition of servitude." However, many discriminatory practices were put in place in subsequent years, particularly in the South, which denied African Americans the right to vote. These included being required to take a literacy test, which they often failed, in large part due to centuries of oppression and poverty, which had led to high illiteracy rates.

The Voting Rights Act of 1965 banned the use of literacy tests, provided for federal oversight of voter registration, and authorized the attorney general to investigate the role of poll taxes in elections. However, despite the passage of the Voting Rights Act, the law was not enforced vigorously and was often ignored, particularly in southern states and where large numbers of African Americans lived.

Efforts to deny African American and other minority populations the right to vote continue today through various strategies, including closing polling places; requiring voters in targeted—usually minority—districts to travel large distances to vote; and dis-enrolling registered voters through "disenfranchisement by typo," which led to many registered voters being required to send additional proof of who they were based on a minor discrepancy in, for example, the spelling of their names.

ica, and Africa since the 1980s. Nearly 12 million Mexican-born people are currently living in the U.S., but large numbers of immigrants have come from other places, including three million from India and 1.9 million from the Philippines.

Before the passage of the 1965 Immigration Act, only about 4% of the U.S. population was foreign born. By 2000, the percentage of the population that was foreign born had risen to about 13% and nine out of 10 immigrants came from non-European countries. Also, one in four children had at least one foreign-born parent.

Immigrants from Central America, including Mexico, initially came to work on farms, which is typically seasonal work. However, as the service sector in the U.S. economy grew, the demand increased for workers in restaurants, for house and office cleaning, and for childcare, which are typically year-round jobs rather than seasonal. For many years, there was limited enforcement of immigration laws and employers found these workers to be hard working and willing to work for less than U.S.-born workers. However, the demand for these types of workers varied according to the economy.

Since 1996, immigration policy has moved away from the goal of family reunification to a policy of detention and deportation, particularly of male immigrants from Mexico and Central America (Korducki, 2018). According to the Department of Homeland Security (2016), the rate of deportations rose from 211,098 in 2003 to 433,034 in 2013, and was then 340,056 in 2016. This number does not include immigrants who left the U.S. on their own initiative ("self-deported") or were turned away or returned to their home country at the U.S. border. In some cases, U.S.-born citizens were improperly deported simply because they were Latinx or were thought to look like they were Latinx.

The deportation rate was particularly high between 2009 and 2015, when Barack Obama was president—about 2.8 million people were deported, according to Gonzalez-Barrera and Lopez (2016). While President Obama claimed to be focused on the deportation of "criminal aliens," undocumented farmworkers working with H-2A seasonal farmworker visas were disproportionately deported under his administration (Portes & Rambaut, 2014). Ironically, many of these people were the same type of workers that were being recruited by the H-2 visa program to work in the United States on a temporary basis.

It is important to note that deportees have included individuals who have spent the majority of their lives in the U.S., having come as young children. These include former American soldiers—veterans—who got deported after their service because they had permanent residency cards and got convicted of a felony, many of them nonviolent (Horton, 2019; United States Government Accountability Office, 2019). Upon deportation, veterans were sometimes forced to leave behind family members, including children, who have had to survive without the deportees' economic support. Also, deportees have often returned to countries where they have faced extortion and physical threats by criminals, militias, and government forces.

Shortly after taking office in 2017, President Trump signed a number of executive orders that are part of what has come to be known as the administration's "zero tolerance" policy toward immigration. These orders authorized a number of initiatives, including the following:

- Withholding funds from sanctuary cities (i.e., municipalities that decline to provide information to the Department of Homeland Security about the immigration status of residents). A federal judge in October 2018 ruled this unconstitutional.

- Authorizing the hiring of 10,000 additional Immigration and Customs Enforcement (ICE) officers (Valverde, 2017).
- Suspending the entry of citizens from seven predominantly Muslim countries (Iran, Iraq, Libya, Somalia, Sudan, Syria, and Yemen), even people who had already been issued visas. Iraq and Sudan were later removed, and two non-predominantly Muslim countries, North Korea and Venezuela, were added, which was considered to be "window dressing" (Gerstein & Lin, 2018).

In addition, Trump's 2018 budget called for $4 billion to be used in the construction of a barrier at the U.S./Mexican border; he increased this sum to more than $5 billion in 2019.

U.S. citizens are not of one mind regarding these policies. According to a Washington Post-Schar School poll held in July 2018, 59% of Americans did not agree with the Trump administration's "zero tolerance" stance toward immigration (The Washington Post, 2019). Resistance to the current climate of intolerance and xenophobia is manifest in a variety of actions, including ongoing protests, state and local policies that challenge ICE actions, and the growth of the sanctuary movement. Several states, cities, and school districts have declared themselves sanctuary states, cities, and school districts—they are typically places that are home to many immigrants. One school district's sanctuary statement can be found in Appendix 1.

While immigrants initially settled in urban regions in five states in the 1980s (New York, Florida, California, Texas, and Illinois), they are now settling in many more places, with significant numbers living in regions previously populated by very few immigrants, such as the Midwest and South (Blau & Mackie, 2017). For example, meat and poultry processing plants that have been established in midwestern states over the course of the last 20 years rely on immigrant labor. While California continues to draw the greatest number of immigrants to the U.S., the percentages have declined in recent years due, in part, to changing labor demands.

Circumstances That Lead Immigrants to Leave Their Home Countries

Immigrants come to the U.S. for a variety of reasons. Very few come simply to enjoy a better economic life. As NPR correspondent, Tom Gjelten, said, "It takes a lot to convince people that they should leave the country of their birth, the only country that they know, their family, their community, and go to a distant country . . . where they're going to be complete strangers. It takes a lot to drive people out of their home country" (Gjelten, 2016).

Many immigrants have faced economic crises in their home countries, which, in some cases, threaten to force them into extreme poverty. Criminal violence (e.g., devastating murder rates, gang activity, kidnapping, and extortion) is a phenomenon that also compels immigrants to leave their home countries. Another cause is the rise of political authoritarianism characterized by autocratic rulers and dictators deploying security forces to carry out acts of violence on those opposing or accused of opposing their authority. In many countries, including several in Central America, the Middle East, and North Africa, civil wars have led to many deaths and the movement of people away from their home countries to safer locations, including the U.S.

These circumstances are reflected in the following brief account of the experiences of María Antonia Larios Soto and her family:

> María Antonia is a Guatemalan mother whose child, Wilson, was taken from her when they crossed the Mexican/U.S. border in Arizona to seek asylum. After she was reunited with Wilson, she was granted permission to stay in the U.S. for one year on a humanitarian parole. When explaining her decision to leave Guatemala, she said, "We don't come here just because we want to live fancy lives. We come here to be safe and give our children a better life. Our lives are always at risk over there. When you leave your house, you don't know if you will come back alive or in a coffin. It's the worst. That's how it is in our country. (Bogado, 2018)

These types of experiences have been encountered by many thousands of immigrants. Desperate conditions in their home countries cause them to risk a lot, and the building of a border wall is unlikely to deter them. Also, as Romero and Dickerson (2019) of *The New York Times* reported, U.S. border and rigid immigration policies have led to immigrants being pushed into more remote, isolated desert areas on the southwest border, where many of them die.

Immigrants face economic challenges once they arrive in the U.S. Compared with the U.S-born population, they often take lower-paying jobs with few, if any, benefits, often living day-to-day with no economic buffer during periods of unemployment. The increased threat of deportation has led to numerous issues and concerns that undocumented families, in particular, face while living in the U.S. They are vulnerable to a number of abuses, including inhumane treatment by employers, landlords, police, criminals, and others. In addition, families face psychological trauma as they negotiate a life under the constant threat of deportation. This has been exacerbated by zero tolerance immigration policies, which often cause emotional trauma and fear among targeted communities. Many accommodate their lives in uncomfortable ways in an effort to avoid detection. For example, Hagan, Eschbach, and Rodriguez (2008) report that parents may never travel together for fear that if they are arrested or detained, their children will be left on their own with no one to care for them. Even when children are reunified with their families, many newcomer children have to readjust to living with parents and family members they do not know well, including parents' new partners and half-siblings. In some cases, children have been put up for adoption without the permission of their parents and if they are reunited, they often face the trauma of not remembering their biological family members.

The Impact of U.S. Economic and Foreign Policy on Immigration

U.S. military interventions have contributed to social, political, and economic upheavals in many parts of the world and have driven migrants to leave their home countries. For example, from 1961 to 1973, the U.S. was at war in several countries in Southeast Asia (i.e., Vietnam, Cambodia, and Laos). In a 2018 article in *The New York Times*, history professor, Christian G. Appy, argued that the Vietnam War was not a civil war as it was reliant on so much U.S. military and monetary support; instead, he asserts it was "an American war that exacerbated Vietnamese divisions and internationalized the conflict." Appy also points out that the U.S. has a lot to account for: "Our leaders, then and now, have insisted that the United States is 'the greatest force for good in the world' that wants nothing for itself, only to defeat 'terror' and bring peace, stability and self-determination to other lands. The evidence does not support such a claim."

As a consequence of the Vietnam War, millions of Vietnamese, Cambodians, and Laotians were displaced and fled their homelands. They frequently left in flimsy boats and often had to face hunger, disease, pirates, and storms at sea; many died while fleeing. If they were lucky enough to land and were placed in a refugee camp, the conditions were often very difficult, including not being allowed to work and unhealthy living conditions. The Orderly Departure Program (ODP) was created in 1979 to provide a safe and orderly way for Vietnamese refugees to leave their homeland and be resettled abroad in the U.S. and other countries, such as Canada. Between 1980 and 1997, almost 500,000 Vietnamese were resettled in the U.S. under the ODP program (Miller, 2015).

It is important to recognize the impact of U.S. economic and foreign policy on why immigrants have left and continue to leave their countries. Driven by an ideology of U.S. exceptionalism, which is the belief that the uniquely privileged position and influence of the U.S. in the world must be maintained at all costs, the U.S. has tended to undermine, both openly and covertly, governments that are not aligned with U.S. political and economic interests, even when those governments aim to improve the lives of ordinary, often impoverished, people. As a consequence, the U.S. has often supported right-wing dictators and authoritarian governments. Also, the U.S. has a history of taking care of the interests of large U.S. corporations, such as United Fruit in Guatemala and Honduras, rather than the rights and interests of the majority local population.

Nowhere has this type of intervention been more evident than in Central America, where the United States has funded military coups and economically exploited an entire region (Korducki, 2018). For example, the U.S. funded much of El Salvador's right-wing military regime during the 1980s and 1990s, which committed more than 85% of the murders, kidnappings, and tortures over a 12-year period. This contributed to the social and political upheaval that has made life in that country untenable for many years for so many Salvadorans. As a consequence, immigrants from El Salvador continue to flee to the U.S. Figure 1.3 summarizes some of the U.S. interventions in countries around the world since World War II.

In 2018, immigrants from predominantly Honduras gathered to move north in a large group, called a *caravan*, in order to reduce the likelihood of being robbed and physically and sexually assaulted on their way to the U.S., as so often happens (Associated Press, 2018). In a 2018 visit to the San Francisco Bay Area, Father Ismael Moreno (known as Padre Melo), a Honduran priest, human rights activist, and director of *Radio Progreso*—one of the country's only independent sources of media—spoke about causes of this exodus from Honduras (Silber, 2018). He said that they include poverty (20% of the population lives on less than $2 a day, and Honduras is currently the poorest country in the Western Hemisphere); homicides (the homicide rate in Honduras is one of the highest in the world); and a government that has become

FIGURE 1.3: Sample of U.S. Interventions in Countries Since the End of World War II

1953	**Iran**—supported a coup d'état that removed the democratically elected government of Prime Minister Mohammad Mosaddegh. The motivation was related to oil.
1954	**Guatemala**—overthrew the democratically elected government of Jacobo Arbenz, which led to several decades of right-wing dictatorships.
1957	**Philippines**—used secret funds to help Christian parties in the 1957 elections.
1957–59	**Indonesia**—the CIA attempted on several occasions to weaken the Indonesian economy and destabilize the democratically elected government.
1961–present	**Cuba**—failed Bay of Pigs invasion, which was designed to overthrow Cuban president, Fidel Castro. Led to decades of economic sanctions and embargoes, which continue.
1961–1964	**Brazil**—helped destabilize the democratically elected government and supported the 1964 coup d'état, which led to the arrest of thousands of political opponents.
1963–1973	**Vietnam**—was behind the coup d'état that led to the assassination of President Diem, president of South Vietnam. Then, from 1965-73, at war with N. Vietnam.
1965–1966	**Dominican Republic**—in the Dominican Civil War, intervened to oppose rebels whose goal was to restore the first democratically elected president.
1965–1967	**Indonesia**—encouraged the Indonesian army to respond with force to supporters of President Sukarno, which led to the deaths of millions of leftists.
1971	**Bolivia**—supported the coup d'état led by General Hugo Banzer, which toppled left-leaning President Torres (and led to his assassination in 1976) and led to a reign of terror.
1973	**Chile**—worked to overthrow (and assassinate) democratically elected President Allende and replace him with the dictator, General Pinochet, leading to years of extreme oppression.
1973–1983	**Argentina**—backed state terrorism by right-wing death squads in the "Dirty War," which led to the disappearance of about 30,000 people.
1979–1989	**Afghanistan**—supported jihadi guerrillas, who became known as the Taliban and who were fighting the Afghan government and its Russian supporters.
1980–1992	**El Salvador**—supported the Salvadoran military in its violent persecution of supporters of impoverished farmers/*campesinos*—more than 75,000 civilians were killed, many in massacres.
1982–1989	**Nicaragua**—armed, trained, and funded the *Contras,* a right-wing militant group dedicated to toppling the Nicaraguan government, which led to many deaths.

1983	**Grenada**—invaded this tiny island to remove the Marxist government, an action that the U.N General Assembly called "a flagrant violation of international law."
1989	**Panama**—invaded the country and brought the president, General Noriega, to the U.S. for trial.
1991	**Haiti**—ousted democratically elected President Jean-Bertrand Aristide with a CIA-backed military coup. The U.S. then arranged for him to be reinstated four years later, only to later remove him from the country by air.
1991–present	**Iraq**—invaded and engaged in long-lasting war in Iraq, in which approximately 600,000 Iraqis and more than 4,000 U.S. service members have been killed.
1992–1996	**Bosnia and Herzegovina**—provided a humanitarian relief operation during the war in the former Yugoslavia.
2001–present	**Afghanistan**—invaded in 1992 and is still at war in Afghanistan.
2004–present	**Pakistan**—sent drone strikes in N.W. Pakistan.
2009	**Honduras**—supported the coup-d'etat that overthrew democratically elected President Zelaya.
2014–present	**Syria**—supported the opposition in the Syrian civil war with airstrikes, downing of planes, weapons, and on-the-ground training of opposition troops.
2010–present	**Yemen**—supported Saudi Arabia's involvement in the Yemeni civil war.

increasingly authoritarian and corrupt since President Juan Orlando Hernández took power after a coup d'état in 2009 that the U.S. supported.

The U.S. has also vigorously pursued trade agreements that have led to the restructuring of several economies around the world that guarantee economic dependence on the U.S. through trade imbalances and the influx of American goods, which ultimately weaken domestic industries in many developing countries. For example, after the North American Free Trade Agreement (NAFTA) was implemented, many Mexican farmers who once supported themselves by selling their products in local markets had to compete with large U.S. companies that charged much less for the same products (Bacon, 2012). Consequently, farmers were forced to charge less for the same product and were unable to make ends meet. The ensuing poverty has driven many to immigrate to the U.S.

An unexpected consequence of these trade agreements and economic policies has been the establishment of drug trafficking in many impoverished areas. With local businesses failing in several countries due to policies favoring U.S. companies, many individuals have turned to the drug industry as a source of employment. In some cases, that industry has made it almost impossible for people to refuse to become involved. For example, Markham (2017) describes occasions when young people have been threatened by physical violence and death if they did not join gangs that engage in illicit activities, including the sale and transport of drugs.

Immigrants' Journeys

Immigrants take a variety of routes when coming to the U.S. Those who come legally tend to cross borders with little trouble, although interviews with immigration officers can be humiliating; many of them enter at airports. Asylum seekers requesting refugee status and those entering without documentation tend to experience very difficult, if not dangerous, journeys, characterized by kidnappings, extortion, violence, and rape. While en route, they may find themselves walking thousands of miles and crossing multiple borders. In the case of those fleeing war in the Middle East, they may have traveled in the Mediterranean Sea in leaky boats that are unseaworthy and may have sunk. The strategy of traveling in large numbers through Central America and Mexico, in *caravans*, saves migrants from paying coyotes exorbitant fees to guide and hide them during their journeys, as well as providing them with a form of protection through numbers.

Refugees, asylum seekers, and other migrants may live in many different places while traveling to the U.S. Indeed, we know many who have lived in detention centers, refugee camps, shelters, and houses in multiple countries. While detention centers and refugee camps provide temporary residents with shelter and food, they are not intended to meet more than their basic needs. Zook (2016) describes how refugees cannot be forced to leave camps, which creates an implicit desire among those who run camps to make them "bad enough to make refugees want to go home, but not bad enough to skirt human rights violations."

Many immigrants face very taxing experiences when they reach the border. In recent years, many thousands have been placed in detention centers and thousands of children have been separated from the adults with whom they were traveling, usually a parent. Family separation can cause severe trauma for young children, some of whom are under the age of two and are unable to advocate for themselves.

Some Common Myths about Immigrants

A number of myths about immigrants and their impact on U.S. society claim that they are undeserving, deviant, and dangerous. In the following pages, we explore some of the more common myths.

Myth 1: *Immigrants are taking over the U.S.*
Reality: *The percentage of immigrants in the overall population is less than it was in the past.*

The largest wave of immigration to the U.S. occurred between 1900 and 1930, when immigrants made up between 12% and 15% of the total population. While there are more immigrants living in the U.S. than ever before, the percentage of immigrants in the overall population is less than it was during other times in history. Sixty percent of immigrants have lived in the U.S. for at least 15 years.

Myth 2: *The number of undocumented immigrants keeps on growing.*
Reality: *The number of undocumented immigrants fluctuates greatly.*

While the number of undocumented immigrants has risen since 1995, when about 5.7 million lived in the U.S., there have been declines in this population, largely in response to economic downturns and depressed labor markets. While approximately 11.3 million undocumented immigrants live in the U.S. today, this is down from the 12.2 million who lived here in 2007.

Myth 3: *The majority of immigrants in the U.S. are here illegally.*
Reality: *The great majority of immigrants living in the U.S. are here legally.*

A majority of immigrants in the U.S. are documented, including around 47% who are naturalized citizens.

Myth 4: *Immigrants are a drain on the U.S. economy.*
Reality: *Overall, immigrants have a positive impact on the U.S. economy.*

Immigrants make important contributions to the U.S. economy. For example, immigration is responsible for raising the Gross National Product (GDP) (Cassidy, 2018). Also, as Farlie (2012) reported, immigrants have stimulated economic growth by starting up significant numbers of businesses; in 2011 they started 28% of new businesses in the U.S. while accounting for just 12.9% of the population.

Annually, immigrants pay billions of dollars in taxes. When considering the fiscal contributions of immigrants, it is important to note that, in many cases, immigrants pay more in taxes than the cost of services that they receive. Moreover, as Cassidy (2018) reported when summarizing a 2016 study by the National Academies of Sciences, Engineering, and Medicine, the children of immigrants contributed more taxes on a per capita basis than their parents or other native-born Americans.

Myth 5: *Immigrants take jobs from Americans.*
Reality: *Immigrants tend to take jobs that Americans either do not want or are not qualified for.*

The evidence indicates that immigrants tend not to take jobs from U.S-born citizens (Anti-Defamation League, 2015). Many take jobs as low-income manual laborers and in service jobs, such as working in restaurants and providing childcare and eldercare. By and large, these are jobs that U.S.-born Americans do not want because they do not pay enough and/or are physically difficult. Immigrants also take jobs that require skills and training that American workers lack, such as in science, technology, engineering, and math (STEM) fields.

Myth 6: *Immigrants tend to have criminal and violent tendencies.*
Reality: *Immigrants are less likely than U.S.-born citizens to commit crimes or be incarcerated.*

According to recent studies, immigrants, regardless of their country of origin, documentation status, and number of years of education, are less likely than U.S.-born citizens to commit crimes or be incarcerated (Anti-Defamation League, 2015). In a large-scale study, Adelman, Reid, Markle, Weiss, and Jaret (2017) found that, in almost 70% of 136 metro areas studied between 1980 and 2016, the immigrant population increased, but crime stayed stable or actually fell.

CHAPTER 2

Welcoming Newcomer Students

AS WE HAVE DESCRIBED in Chapter 1, an increasing number of immigrant families have experienced trauma prior to and during their journey to the U.S. Many are dealing with the aftermath of harrowing events including violence, extortion, and extreme poverty. Once they arrive in the U.S., challenges continue as they struggle to earn a living, find housing, and put food on the table. Further, xenophobia and anti-immigrant sentiments that are currently on the rise in the U.S. are contributing to the fear, mistrust, and psychological distress felt among immigrant communities (Langhout et al, 2018).

Many newcomer students suffer emotional challenges and economic insecurity as a consequence of having been separated from family members due to deportation or detention of a caregiver/parent and/or having to flee desperate situations in their home countries. The threat of deportation can also contribute to anxiety and psychological stress among youngsters. As researchers have found, immigrant children who have witnessed or heard about immigration raids often feel abandoned, isolated, fearful, traumatized, and depressed (Adames & Chavez-Dueñas, 2017). Researchers have also found that the threat of deportation may lead to poorer school performance on the part of immigrant children (e.g., Brabeck & Xu, 2010).

Because many newcomer children are separated from their caregivers/parents or forced to emigrate alone or with someone who is not a parent, immigrant families do not necessarily fit the traditional mold of parents and children. Once in the U.S., newcomers' caregivers may be older siblings, aunts, uncles, grandparents, or family friends, and they may not know these individuals well or even at all. Newcomer children may be missing a parent or close relative that they left in their home country and struggling with their role in new or reconstituted family units.

In this chapter, we will describe what advocacy-oriented teachers need to know and do to make sure that schools and classrooms are safe, nurturing, and welcoming environments for newcomer students and their families. The chapter will address the following topics:

- Newcomers' initial welcome to school;
- Newcomers' rights and protections;
- Learning about newcomer students;
- Addressing newcomer students' socio-emotional circumstances and needs; and
- Establishing a welcoming and nurturing classroom and school community.

Newcomers' Initial Welcome to School

Imagine dropping your child off at an imposing building that, while called a "school," is unlike the schools you or your children attended in your home country. Hundreds of children roam the hallways and a huge asphalt yard, shouting in a language you cannot understand. A bell rings and the students file into 30 different classrooms. School personnel speak to you in an unfamiliar language and ask you to sign papers you cannot read. You drop your child off in one place—an office—but you do not know where to find your child at the end of the day. You know children are required to go to school and you hope your child will learn English and adapt quickly, but you are nervous leaving your child in such an unfamiliar environment. Imagine how your anxiety would be compounded if you had already been separated from this child for months or years while you were in immigration detention centers or were in the process of obtaining legal documentation (and had yet to obtain this documentation). You may wonder, "Are these American strangers to be trusted?"

When a newcomer family arrives at a school, school personnel and teachers can engage in a variety of practices to welcome them and ease this transition. Caregivers/parents and students must be greeted warmly and given an orientation to the school in their native languages, if they do not speak English. During this initial orientation, we advise school personnel to do the following:

- Learn and use a few phrases, including greetings, in newcomers' home languages when meeting newcomer families and students. In the case of those languages for which you do not have access to translators, try using the Internet to come up with some appropriate phrases.
- Make it clear that you are eager and happy to have caregivers/parents and their children as members of your school community.
- Inform caregivers/parents where they can obtain translation services (e.g., from the district). (See the section in Chapter 9, "Communicating with Caregivers/Family Members," regarding tips for getting support with translation.)
- Provide caregivers/parents and students with a tour and an explanation of school norms and expectations that may be unfamiliar, including:
  - Pick-up and drop-off procedures;
  - Whether or not students are expected to wear uniforms;
  - Whether meals are available to students and what can be done to reduce or waive the cost of meals;
  - What services are available at the school (e.g., after-school care, medical, dental, counseling);
  - School policies regarding student behavior; and
  - How to contact teachers and office staff.
- Introduce caregivers/parents to their children's teacher(s) and school-community liaison(s). We have worked with teachers who visit students and their families at home prior to or soon after they are enrolled. (See the section, "Making home visits," in Chapter 9.)
- Pair students and family members with other members of the school community. A newcomer student can be paired with a peer buddy who can, for example, give the newcomer student a tour of the school, help orient the student to the school, find classes and the bathroom, and/or negotiate the cafeteria system. The school can also recruit families to be buddy or host families for newly arrived families to help orient them to the community.
- Provide invitations to school-wide events and meetings intended for caregivers/parents (e.g., back-to-school nights, Parent Teacher Association [PTA] meetings, meetings related to immigrant rights,

parent-teacher conferences). Invitations and information about events and meetings should be in family members' native languages.

- Describe ways that caregivers/parents can participate in the children's schooling, including in decision making regarding the curriculum, school budget, and school policies (e.g., via participation in organizations like the PTA or School Site Council [SSC]). In some states, like California, caregivers/parents of English learners participate in special committees to advise the principal and staff about programs and services for English learners. Members of these committees are provided with opportunities to receive training to support them in this activity. For additional information about California's English Learner Advisory Committee, go to https://www.cde.ca.gov/ta/cr/elac.asp.

Newcomers' Rights and Protections

Newcomer families need access to all sorts of information related to the schooling of their children and the wellbeing of their entire family. Schools are often the first place where newcomers gain access to this information. Some districts have established community centers around schools, where a library, clinic, various social service agencies—including those providing mental health and legal services as well as basic necessities—are located on the same campus as the school. Descriptions of community schools are available at the Coalition for Community Schools at http://www.communityschools.org/aboutschools/national_models.aspx. Many school districts throughout the country have a variety of practical resources for newcomer families. It is helpful to know what resources are available in your school and district so that you can inform families about them. Here we provide an overview of the kinds of information that we recommend including in orientations, as well as literature we recommend giving to newcomer caregivers/parents, who may be unaware of these resources. Because many families are focused on a number of pressing needs (e.g., obtaining employment, housing, food, healthcare, and other basic goods and services), they may not act upon this information when they first enroll their children in school. For this reason, it is important to provide parents with information of this kind on an ongoing basis.

Educational Rights, Policies, and Regulations

There are a number of rights and policies that relate to the schooling of newcomer and immigrant students. In order to effectively welcome, work with, and inform newcomer students and their caregivers/parents, we believe that it is important for teachers to be familiar with the following rights and policies, which are described more fully in a U.S. Department of Education publication, *Newcomer Toolkit* (2016, 2017):

- According to the Family Educational Rights and Privacy Act of 1974 (FERPA), schools cannot share student information, including their citizenship status, if they know it, without parental consent. Given the current political environment, this issue may prevent newcomers from even approaching government institutions like schools and enrolling children in school (Langhout et al., 2018). According to the U.S. Department of Justice, Civil Rights Division, and the U.S Department of Education, Office for Civil Rights (2015), this prohibition against the schools' sharing such information must be communicated to newcomers' caregivers/parents in a language they can understand.

- Schools cannot require caregivers/parents to apply for or reveal their Social Security numbers (U.S. Department of Justice, 2014). Some school districts ask for children's Social Security numbers so that they can use them as identification numbers. If a school or school district asks for a student's Social Security number, it must: (1) inform caregivers and the students that providing the number is voluntary and that refusing to do so will not prevent their children from enrolling in or attending school, and (2) explain how the number will be used.

- Schools need to inform caregivers/parents about what their child is learning and doing at school as well as provide regular reports of their progress.

- Schools need to inform caregivers/parents about testing policies and practices. (See Chapter 4.)

The New York City Department of Education (NYCDOE) provides caregivers/parents of English learners with a Bill of Rights at https://www.schools.nyc.gov/multilingual-learners/process/bill-of-rights-for-parents-of-english-language-learners. The following is an abridged version:

ABRIDGED VERSION OF THE NEW YORK CITY DEPARTMENT OF EDUCATION BILL OF RIGHTS FOR PARENTS OF ENGLISH LANGUAGE LEARNERS

As the parent or guardian of an English Language Learner, you have the right for your child to receive a free public education in the school district where you live. This is true regardless of your or your child's immigration status or what language you speak. You also have the right to:

1. Enroll your child in school without being asked to share your or your child's immigration status.
2. Have an interpreter or translator help you communicate with your child's school about your child's education.
3. Have your child placed in a bilingual education program when there are 20 or more students in the same grade who speak the same language. You may opt out your child from a bilingual program. However, the child must be placed in a bilingual or English as a New Language program within ten school days of enrollment.
4. Be notified in writing in your language and English about your child being identified as an English Language Learner and being placed in either a bilingual or English as a New Language program.
5. Meet with school staff to learn about New York State standards, tests, programming, and school expectations for English Language Learners; this meeting must occur before your child's final placement in an educational program and must be conducted in your language.
6. Receive information about your child's English language development (and home language development if s/he is in a bilingual education program).
7. Meet with school staff at least once a year to discuss your child's progress in school.
8. Have your child get the same support services and access to school activities that the school gives to all students.

Social and Economic Services for Newcomers

Newcomers tend to face economic struggles when they arrive in the U.S. In fact, most of their time may be dedicated to securing food and shelter, which may make it hard for them to focus on other issues. While native-born citizens and people who are documented are able to obtain certain economic and social benefits such as healthcare and economic support, it is more difficult for those who do not have documentation.

Caregivers and parents may ask teachers and other educators for information about how to obtain public health services and private insurance. Obviously, this is an extremely important concern, but the laws and regulations in this complicated and ever-changing area of law are beyond the scope of this book to address. The best way to inform yourself about these issues is to speak with a lawyer who specializes in healthcare and/or immigration law, but if that is not a viable option, you can find useful information at https://www.healthcare.gov/immigrants/coverage/. There is also some useful information at https://www.healthinsurance.org/obamacare/how-immigrants-are-getting-health-coverage, but please be aware that this site is primarily a commercial site that provides quotes from companies interested in selling health insurance. It is helpful to have information available about organizations, such as churches and nonprofits, that provide those in need with food, clothing, and other necessities. Schools may have this information at hand. The following list includes organizations that provide services to immigrants regardless of their status:

Hispanic Federation	https://hispanicfederation.org
Catholic Legal Immigration Network	https://cliniclegal.org
Lutheran Immigration and Refugee Service	https://www.lirs.org/mission-and-vision
International Rescue Committee	https://www.rescue.org

Information Regarding Newcomers' Immigration Options

The immigration status of newcomer children and their families contributes to a great deal of concern, anxieties, and other issues that threaten their well-being. Members of immigrant families may have different statuses. Citizens, permanent residents with Green Cards, and those who are undocumented are often members of the same family and may be living together. A number of agencies recommend that undocumented immigrants find out what protections and options they may be able to obtain. Many districts employ outreach personnel, including family or home-school liaisons, who have access to this information. Resources available to all immigrants, regardless of their immigration status, are available at the following sites:

The Immigrant Legal Resource Center	https://ww.ilrc.org
Immigration Advocates Network	https://immigrationadvocates.org
Immigration Law Help	https://www.immigrationlawhelp.org
American Civil Liberties Union	https://www.aclu.org

What to Do If Family Members Are Approached or Detained by ICE Officials

ICE officers have been known to engage in racial or ethnic profiling when detaining people from all walks of life, including documented as well as undocumented immigrant people. Indeed, we have known of several U.S. citizens detained by ICE agents who suspected they were undocumented immigrants. According to St. John and Rubin (2018), ICE has wrongly identified at least 2,840 United States citizens as possibly eligible for deportation since 2002. At least 214 of these people were taken into custody for some period of time, according to ICE records analyzed by the Transactional Records Access Clearinghouse at Syracuse University. Some were military veterans who were deported for traffic violations and nonviolent crimes (e.g., possession of marijuana, fraud).

All immigrants (both documented and undocumented) and, if possible, their children, must know that they have rights, if they are approached by ICE officials. A number of organizations have prepared guidelines for immigrants who are approached by ICE officers and/or local police. The following list of rights is a brief version of the ACLU guidelines at https://www.aila.org/advo -media/tools/psas/know-your-rights-handouts-if-ice-visits as they existed at the time this book went to press. If you have specific concerns or questions about specific situations, you should seek advice from an immigration lawyer and not rely on this or any summary description of the laws and regulations in this complicated and evolving area of law.

- *If ICE agents or police officers come to their home,* immigrants do not have to open the door unless the agents show them a search warrant signed by a judge that has their correct name and address on it. (An ICE deportation warrant does not entitle the agents to enter the home.) Agents and police officers can slide these warrants under the door or show them through a window.
- *If ICE agents or police officers stop an immigrant in public,* unless the

immigrant is actually being arrested, they do not have to consent to a search.

- *In either case:*
  - They have the right to remain silent, but if they choose to do so, they should say so out loud to the agents or officers.
  - They are advised to give the agent or police officer a "red card" or "know-your-rights" card. "Red cards" can be obtained in a variety of languages on the Immigrant Legal Resource Center website: https://www.ilrc.org/red-cards. If immigrants are confronted by ICE agents or police officers at their home, the card can be slipped under the door.
  - They have the right to speak to a lawyer immediately if they are detained or taken into custody. If they don't have a lawyer, they can ask the immigration officer for a list of all pro bono lawyers (i.e., lawyers who work voluntarily and without payment) in the area.

It is important that immigrants have specific documents with them at all times, including a work permit or Green Card if they have one; an ID or driver's license; the telephone number of someone who knows of their plans or wishes regarding their children, in case they are detained; and who to contact for an immigration attorney. It is advisable that they do not carry any documentation about their country of origin or false identity documents, including falsified immigration documents.

Given the danger and insecurity many immigrant families face, it is important that caregivers/parents plan for the possibility of being detained or being the target of an unanticipated sweep. Many schools let caregivers/parents know if ICE officials are in the area or have been on school grounds via robocalls. Teachers and schools can help caregivers/parents develop a plan that addresses the following:

- Caregivers/parents need to make decisions about who will care for their child if they face deportation. This includes whether or not the caregiver/parent wants their child to stay in the U.S. and with whom. When deciding on who will take care of children, it is important to consider the immigration status of that individual. Caregivers/parents should consider individuals who are U.S. citizens or who cannot be deported.

- Caregivers/parents need to provide the school with updated contact information regarding who will take care of their children, if they are unavailable. They need to make sure that the school and an adult who may be caring for their children have written information regarding their children's medical conditions, including any allergies they may have, the medicines they take, health insurance information, and their doctor's contact information. In states like California, caregivers/parents should consider having adults who assume the role of caregiver fill out a Caregiver's Authorization Affidavit. (For a copy of the affidavit, visit: https://www.lsc-sf.org/wp-content/uploads/2015/10/CAA-with-Instructions.pdf.)
- If at all possible, caregivers/parents need to inform their children and other family members residing in the U.S. of their plans regarding possible deportation. This needs to be done in a manner that is reassuring to children so that they know that a trusted person will care for them if the caregiver/parent is not available.

There are a number of resources that can be referenced for developing materials and orientations that help newcomer families better understand their rights, how to navigate social service agencies, and what they must consider when planning for the possibility of being approached or detained by ICE agents. School districts like the Oakland Unified School District (OUSD) have specific protocols regarding how teachers, principals, parents, and other school staff or school district employees will respond if contacted by ICE. This information is made available to all families with children enrolled in the school district. For an example of the information about ICE posted on the OUSD website, see Appendix 2.

The following websites are also useful when developing materials and orientations for newcomer families:

Immigrant Family Defense Fund	https://immigrantfamilies.org
Immigrant Legal Resource Center	https://www.ilrc.org/family-preparedness-plan
National Immigration Law Center	https://www.nilc.org/get-involved/community-education-resources/know-your-rights/
Informed Immigrant	https://www.informedimmigrant.com/guides/

Learning about Newcomer Students

When newcomer students arrive in schools, it often takes teachers time to learn important information about them. It may take a few days, for example, to realize that a newcomer is an emerging reader in their native language, has not yet studied division, or is struggling with trauma from family separation. To learn about newcomers, we recommend that teachers engage in a series of initial assessments that can help them tailor their instruction according to students' needs and experiences. These assessments include:

- *A conversation with the family to learn about the students' educational history and immigration journey, family, and language background.* The following suggestions can be helpful:
    - The conversation should be done sensitively and in the family member's home language, with the help of an interpreter, if needed.
    - Families must be assured that certain information will be kept confidential and they are welcome and safe at the school regardless of their immigration status.
    - The sample questions on the next page provide an idea of the kinds of issues school personnel might ask about. However, what is crucial is that this is a welcoming conversation, that the student and family member or caregiver feel safe, and that you are building a trusting relationship. To ease this, it can help if you have the conversation in a parent center or lounge area with a sofa and comfortable seating and offer beverages and snacks.
- *A one-on-one reading assessment in the newcomer student's native languages, as well as in English if the newcomer speaks or understands some English.* The school or district may have an adopted assessment in the native language of students, such as the *Evaluación del Desarrollo de la Lectura* by Ruiz and Cuesta (2000) (the Spanish version of the *Developmental Reading Assessment*) or *Sistema de Evaluación de la Lectura* by Fountas and Pinnell (2012). If not, school personnel with knowledge of a student's native language can ask the students to read a book in the native language, do a running record, and then ask the student to retell the text. (See Chapter 6 for information on how to conduct a running record.)

EXAMPLE OF NEWCOMER STUDENT INTAKE
INTERVIEW GUIDELINES AND QUESTIONS

I'd like to ask you some questions so that I can better get to know you and _____ (child's name). This will help me be a good teacher for _____ (child's name).

If parent says yes, continue with the interview.

Personal History:

1. How are you/your family doing?
2. What language(s) do you speak at home?
3. Where was your child born?/Where were you born? (Country and city/town, or other location)
4. When did your child arrive in the U.S.?/When did you arrive in the U.S.?
5. Where did you live before coming to the U.S.?
6. Did you live anywhere else in the U.S. before you came to _____ (name of the community where school is located)?
7. When did you arrive in _____ (name of the community where school is located)?
8. With whom do you live?

Schooling and Academic History (Asked of students or, if students are too young, of caregiver/parent about the child):

9. Did you go to school in your home country?
10. Did you like going to school in your home country? What did you like best?
11. How old were you when you first began going to school?
12. What language(s) did teachers use with you when you were going to school in your country? Did you also use that/those language(s)?
13. How many days a week did you go to school?
14. How many students were in your class?
15. What subjects did you study in school?/What did you do in school?
16. Did you go to school every day or did you miss days? Why did you miss school days?
17. What do you like to do? (e.g., music, arts, theater)
18. How do you feel about going to school here?
19. What would help you feel good/better about going to school here?

- *A writing sample in the newcomer's native languages and in English, if the student is able to do this.* We recommend giving a simple prompt, such as asking newcomers to write a story from their imagination or providing an intriguing picture and asking them to write a story about it.
- *A diagnostic math assessment,* such as the following, which is an assessment that tests from counting skills up to middle school math skills: http://excelmath.com/downloads/placement_test_spanish.pdf. Students should be asked to complete as much as they can and stop or skip problems they don't yet know how to do.

In the absence of a centralized school or district intake system, many teachers have developed ways to informally assess and get background information on newcomer students who have been recently enrolled in their schools. For example, when new students arrive in Laura's class, she asks them to write her a letter introducing themselves. She provides a set of questions to help give them ideas about what they can write about. Newcomers write those letters in their home language. This provides Laura with some key information about her newcomers' families, experiences, and native language literacy. One of Laura's colleagues prepares a letter in Spanish, in which she introduces herself. When newcomers arrive, she shares this letter with them so they can get to know her a bit and to provide a model for their own letter.

Teachers can also learn about their newcomer students by being alert to how they behave. For instance, as we observe newcomers at play, we can become aware of the customs and practices that are part of their everyday lives outside of school. For example, when Cindy (Lucinda) taught preschool in a largely Mexican immigrant community, she learned about celebratory events as she watched children enact these events while playing with one another. During times of the day when teachers played Mexican *ranchera* music, her students arranged chairs along the walls of the classroom, leaving an empty circular space in the center. They then sat down on the chairs. After a few minutes, some children would get out of their chairs, approach another seated student, take that student's hand, lead them out into the circular space, and begin dancing together. Later, Cindy observed a similar scenario when attending a dance that her students' parents organized as a fundraising activity for the school.

Teachers also learn a great deal about newcomer students when making home visits and/or attending community and family events. Chapter 9 provides a detailed description of the ways teachers can engage with family members during these visits.

There are a number of very compelling and informative accounts about immigrants to the United States. There are also several recent films that address these topics. The following lists provide summaries of books and films that we think are particularly useful:

Books

- *Lives in Limbo: Undocumented and Coming of Age in America* by Roberto Gonzalez (2016). This account follows 150 undocumented young adults in Los Angeles. Gonzalez documents the challenges and injustices that undocumented immigrant children have faced growing up in the U.S. Despite the fact that the U.S. is the only country that they know, they are denied the rights and benefits that their native-born peers enjoy.
- *Tell Me How It Ends: An Essay in Forty Questions* by Valeria Luiselli (2017). Luiselli shares young asylum seekers' responses to interview questions that they are asked upon their arrival to the U.S. Luiselli, who was charged with the responsibility of interviewing these children or translating at their interviews, weaves their responses into a compelling account of the dangers and challenges they face while traveling to and living in the U.S.
- *The Far Away Brothers: Two Young Migrants and the Making of an American Life* by Lauren Markham (2017). This book chronicles the journeys of two unaccompanied minors, brothers Ernesto and Raul Flores, as they make their way from their home in Mexico to Oakland, California. Markham provides a poignant and eye-opening account of the trials they and their families experienced as they traveled across the border. Along the way they faced violence, detention, and encounters with immigration authorities. Once they arrived, they had to navigate a new culture, school, and economic challenges as they confronted their uncertain futures.
- *This Land Is Our Land: An Immigrant's Manifesto* by Suketu Mehta (2019). This well-researched book provides a global perspective on immigration, through analyzing the causes of immigration from different continents to the U.S. and Europe, and links immigration

to the history of colonialism. Mehta also details the ways in which receiving countries benefit from immigration.

- *Enrique's Journey* by Sonia Nazario (2006). In this book, Nazario describes the journey of 17-year-old Enrique from Honduras to the U.S., in search of his mother, who immigrated to the U.S. 11 years earlier. Throughout his perilous journey north, Enrique faced almost insurmountable dangers as he traveled alone, clinging to freight trains and going by foot.

Films

- *Documented*, produced and directed by José Antonio Vargas (2013). This documentary chronicles the immigration story of the Pulitzer prize-winning journalist, José Antonio Vargas, who came from the Philippines to the U.S. as a child. Vargas describes his experiences and the impact they had on his life and emotional wellbeing, as well as his subsequent work as an immigration activist.
- *This Is Home*: *A Refugee Story*, directed by Alexandra Shiva (2018). In this documentary, the viewer meets four Syrian refugee families who arrive in Baltimore, Maryland. With a limited amount of time to be able to negotiate their lives in an unfamiliar setting, the families find themselves having to contend with the travel ban, which constrains their economic and social opportunities.

Newcomers Students' Socio-Emotional Circumstances and Needs

According to the American Psychological Association (2015), as well as a growing number of researchers, immigrant children who have experienced trauma, fear, and separation from their families are subject to psychological stressors and mental health issues. Many have been found to suffer from post-traumatic stress disorder (PTSD), anxiety, and depression. When beginning school in a new country, feelings of anxiety can be overwhelming, particularly for those who have experienced violence and insecurity in their home countries, a difficult journey to the U.S., family separation, economic challenges, and/or discrimination once they arrive, including in school. Teachers need to be alert to signs of socio-emotional distress in their students, including the following:

- Shaking and trembling
- Appearing withdrawn or listless
- Displays of aggression and/or anger
- Reports of not sleeping at night
- Crying or outbursts, and it is difficult to console the student
- Signs of self-inflicted harm (e.g., cutting)
- Dramatic changes in behavior

If you notice any of these signs or suspect that a student is in distress, immediately seek help from school or district administrators, a school-community liaison, and/or school district support staff. They may tell you to refer children for special education services, so that children can be further assessed to determine if they may be given Individualized Educational Programs (IEPs or 504 plans) that address psychological or socio-emotional issues. School and district administrators and school-community liaisons may also connect students with counselors, medical providers, and social workers who are available via community clinics and local hospitals. In the case of undocumented children, schools may be the only means through which they can obtain affordable health services, including mental health treatment.

Establishing a Welcoming and Nurturing Classroom and School Community

All students benefit from being part of school and classroom communities where members trust, respect, and care for one another. Indeed, a number of researchers have found that strong and productive relationships among students and teachers foster students' academic achievement and socio-emotional wellbeing (Langhout et al., 2018). In the following scenario, Mr. Navarro involves his students in a number of approaches intended to help establish a caring and nurturing classroom community.

SCENE: A fourth-grade morning meeting

PARTICIPANTS: 29 fourth graders from a variety of different backgrounds. Four of these students are newcomers who came to the U.S. within the last six months.

Mr. Navarro stands at the door as his students enter the room. As students walk in, they choose if they want to greet their teacher with a high five, fist bump, hug, or wave. This allows him to gauge how students are feeling that morning. When Samuel comes in with tired eyes peeking out from under his hoodie and waves slightly, Mr. Navarro smiles, waves back, and makes a note that he should check in with Samuel later on. Students place their backpacks at their desks and form a circle on the carpet. On the board, Mr. Navarro has posted the following agenda for their morning meeting:

- Greeting: weather
- Morning letter
- Learning target: I can collaborate with my group
- Initiative: paper towers
- Debrief
- Collaboration goals

When the students are all gathered on the rug, Mr. Navarro welcomes them: "Today, let's check in with weather. Different kinds of weather might represent different feelings. What's one kind of weather?"

"Sunny," says Jessica. Mr. Navarro starts a chart labeled *Weather* and writes *sunny* with a picture of a sun.

"Rainy," offers Melinda. Mr. Navarro adds *rainy* and a picture of a rain cloud.

The class continues brainstorming types of weather and, in a few minutes, has a chart with several types of weather, including foggy, cloudy, hailing, rainbow, and snow, along with corresponding pictures.

"This morning in the circle, you're going to choose one kind of weather that shows us how you're feeling. For example, today I feel foggy (*he points to the word and picture for foggy*) because I'm a little sleepy this morning (*he rubs his eyes and yawns indicating that he's sleepy*). First, let's share with our partner." He strategically has his four newcomer students seated with helpful students who can support them in choosing a weather word that represents how they're feeling. Then the students go around the circle sharing a weather system and, in most cases, explaining how it represents their current mood.

Ana, a newcomer from Guatemala, shares, "Sun because . . . I . . . happy. Es el cumpleaños de mi hermanito y vamos a comer pastel esta noche (*It's my little brother's birthday and we're going to have cake tonight*)."

"You feel sunny because you're happy today. It's your baby brother's birthday and you're going to celebrate with cake. How old is he? Is he one or two years old?" Mr. Navarro asks, showing one and two fingers.

"Two," answers Ana, showing two fingers.

Next, Fatima, a newcomer from Yemen, shares. "Cloudy," she says. "No happy." Fatima does not elaborate in her home language because she knows Mr. Navarro and most of her classmates will not understand. However, Mr. Navarro elaborates on Fatima's contribution and makes a mental note to watch her and check back in with her later. "I'm sorry you're not feeling happy today. Thank you for sharing with us. I hope you feel better later today."

After the class finishes sharing in the circle, Mr. Navarro directs their attention to the daily letter, which the class reads chorally:

Dear Class,

I'm so excited today because we are starting our science project. You've learned a lot about energy this month, and now you'll start designing and making a car that moves with electricity. I've gathered lots of different materials you can use, like wires, batteries, Legos, tape, and toy cars. You'll be doing this project in your science groups, so you'll have to collaborate and work together.

Sincerely,

Mr. Navarro

The students buzz with excitement and look at the materials Mr. Navarro takes out to help his students understand the task they will complete. Then he introduces the cooperative activity or challenge, known as a *cooperative initiative*, which his students will engage in today. Twice a week, the class participates in cooperative initiatives that are focused on different socio-emotional learning (SEL) goals. Mr. Navarro strategically chooses initiatives and SEL goals that will support students with their academic work later in the day. Recently, the students have conducted several science experiments in their groups, and he's observed some challenges with collaboration, such as one or two students taking over and not allowing newcomers to contribute and conflicts about turn taking and how to go about a task. He has chosen an initiative to help students practice collaborating in their science groups with a non-academic task.

"Today in your group, you're going to get 10 pieces of paper and your mission is to work together to build a tower that will stand up by itself. You won't get any tape or glue, so you'll have to be creative," Mr. Navarro explains, showing the materials and gesturing to help his newcomers understand. Then he explicitly mentions the challenges students have had collaborating. "Sometimes, it's hard to work together. We can have trouble sharing materials or deciding together what we want to do. We can't always get our way when we work in a team. We also need to make sure everyone gets to participate and that one person isn't taking over. While you're building, I'm going to walk around and observe how you're collaborating. What does it mean to collaborate well? What will I see and hear when I'm walking around if your group is collaborating?"

Mr. Navarro creates a chart with the class labeled "Collaboration." As the students suggest ideas about how to collaborate with one another, he lists them on the chart and annotates each item with an image. After a few minutes, the class, with Mr. Navarro's help, has generated the following chart:

FIGURE 2.1: Collaboration Chart

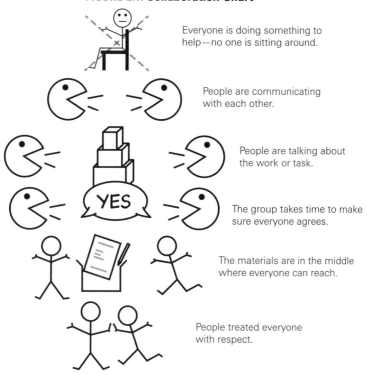

Everyone is doing something to help—no one is sitting around.

People are communicating with each other.

People are talking about the work or task.

The group takes time to make sure everyone agrees.

The materials are in the middle where everyone can reach.

People treated everyone with respect.

Mr. Navarro gives the class 10 minutes to create their towers. As students work together, he walks around, jotting down notes on his clipboard. He avoids directing the students' work or mediating for them if things get tense. The groups buzz with activity and he sees two newcomers, Samuel and Fatima, start to perk up and engage actively with their groups. At the end, the students come together and compare their towers. They celebrate the groups whose towers are still standing. Although some towers fall, they know this was a game and groups giggle as their towers fall apart. Mr. Navarro keeps a lighthearted tone and emphasizes the process of their collaboration rather than the product. He brings the class together to the carpet to debrief their collaboration. First, he gives them a few minutes to talk in their groups about two questions: What went well? What was challenging?

When Mr. Navarro brings the class together, students use their collaboration chart to debrief their work together. He also adds specific observations of things he saw students doing well in their collaboration to affirm and extend their ideas. He says, "I noticed that Table Two divided up the task so everyone had something to do. Fatima and Javier were folding papers into square tubes, and Melissa and Helen were putting them together. Everyone was busy helping the whole time. I also saw at Table Four, they had a hard time deciding how to start because Michelle had one idea and Sarahi had another idea. Then Sarahi said, 'We're running out of time, so let's just try it your way, Michelle.' She compromised and then they could get started." Mr. Navarro adds *Divide up tasks*, *Compromise*, and *Negotiate* to the class collaboration chart and says, "I also noticed that there were times when students used different languages during the activity. For example, Fatima asked Sarahi a question in Arabic. I'm thinking that Sarahi's answer was helpful for Fatima." He adds *Use different languages to help everyone understand and complete the activity* to the chart.

To close out the morning meeting, Mr. Navarro gives each child a sticky note and asks them to write a collaboration goal for themselves. He asks, "What is something you need to work on today in your science group? Maybe you need to work on listening to other people, or maybe you need to work on being more involved or asking for help?" He charts possible goals and asks for other ideas from the class. Then each student writes their own goal and shares it with their group. They leave the sticky notes on the tables to remind themselves of their goals. After science time, they will reflect on their goals and set new goals for tomorrow's science work.

Key principles underlying the above scenario include the following, which are discussed below:

- Check and reconsider assumptions and biases.
- Foster trust, empathy, and belonging.
- Celebrate newcomers.
- Foster agency and activism.
- Engage in restorative approaches to conflict and discipline.

Check and Reconsider Assumptions and Biases

Newcomers are unfamiliar with many of the customs and practices that many people who are born in the U.S. share or know about. Further, they are not a monolithic group. Rather, they come from many different countries and cultural backgrounds. We cannot assume that they share the same immigration story or immigration status. And, they certainly don't share the same customs, academic experiences, or histories. It is important that we don't rely on any stereotypes or biases we may have about newcomers, including their race, ethnicity, religion, and gender. Further, we must be careful not to privilege our experiences and practices over those of other communities. For example, Mr. Navarro in the scenario above has had few opportunities to work with female Muslim students. When first encountering students like Fatima, who wore traditional head scarfs, he assumed that Fatima would be shy, quiet, and hesitant when participating in class because he thought the use of head scarfs among Muslim women and girls was a sign of female submissiveness. As he stated when describing his assumptions, "I thought girls who used head scarfs would be docile and likely to do whatever I or any male students told them to do." However, he learned that Muslim students like Fatima were often willing contributors to class discussions, unafraid to express viewpoints that may not be shared by Mr. Navarro or her peers.

Bias is also reflected in what many of us consider to be normalized views about children and child raising. For example, we have often found that many people from mainstream cultural communities, including teachers, assume that the child-raising experiences thought to be associated with mainstream communities are not only the norm, but necessary, if children are to learn. Consequently, they may hold steadfast views about the practices that they think are essential for children's learning and those that are to be discouraged or, worse, deplored. For example, drawing on her work examining language socialization practices in Anglo and Latinx communities, Ana Celia Zentella (2005) argues that many teachers and members of the public at large think that reading to children, a practice common in many mainstream Anglo communities, is an essential child-raising activity and a hallmark of good parenting. However, this practice was not prioritized in the Puerto Rican community in New York, where she was raised. Instead, letter writing and completing one's homework were valued literacy practices in her home. She states that, when individuals view mainstream practices as the norm, they often discount or even demonize the practices and cultural views that non-mainstream children bring to school.

Bias can be addressed in classrooms by making sure that students from marginalized populations are viewed as capable and contributing members of the classroom community. For example, Mr. Navarro noticed that some of his students took over activities and did not allow newcomers to contribute. He decided to emphasize the contributions newcomers made to groups in order to increase their social and academic status in the class. He also focused students' attention on assessing the collaborative aspect of their work together so that they would encourage and value the contributions of all students.

Bias is also reflected in the collection of books and materials that are present and used in classrooms. We can address bias when selecting books and materials by considering the guidelines described in Chapter 6.

Foster Trust, Empathy, and Belonging

There are a number of approaches and activities that we and others have used that are intended to help students engage with others and, in so doing, gain an appreciation and understanding for different perspectives; foster a sense of belonging in the context of a safe and caring community; and conceive of one another as equally valuable participants in joint endeavors. Such activities include the following:

- *Cooperative learning activities,* such as the one described in Mr. Navarro's class, in which students engaged with one another to accomplish a task or activity. In the case of newcomers new to English, it is important to develop activities that they can engage in without having to rely exclusively on spoken or written language to make meaning. For example, Mr. Navarro used a cooperative initiative or challenge in which students collaboratively constructed a tower. As they engaged in this activity, they had opportunities to work with a diverse group of learners to accomplish a joint goal and, in the process, foster friendships, a sense of community, and belonging (e.g., newcomers were not paired with students from similar backgrounds, with students deemed to be roughly the same in terms of their academic ability, and/or with students who spoke the same language). As they jointly assessed their work, students reflected on and gained access to others' perspectives in order to focus on the challenges and successes they had collaborating with one another. They also gained insights into the varied resources that different students brought to the activity. This was of particular concern to Mr. Navarro because he wanted to make sure that students did not privilege the contributions of some students over others, which can contribute to establishing social hierarchies within the classroom community. For that reason, he made sure to offer his own observations about students' contributions when he pointed out the different ways students collaborated (e.g., by compromising, by focusing on a particular task). Examples of other cooperative activities can be found in Appendix 3. Regardless of the cooperative activity used, it is important that we, like Mr. Navarro, engage students in debriefing those activities.

- *Icebreakers and greetings* that explicitly welcome each child into the room and foster a sense of belonging among newcomer students. In addition, we can use greetings to gauge how students are feeling early on in the school day. In the case of the previous scenario, Mr. Navarro greeted each child nonverbally via a signal of the child's choosing (e.g., a high five or fist bump) and asked them to share how they were feeling by choosing a weather condition that matched their mood.
- *Discussion activities* linked to academic tasks, like book discussions (see Chapter 6).

Celebrate Newcomers

In order to convey to students that their classrooms and schools are welcoming and inclusive spaces that foster a sense of belonging and trust, teachers acknowledge and celebrate who their students are. Students need to see their school and classroom as their space, a place where they feel they belong and that reflects their identities and interests. In the previous scenario, Mr. Navarro enacted this principle when he explicitly called attention to the contributions that newcomers Fatima, Javier, Ana, and Sarahi made when working in their groups, including occasions when they used languages other than English. Despite not understanding what Fatima and Sarahi said to one another in Arabic, he conveyed a positive message about their use of that language when he said that he was sure that what Sarahi said in Arabic was helpful.

Additional practices aligned with this principle include the following:

- Display art, photos, and other objects from students' home countries in classrooms and throughout the school.
- Make sure that culturally responsive books in students' home languages are available in the school library and students' classrooms. See Chapter 6 for a list of publishers and distributors of bilingual books and books in languages other than English.
- Provide opportunities for students and families to share their cultures with others via music, singing, storytelling, art, and cooking. See Chapter 9 for suggestions.
- Ask children to plan and decorate the classroom in ways that reflect their interests and identities.

It is important that we are aware that some newcomer students and their family members may not want to share information about their home countries and cultures and immigration journeys. Consequently, we need to let family members know that we would like to draw on this information when working with students and ask them for their permission to do so.

Foster Agency and Activism

When we encourage students to assume an active role in their learning and classroom community, students see themselves as being responsible for and in control of what they do. In the previous scenario, this sense of agency was fostered when Mr. Navarro had the students articulate what quality collaboration looks like. He also had the students set their collaboration goals for their science work, giving them space to reflect on what they felt they needed to work on. Throughout this book, we advocate for providing students with opportunities to exercise agency as they make choices about what they read, write, and talk about.

As we mention in Chapter 8, when the curriculum focuses on issues of social justice, students see themselves as actors or agents when it comes to fostering a society that is committed to the wellbeing and equality of all its members. As we describe in Chapter 1, like other students from marginalized communities, many newcomers have experienced the kind of oppression that has constrained their voices, rights, and individual and collective freedoms. By addressing social justice issues in the classroom, we can help to foster and, in some cases, restore agency and hope to newcomers who have struggled with oppression.

Engage in Restorative Approaches to Conflict and Discipline

Over the course of the last few decades, zero tolerance policies to discipline have been promoted in many schools serving immigrant students and students of color. These policies, which began to gain momentum as a response to school shootings in the 1990s, are grounded in the assumption that youngsters' unwanted behaviors would be eliminated when met with harsh punishments (Ginwright, 2016). Critics of these policies have argued that instead of improving school climate and contributing to safety, they foster a climate of defiance and retribution that may contribute to or further intensify tensions between teachers, students, school administrators, students' families, and community members. When enacted in schools serving student populations that have experienced discrimination and oppression, these approaches are particularly damaging.

A crucial part of restorative justice is building a strong classroom community so that when conflict or challenges arise, there is something to restore and there are relationships to work through those challenges. In the previous scenario, Mr. Navarro took time each day to welcome each student into the room and to build a strong learning community. He planned and facilitated activities so students could develop positive relationships with one another. He also utilized a restorative approach when he was honest about how collaboration is challenging and had students reflect on what was difficult in a way that did not blame one another. Challenges were not seen as the fault of particular individuals, but as something inherent to collaboration. Mr. Navarro created a space to talk about this proactively and for the students to name what productive collaboration looks like and to practice it in a non-academic activity where differences in academic status often make collaboration more charged. Mr. Navarro supported students in taking a growth mindset toward their and others' development by setting collaboration goals. The ethos is that everyone has something to work on and is in development as human beings; no one has reached perfection. To learn more about restorative approaches, please visit the following websites:

- https://www.ousd.org/cms/lib/CA01001176/Centricity/Domain/134/ BTC-OUSD1-IG-08b-web.pdf
- https://www.weareteachers.com/restorative-justice/

Additional Resources

The following websites contain information that you may find useful as you prepare to welcome and foster a caring and productive classroom community.

- *U.S. Department of Education Newcomer Toolkit:* https://www2.ed.gov/ about/offices/list/oela/newcomers-toolkit/index.html
- *Building Welcoming Schools: A Guide for K-12 Educators and After-School Providers (Welcoming America):*https://19lwtt3nwtm12axw5e31ay5s -wpengine.netdna-ssl.com/wp-content/uploads/2018/02/WR_ K12Toolkit_Final.pdf

- *Creating a Welcoming Classroom for ELLs and Immigrant Students: Strategies and Resources*: http://www.colorincolorado.org/teaching-ells/ creating-welcoming-classroom/creating-welcoming-environment -ells-and-immigrant
- *Support for Immigrant and Refugee Students: A Guide to Creating Safe and Welcoming Schools for Immigrant and Refugee Students in California:* https://19lwtt3nwtm12axw5e31ay5s-wpengine.netdna-ssl.com/wp -content/uploads/2018/04/SIRS_Guide_to_Safe_and_Welcoming_ Schools_With_Cover.pdf
- *Oakland Unified School District's Family Orientation Videos:* These videos are intended for newcomer families and are available in several languages. They explain how elementary, middle, and high schools are organized in the U.S., how newcomer programs are typically structured in the district, and how to enroll children in school: https:// sites.google.com/ousd.k12.ca.us/newcomer-toolkit/whole-child/ orientation-videos?authuser=0

CHAPTER 3

Foundational Understandings about Second Language Learning and Teaching

BEFORE WE TALK ABOUT how to teach language, we need to take a moment to think about what language is. Is language a collection of words and grammatical structures? Does being proficient in English mean that you can define many words and have learned how to conjugate verbs correctly? If one takes this view of language, teachers may engage students in memorizing lists of words and practicing grammatical forms. This form-focused view of language is all too common in schools and programs that serve English learners. In contrast, we view language as a resource for participation and action. Language is essential for getting things done and participating in a range of activities that are vital to carrying out our daily lives, from negotiating the rules to a game on the playground to figuring out which bus will get us home. Language also enables us to make sense of our experiences and interactions with others and plan for future activities.

So what does this view of language mean for how young people learn a non-native language? We argue that children and adolescents learn non-native languages in a similar way to how they learned their native language: through using it in everyday activities. Most of these activities involve young people in communicative interactions with others. To help understand what we mean, let's examine the following exchange, which involves two five-year-olds at recess time. Alison is a native speaker of English and her companion, Kenji, is new to English, having moved to the U.S. from Japan a month earlier. They have been playing catch during recess on the yard outside their kindergarten classroom and the yard supervisor has blown the whistle, indicating that recess time has ended. Kenji is standing on the playground holding Alison's ball.

> **ALISON**:   That's mine. *(Reaching for the ball)*
>
> *(Kenji moves the ball out of Alison's reach.)*
>
> **ALISON**:   That's mine! *(She frowns, shoves Kenji, and reaches for and grabs the ball out of Kenji's hands).*

When Alison first says, "That's mine," her intention is to get Kenji to hand her the ball. Recess is ending and she wants to make sure to collect her ball so it doesn't get mixed up with other recess equipment. When Kenji doesn't comply, Alison responds forcefully by shoving him and grabbing the ball. After repeated exchanges like this one, Kenji learns that "that's mine" means someone really wants what he is holding and that he should hand it over. In other situations, when a child says "That's mine," he responds by giving the desired object to that child. He also says "That's mine" in order to obtain something that he wants.

As the above exchange illustrates, the immediate context, as well as the nonverbal cues, actions, and objects that are part of an interaction, enabled Kenji and Alison to understand each other and convey meaning. This illustrates how second language learners like Kenji are actively engaged in the language learning process. The fact that the youngsters have been tossing a ball back and forth influences the meaning they glean from the interaction. It's clear that Alison's reference to "That's mine" isn't a reference to the sweater she's wearing. Alison's angry expression and forceful action (i.e., grabbing the ball) also help convey to Kenji what Alison's intentions are when she says "That's mine."

As newcomers participate in activities and conversations with others, they learn language, along with many other things, like the norms and practices of their new cultural communities (e.g., who do you make eye contact with and when), how to accomplish a specific skill or activity (e.g., how to play the latest video game), or knowledge that is valuable in their community (e.g., which are the safest walking routes). Initially, they may participate as observers or by relying on gestures, expressions, and other nonverbal cues. Over time, they will begin using more and more English words and phrases, in combination with nonverbal cues, to participate and engage with those around them. For example, in the following exchange recorded in a second-grade classroom, seven-year-old Ali, who recently emigrated with his family from Yemen to San Francisco, and two other children, Joaquín and Mary, are tablemates. Their teacher has asked them to work together to draw a map of their school. Joaquín and Mary are both bilingual and the children of immigrants; Joaquín is of Mexican descent and speaks Spanish and English, while Mary, who knows Mandarin and English, came to the U.S. from Taiwan when she was a baby.

MARY: Let's draw the outside garden over here. *(Mary points to a corner of the butcher paper they are drawing on.)*

JOAQUÍN: The tomato patch goes here. So I'm gonna make the tomatoes red and the plants green. *(He starts drawing green plants with red spheres on them.)*

ALI: No. No. Red no. *(Ali points to the red sphere on Joaquín's plant.)*

JOAQUÍN: What do you mean? Tomatoes are red. *(Joaquín picks up his red crayon and places it in front of Ali.)*

ALI: Green. Green. *(Ali picks up a green crayon and places it in front of Joaquín.)*

MARY: He already colored in the green part of the plant. *(Mary says this while pointing to the green part of the plant that Joaquín drew. Joaquín continues to draw red spheres on his tomato plants.)*

ALI: Now . . . Today . . . No red. Green. Green. *(Ali points to the window where the tomato plants are in view.)*

JOAQUÍN: Oh. I see. The tomatoes aren't red now. They're green. Later they'll turn red.

ALI: Yes. Later red.

MARY: We should date our map so that people will know why the tomatoes are green.

A month prior to this exchange, Ali spent most of his time observing his tablemates, occasionally laughing at their antics. Gradually, he made efforts to speak with Joaquín and Mary, who were also eager to interact with him. In this exchange, Ali is doing all that he can to make sure they understand him while they work together drawing a map of their school. Further, Mary and Joaquín ask questions, use gestures, and engage in actions that Ali responds to. And they, in turn, respond to him. Also, Ali takes up and uses the language of his peers, as when he says "Later."

In analyzing both Kenji's and Ali's interactions, we want to emphasize their agency in both making sense of English and using language to participate in meaningful activities. Even when newcomers are not yet speaking much English, as in the case of Kenji and Ali, they are actively making sense of the language and actions of those around them. As they begin to understand and speak more, the efforts ELs make to process the language around them is evident in their verbal contributions. In some cases, they rely on what they know about language from their native language. For example, Spanish-speaking newcomer Angelina relies on Spanish grammar when she says "I have 10 years" (in Spanish, *Yo tengo diez años*) or "This is the car of my dad" (in Spanish, *Este es el carro de mi papá*). English learners' active engagement is also evident in their use of ungrammatical forms like *runned* or *buyed*. Their use of these forms suggests that they are overgeneralizing their knowledge of the regular past tense based on their experience with past tense verbs like *walked*, *played*, and *learned*.

Children and young people learn non-native languages as they engage in and make sense of activities, particularly those that matter a lot to them. They assert their agency as language learners through their participation in interactions with others, involving both verbal and non-verbal actions, which enable them to work together to accomplish an activity. As they develop in the non-native language, their participation also develops, and they may take on more leadership in situations or communicate more nuanced meanings.

Myths and Realities Regarding the Learning/ Teaching of Languages and Literacy

In contrast to the meaning- and activity-based perspectives on learning and teaching that we describe in this book, many schools and districts serving English learners, including newcomers, draw on very different assumptions about second language learning. These assumptions have become taken-for-granted beliefs that influence the way schools teach and work with newcomers. We address these assumptions in the following discussion of prevailing myths about second language learning.

Myth 1: *Being proficient in English or any language means correctly using its grammar and vocabulary.*

Reality: *Being proficient in a language means being able to communicate and participate in activities in that language.*

When it comes to knowing a language, users know so much more than grammar and vocabulary. We know which ways of using language or language practices are suitable in certain settings or with certain people. For example, in communities where we have lived, the language used at home with one's siblings is not the same as the language that is used with an elder at a formal event. For example, a greeting to a sibling may consist of a simple "Hey. What's new?" while a more formal "How do you do? It's such a pleasure to meet you" is appropriate when greeting your grandmother's friend for the first time.

It is important to note that these language practices vary across communities. For example, in Laura's family, taking leave of companions at a party among middle-class Colombians entails shaking the hand of each companion and saying something complimentary about the time you have spent with that individual and/or your wish to see them again (e.g., *Tanto gusto en verte*/ So nice to see you. *Espero que nos veamos pronto*/I hope to see you again soon). In contrast, leave-taking in a similar setting in the predominantly white, middle-class community where Cindy grew up entailed thanking the host and briefly saying goodbye to those you encountered on your way out of the door.

Using correct grammar and vocabulary is not necessarily associated with being able to communicate in English. Learners who have had access to a curriculum that focuses on the correct production in English of, for example, pronouns, verb tenses, and word order, do not necessarily learn how to use English in real-world contexts. Take the case of 10-year-old Bao, who took English each year while attending elementary school in China. The English curriculum at her school was organized around a set of grammatical structures that were introduced to her via dialogues she was required to memorize. Once she and her classmates memorized the dialogue, the teacher focused students' attention on the different structures contained in the dialogue. For example, she would have students complete worksheets on which they would fill in blanks in sentences by providing the correct grammatical form, such as a verb tense (e.g., *Yesterday I (walk)* _____ *to the store with Mary.*). Bao was among the most accomplished students in her class, earning As. To Bao's surprise, her experiences in school did not help her once she immigrated to the U.S. Having had no experience using English to accomplish real-life activities, she was unable to communicate with her classmates. For example, she could not ask for directions to the bathroom or understand classmates' questions about where she came from and whether or not she wanted to play with them.

Many non-native English speakers whose English may not be grammatically correct all the time may be able to use English in ways that native speakers may not be able to. For example, Antonio, a Spanish speaker who came to the U.S. as a young adult, often reverses adjectives and nouns, resulting in utterances like *paper toilet* instead of *toilet paper* or *control remote* instead of *remote control.* However, as an economist who has worked for 40 years writing reports in English that explain and project his company's expenditures, he is viewed as an expert. Indeed, part of his job is to review and edit the writing of his colleagues, including those who grew up speaking English.

Myth 2 : *Being bilingual is the same as being a native speaker of two languages. That is, a bilingual person is someone who has fully mastered two linguistic systems.*

Reality : *The language abilities of bilingual or multilingual people vary depending on the contexts and situations in which they use language.*

Consider your own linguistic repertoire. Even if you speak only English, do you use language with equal facility in all contexts and situations? Are you just as effective when explaining the intricacies of building a new foundation for a house as you are when talking about what you did on a family vacation? The same holds for bilingual and multilingual people growing up in environments in which different languages are used in different settings and situations. For example, Cindy routinely uses Spanish with family members in Bogotá, Colombia, and is quite adept when it comes to using Spanish to talk about topics they routinely discuss, such as household activities and the health of different family members. However, English is the language she uses when talking with colleagues about language policy, a topic she has read and written about in English. Not surprisingly, she struggles when it comes to using Spanish to talk about language policy.

When teachers encounter newcomer students who are particularly adept at using English for certain purposes and in certain contexts, we cannot assume that those same children are as adept in other contexts. For example, although six-year-old May Lim uses English easily and fluently while engaged in play with her friend Rene, she is not as successful when explaining what photosynthesis means in English to her friend Sylvia. Simply put, our language abilities are often stretched across languages largely due to the situations and contexts in which they are used.

Myth 3: *Newcomers cannot learn academic content in English until they are proficient in the language.*

Reality : *Newcomers can learn about many things as they learn English. As they do, they gain access to knowledge that enhances their English.*

Teachers and school-based personnel often claim that they can't include newcomers in English-medium content-area classes and activities until they have learned English. This can lead to newcomers being left out of classroom activities. For example, we have observed in classrooms where newcomers work alone, drawing, coloring, filling out simple worksheets, or using online language-learning apps while the rest of the class is participating in, for example, science experiments or book discussions.

As we describe in the chapters that follow, meaningful activities can provide newcomers with rich opportunities for engaging with and learning both content and English if teachers differentiate and scaffold instruction in ways that accommodate newcomers. By putting off content instruction, we are denying newcomers access to the academic experiences that are available to other students. Also, many newcomers who have been educated in their home countries often come with considerable content knowledge, which they can draw on while learning content in English.

Myth 4: *Teachers should not allow newcomers to use their native language in the classroom as that will retard their English language development. After all, the more exposure youngsters have to English, the better.*

Reality: *When used purposefully and strategically, newcomers' native languages can support their academic and English development and help them feel comfortable in a new school setting.*

It can be very helpful for newcomers to have opportunities to use their native language to make meaning of talk and text in English. For example, in the following scenario, Anita and Felipe use Spanish to make sense of a text they are reading in English.

SCENE: A fifth-grade independent reading time

PARTICIPANTS: Felipe is from a mountainous part of Ecuador near Quito. Anita is from Northern Mexico. They are both fifth graders and have been in the U.S. for a little over a year. They both speak Spanish.

SCENARIO: Felipe and Anita are reading a section in English from *In My Family/En Mi Familia* by Carmen Lomas Garza. It is called "Cleaning Nopalitos" and is accompanied by a colorful picture of a gray-haired man and his granddaughter. The man is using a knife to cut off the thorns from a nopal, or prickly pear cactus, which then fall into a nearby bucket. A plate of nopales without their thorns is on a table to his side. Felipe and Anita are taking turns to each read a few lines.

FELIPE: (*Reading*) "He's shaving off the thorns . . ." *¿Qué son las cositas que está quitando?*/What are the things he's taking off? (*He points to the thorns in the picture on the accompanying page.*)

ANITA: *Son las espinitas. Los thorns*/They're the spines. The thorns. *¿No sabes que estes son nopales y tienen espinas?*/Don't you know that these are prickly pear cactuses and that they have spines? (*Anita points to the picture of the nopal that is being shaved.*)

FELIPE: *¿Nopales?*/Prickly pear cactuses? *¿Qué son nopales?*/What are prickly pear cactuses?

ANITA: *Es una planta que trae espinitas.*/It's a plant with spines.

FELIPE: *Nunca he visto esta planta.*/I've never seen that plant. *¿Qué van a hacer con esta planta?*/What are they going to do with that plant?

ANITA: *Van a cocinar estos pedazos y luego los comen.*/They're going to cook these pieces and then eat them. (*She points to the plate of nopales that have been dethorned.*)

FELIPE: *¿De veras?*/Really? *Yo no como plantas con espinas.*/I don't eat plants with spines) *¿Qué tal son?*/What do they taste like?

ANITA :   *¿Los nopales?*/Prickly pear cactuses? *Son sabrosos.*/They're delicious.

As can be seen in this scenario, Felipe's understanding of the text was helped enormously by being able to converse with Anita in their shared language, Spanish. It is likely that when he encounters other texts in which the prickly pear cactus is mentioned (which is not uncommon in books for children set in the southwestern U.S.), he will come already knowledgeable about what it is, how it is used, and how it is prepared. Being able to use one's native language in order to make meaning, to clarify, and to contribute to classroom discussions is a very important resource for newcomers. Also, providing students with opportunities to use their native languages in school helps them to develop and sustain the languages and cultural practices they bring to school.

Myth 5: *The four major language modalities must be taught separately and in a specific order, from listening (aural, receptive) to speaking (oral, productive) to reading (receptive) to writing (productive).*

Reality: *All modalities can be learned and taught in tandem and can complement one another.*

While it is true that listening often precedes speaking, it would be a mistake to limit newcomer students' learning experiences to just listening exercises or activities; instead, ELs often develop listening while drawing, writing, and trying out the language and observing the responses of others.

In the case of newcomers who have been educated in another language that has a written form, they often find it helpful to see written English while developing their listening comprehension. For example, when a teacher talks from or refers to charts posted in the classroom or reads from a big book or projected text, newcomers can use the print to help them make sense of the teacher's talk. Spoken language is fleeting, and a newcomer must learn how to parse a quickly flowing stream of English into meaningful chunks to make sense of it. Printed language, in contrast, can be re-read and pondered, allowing students more time to make sense of it. In print, it may also be easier to recognize cognates, words that have the same root in different languages. Cognates often look similar across languages and may sound similar, but they may also sound very different in English and the child's native language.

Myth 6: *Learning a non-native language follows a universal and fixed order.*
Reality: *Language does not develop in a linear or uniform way for all non-native language learners.*

Newcomers take different paths and progress at different speeds as they learn English. While there are certain patterns that tend to characterize it, there is no one path when it comes to learning a non-native language. A variety of factors may account for the variation in language learning processes and trajectories. For example, Wong Fillmore (1976) observed pronounced differences in the English language learning trajectories of five Mexican-descent kindergarten-aged children. All five had no prior knowledge of English before beginning kindergarten. Shortly after entering kindergarten, they began to use entire phrases like *Right here*, *Lookit*, *Wait a minute*, *Lemme see*, *Gimmee*, and *You know what?*, which sounded very much like their English-speaking peers. The most prolific user of these phrases or formulae, Nora, was also extremely outgoing and friendly. She spent much of her time playing with her English-speaking peers and engaging them in conversations using these formulaic expressions, even though it was clear that she didn't always understand the meaning of the expressions. Nora was also extremely successful as a language learner. By the end of kindergarten, she had surpassed her four non-native

English-speaking peers in her ability to understand and speak English. Wong Fillmore suggests that Nora's outgoing personality and desire to be with and perhaps be like her English-speaking peers contributed to her success as a language learner when compared to her English-learner peers. In working with ELs, we have often found that more outgoing students may be more willing to take risks in speaking English, whereas students who are quieter or shy may speak less early on. However, when they do begin speaking, their English may be more grammatically and semantically accurate.

Being literate in the native language can also affect the paths that newcomers take in acquiring English. Students who come to U.S. schools with strong literacy abilities in their native language often progress more quickly in reading and writing English than peers with little or no literacy in their native language. They also usually have an easier time learning math or science in English because they have previously developed background knowledge in their home countries, as compared to students with interrupted or limited schooling.

It is also important to recognize the varied opportunities newcomers have to engage with English outside of school. For example, a recently arrived child who lives with U.S.-born, bilingual cousins and a bilingual aunt will likely have more access to English than children who live with their newly arrived parents and grandparents who do not speak English.

An important point to make is that language development is not linear and students may go through periods when they appear to regress or backslide. For example, Wong Fillmore (1976) noticed that, while Nora initially used entire phrases that were grammatically correct, her later speech contained more grammatical errors. Upon closer inspection, Wong Fillmore found that Nora had initially memorized entire chunks of language as single units, or formulaic chunks. For example, she memorized the phrase, *How do you do dese?*, which she frequently used with English-speaking peers. Later she used portions of this phrase in utterances that did not conform with English grammar (e.g., *How do cut it?*). Thus, on the surface, Nora's early utterances containing memorized formulae appeared to be more grammatically accurate than subsequent ones that contained the words *How do* and were not part of these memorized chunks or formulae. Teachers may assume that students like Nora have regressed when, in fact, they are making progress.

Teachers must be attuned to the fact that children's language proficiencies are variable and complex and that "errors" are often a sign of language development. Students may first memorize chunks of language, but as they unpack phrases, try out new language, and communicate more complex ideas, their speech can become less accurate. Valdés, Capitelli and Alvarez (2011) examined beginning English learners' story retellings over two to three years. Over time, they found that students' narratives became more complete and complex and incorporated more features of the genre, including dialogue, temporal markers such as *then, next,* and *one day,* and a greater variety of sentence structures and vocabulary. However, as their speech became more elaborated and varied, students made more grammatical errors because they were no longer relying on memorized chunks of English.

Meaning-based Teaching and Newcomers

We began this chapter by arguing for a perspective on language and second language learning and teaching that conceives of language as a means to engage with others and participate in meaningful activity. We then addressed six myths that are prevalent in schools serving ELs. For each myth, we provided a reality that reflects current research and theory on second language acquisition (summarized in the left column of Figure 3.1). We will now discuss six teaching points that align with these understandings about second language development (in the right column of Figure 3.1). These teaching points are foundational to working with newcomers and will be explained briefly below the figure and elaborated on in more depth in the chapters that follow. In 2019, the international professional organization, Teachers of English to Speakers of Other Languages (TESOL), published *Six Principles for Exemplary Teaching of English Learners.* These principles (e.g., create conditions for language learning) are grounded in similar perspectives on language learning and teaching that we explore in this book.

Teaching Point 1: *Instead of teaching language forms and structures in isolation, involve newcomers in activities where they use language to engage in meaningful activity.*

Many of us have experienced language instruction, perhaps in foreign language classes in high school or college, where the focus was on learning discrete features of language, like grammar and vocabulary. We may have practiced how to conjugate verbs, identified the correct word to fill in the blanks in sentences, and practiced formulaic dialogues for different purposes (e.g., meeting new friends, making plans to see a movie). However, when we were actually in a situation that required us to use the language, we found ourselves ill-equipped to communicate fluently. Outside the classroom, speakers talked much faster than our teacher or the speakers in the dialogues we listened to. People outside the classroom had ways of greeting and communicating that didn't match what we'd been taught (e.g., *What's up?* vs. *Good morning. How are you today?*). We couldn't think of the correct verb conjugation or vocabulary fast enough to actually keep up a meaningful conversation. What happened? The problem is we had studied the language, but not how to actually use it for meaningful purposes.

FIGURE 3.1: Understandings about Second Language Acquisition and Related Teaching Points

Understandings about Second Language Acquisition	Teaching Points
Being proficient in a language means being able to communicate and participate in activities in that language.	Instead of teaching language forms and structures in isolation, involve newcomers in activities where they use language to engage in meaningful activity.
The language abilities of bilingual or multilingual people vary depending on the contexts and situations in which they use language.	Create opportunities for newcomers to use language for a variety of purposes and to interact with English speakers.
Newcomers can learn about many things as they learn English. As they do, they gain access to knowledge that enhances their English.	Scaffold newcomers' engagement with rich, age-appropriate content in English.
When used purposefully and strategically, newcomers' native languages can support their academic and English development and help them feel comfortable in a new school setting.	Provide newcomers with opportunities to use all of their language resources in the classroom, including their native languages.
All modalities can be learned and taught in tandem and can complement one another.	Provide activities that use a variety of language modes (speaking, listening, reading, and writing), as well as other modes of expression, such as art and movement.
Language does not develop in a linear or uniform way for all second language learners.	Make instructional decisions based on regularly assessing newcomers' language abilities and needs rather than relying on a scope and sequence described in textbooks.

When planning instruction for newcomers, our entry point should be the goals of the activity we are preparing students to participate in rather than a sequence of grammatical forms or vocabulary we're working through. For example, the third graders in Ms. Tania's class are launching a social studies unit on people who have fought for social justice. Her class includes four newcomer students from Vietnam, El Salvador, and Mexico, as well as 10 other students classified as "English learners." The remaining 10 students are either native English speakers or have been reclassified as Fluent English Proficient (FEP). As she is planning her unit, Ms. Tania thinks through the following questions: *What are the key activities in this unit? What are the language demands of these activities? How will I scaffold my newcomers to participate in these activities and support them to develop the language needed to participate?*

Throughout the unit, Ms. Tania plans a sequence of activities that engage students in inquiry to learn about how and why people have worked for social justice. The class begins by learning about Fred Korematsu, a civil rights activist who resisted the internment of Japanese-Americans during World War II. The class will be using the biographical book, *Fred Korematsu Speaks Up* (Atkins & Yogi, 2017) as an anchor text for their unit. Before reading the book, Ms. Tania uses the *See-Think-Wonder* protocol (Ritchhart, Church, and Morrison, 2011) to study the image that accompanies the first chapter, which recounts Korematsu's experience with racism at a barbershop. *See-Think-Wonder* is often used at the beginning of a unit in order to activate and build students' background knowledge and language, but it can be used at different points in an instructional sequence or unit. There are the following three steps in this activity:

- *Step One: See.* Students study an image carefully (e.g., a picture or photo) and comment on what they see.
- *Step Two: Think.* Students infer information from the image.
- *Step Three: Wonder.* Students ask questions and discuss what they are wondering about the image.

Ms. Tania does not provide much context for the picture, simply explaining that the class is going to read a book about a man named Fred Korematsu. She has strategically planned to launch their study with *See-Think-Wonder* because using an image for their initial inquiry provides an entry point for her newcomers. She has made some intentional decisions about how to scaffold newcomers' participation in the activity and how to use it to surface ideas and language that they will encounter as they read. Students first study the image in their table groups and note what they see. Ms. Tania has placed the newcomer students in groups with students who are bilingual in the newcomers' native languages and are supportive and facilitative so that they can help the newcomers engage in the discussion.

Students then share out with the class in English, and Ms. Tania charts their ideas on a poster with the image pasted to it. She uses arrows to connect the observations to the specific items in the picture to help the newcomers track the conversation. Ms. Tania encourages newcomers to participate through a mix of English and their native language and, with the support of other students, translates their contributions into English on the chart. The class then moves on to what they think or infer from the picture. Again, the students talk in their table groups, followed by a whole-class share-out. Ms. Tania uses another marker to chart what they think, again writing it near the part of the image that elicited that inference. Finally, they move on to questions, first brainstorming in their groups, and then sharing out with the class.

The *See-Think-Wonder* activity generated background knowledge and language, which will help students as they start reading the text. Students observed carefully, inferred and developed hypotheses based on their observations, and posed questions to guide their study. Importantly for the newcomers and other ELs, the class built a rich web of language and environmental print that students could refer to and use as a resource in reading and other later activities.

Because Ms. Tania knew that newcomers might have difficulty with the complexity and length of the text, she prepared a modified, more accessible version of each chapter for her newcomers. (See Chapter 8 for steps to take when modifying text for newcomers and a modified version of one chapter.) She then met with the newcomers in a small reading group to support their reading of the text. After reading the book, the group of newcomers created a captioned picture book of Korematsu's life, using the illustrations that open each chapter and writing an accompanying caption explaining the event in his life and why it was important to his work as a civil rights leader (for an example, see Figure 3.2). Ms. Tania followed a similar routine as the class studied different social justice leaders. The collaborative books her newcomers made were published and became favorites in the class library.

FIGURE 3.2: Page from Fred Korematsu Biography Written by Students

When Fred Korematsu was a teenager, he wanted to get a haircut at a barbershop. The barbershop was in Oakland. The barber was racist and said he doesn't cut the hair of Japanese people.

As we have described, newcomers learn English as they engage in purposeful, language-rich activities. The goal is not to transmit a set of language rules or structures to students. Instead, it is making sure that newcomers learn how to accomplish things (e.g., investigate, read, communicate, and express ideas in English). Even though newcomers have emergent English abilities, it is important that they are intellectually engaged and involved in generating knowledge in collaboration with their peers.

In this approach, teachers can draw students' attention to how English works so that they are also generating knowledge about how speakers and writers use language for different purposes. When Ms. Tania's newcomers were preparing to write the captions for the group book, they studied the captions in other books. They noticed that captions were usually one or two sentences, described key actors and places in the pictures or photos, and explained when the event occurred. After this, Ms. Tania's newcomer students returned to the original *See-Think-Wonder* charts and the texts they had read and highlighted words and phrases that would be important to use as they wrote each caption. She also taught them about past-tense verbs, which they used when describing the photos.

Teaching Point 2: *Create opportunities for newcomers to use language for a variety of purposes and to interact with English speakers.*

Language is learned in interaction, so newcomers need multiple opportunities throughout the day to use English for different purposes and to interact with English speakers who can provide models of how the language works. For example, we described earlier how Ms. Tania engaged all her students, including newcomers, in using English for a variety of purposes as they learned history—making observations from primary sources, inferring and hypothesizing, wondering and asking questions, learning from texts, and communicating their knowledge by writing captions that could teach others about social justice leaders.

When organizing activities for their class, teachers frequently use small groups, pairs, and triads to facilitate the learning of their students rather than relying exclusively on large group instruction. This is a good strategy to use, particularly when newcomers are in the class. However, simply grouping students randomly often doesn't work as the newcomers can end up being isolated without a meaningful role in the group. Instead, it is important to take into account students' socio-emotional and academic strengths and growth areas. Students who are empathetic and facilitative are often good partners for newcomers. Also, students need to be taught how to interact successfully in groups, including how to include and support newcomers. Useful strategies include the following:

- Keep the materials in the center of the table to make sure everyone gets to observe or investigate with the materials.
- Ask and encourage newcomers to share what they think.
- Help newcomers translate their ideas if they don't know how to say something in English.

We have learned that it is very helpful to try out different groupings and observe carefully to see which pairings or small-group configurations succeed. In some cases, our best efforts at pairing students don't work out, despite taking care when placing students. For example, Melissa Granada, a fifth-grade teacher in a large metropolitan school district serving newcomers and English learners from a variety of backgrounds, thought that Margarita, a newcomer from El Salvador, would enjoy working with Elena, a second-generation student of Mexican-American background. She was surprised to observe these two students arguing rather than sharing their writing, which, in the case of Margarita, was a series of pictures. Later, Melissa observed Margarita and May Lim (a native speaker of Chinese) having a very animated exchange in English. While pointing to Margarita's pictures that chronicled her arrival in the U.S., May Lim asked Margarita to name the people and places in her pictures. Margarita was enthusiastically responding to May Lim's questions. Based on what she saw, Ms. Granada made sure to pair the two students in subsequent activities and groupings. After reflecting on what she had observed, Ms. Granada sought her students' input on grouping arrangements. This led her to ask students to complete the following questionnaire from time to time.

1. Do you like working with students in your table group?
2. Do you think your table group works well together?
    a) If you answered **YES** to this question, why do you think your table group works well together?
    b) If you answered **NO** to this question, why do you think your table group doesn't work well together?
3. Name three people who you would like to work with. (One must be someone you have not worked with this year.)

Ms. Granada read the newcomers' responses and, when she didn't quite understand, she talked with them to clarify. She then used these data to arrange groups, which changed several times in the school year.

Ideally, newcomers should not spend their entire day in classrooms where they only speak with other newcomers. Even in newcomer programs or schools, there are ways to create opportunities for newcomers to interact with English speakers, such as: field trips, adult volunteers, high school student volunteers, and service learning projects with English speakers from all walks of life (e.g., working on a neighborhood garden, organizing a recycling project). We have all worked with newcomers in buddy programs, where English-speaking students are paired with newcomers. For example, Cindy and Katharine have participated in cross-aged tutoring programs in which intermediate-grade students read to and documented the literacy and language development of primary-grade students, many of whom were newcomers (Samway, Whang, & Pippitt, 1995; Vasquez, Pease-Alvarez, & Shannon, 1994). In these programs, students read to and interacted with primary-grade students in English in 20–30 minute tutoring sessions. After these sessions, they discussed what transpired with their teachers and the primary-grade students' teachers. They also collected data on their tutoring sessions and drew on their data when writing letters to their tutees' teachers and parents about their tutees' language/literacy development. Laura worked on a project in which undergraduate students and adult community volunteers worked one-on-one with beginning English learners in an after-school program (Valdés, Capitelli, & Alvarez, 2011). The volunteers engaged the children in language-rich activities, such as reading and talking about books and playing games that require talk.

Teaching Point 3: *Scaffold newcomers' engagement with rich, age-appropriate content in English.*

Although newcomers are beginning to learn English, they can still be engaged in learning content through the language, and engaging in age-appropriate content activities can be a venue for language learning, as described in the previous scenario from Ms. Tania's class. It is important to point out that teachers need to scaffold newcomers' participation in content instruction—they will not learn English or content by just being in the room. As we saw in Ms. Tania's history unit, this scaffolding takes intentional planning and attention to newcomers.

Inquiry-based science can also provide rich opportunities for integrated language and content learning. Hands-on investigations and visual models or diagrams help students make meaning of scientific concepts and help to ground the language students are learning. For example, in Laura's seventh-grade science class, students learned about endothermic and exothermic reactions to create their own heating and cooling packs. They first mixed different chemical combinations, taking the temperature before and after mixing to determine if the reactions were producing heat (exothermic) or absorbing heat (endothermic). They graphed their data to see visually how the temperature was either increasing or decreasing as the chemicals mixed. They then read texts with visual models to learn about what was happening at a molecular level in both types of reactions. Finally, they used their investigation data to design their heating and cooling packs, choosing chemicals that would create either an endothermic or exothermic reaction. They created and tested prototypes and used the data to revise their designs to maximize the cooling and heating capabilities of their packs.

Throughout the process, Laura's newcomers were actively engaged with their groups. They were placed strategically with students who would facilitate their involvement. The hands-on activities and use of visual graphs and models supported students to understand the core scientific concepts. At the end of the unit, students wrote up engineering reports in which they explained the science behind their heating and cooling packs. Newcomers completed a modified assignment, creating models of the packs, using arrows and labels to show how the chemicals had mixed and how the molecular bonds had either broken or been formed in order to release or absorb heat (see Figure 3.3).

FIGURE 3.3: **Model of a Heating Pack**

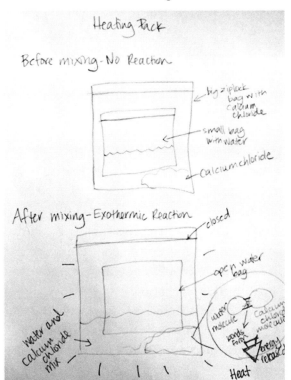

Teaching Point 4: *Provide newcomers with opportunities to use all of their language resources in the classroom, including their native language.*

As newcomers make sense of new content and a new language, they need to be able to draw on all of their intellectual, linguistic, and cultural resources. This means using their native language to access content and engage in conversations on topics they cannot yet address in English. We have encountered many newcomers who have appreciated the opportunity to chat with another student or adult in their native language while in school. Many have told us that they feel much more comfortable or confident when using their native language. They also use their native language to develop friendships with youngsters from similar language backgrounds and gain access to social networks and resources that can help them acclimate to a new country and learn. As a number of researchers have pointed out, identity, as conveyed through language, plays an important role in the academic lives of second language learners.

As we support newcomers in developing English, we want to expand their language repertoire, not replace their native language. There are numerous benefits to being bilingual/multilingual and biliterate/multiliterate, from enhancing one's cognitive abilities, to communicating and maintaining ties to family and cultural identity, to opening up multiple career possibilities as students get older.

As defined by Ofelia Garcia (2009), translanguaging refers to the use and combination of multiple languages among individuals, like newcomers, who are developing bilingualism/ multilingualism. Researchers have described many occasions when newcomers use translanguaging practices (e.g., Orellana, 2009; Valdés, 2003; Vasquez, Pease-Alvarez, & Shannon, 1994). These practices include using bilingual dictionaries or translation software; code switching; translating and interpreting; and using different languages for different modalities (e.g., English for reading and Spanish for discussing and writing about reading). As newcomers develop their abilities to produce English, they will often communicate in a combination of their native language and English. They may also use their native language to make sense of text in English, as we saw in the example involving Felipe and Anita talking about *nopales* earlier in this chapter. Often, newcomers are able to comprehend English far beyond what they can produce, and they can show their comprehension quite effectively via their native language.

While valuing and encouraging the use of students' native languages, we must also ensure that we are providing opportunities for them to take risks and develop new competencies in English. Teachers must make the basis for language choice expectations clear to students. In doing so, we should not pit one language against another, but understand the importance of linking language choices to particular goals. For example, Laura works with Spanish-speaking middle-grade students and is explicit about using Spanish with newcomers to preview an activity. She then explains that she is switching to English and, even though she knows the students won't understand every word she says, she is using English so that they work to expand their abilities in English. They discuss and practice listening strategies that help them gain as much meaning as possible. When they engage in reading activities, she makes it clear that beginning newcomer students may express their understanding in Spanish because this helps her see how they are making sense of the English text. As they move into more structured speaking and writing tasks, the expectation is that students use as much English as possible and she and their peers support them with words or phrases they need to communicate in English.

Teaching Point 5: *Provide activities that use a variety of language modes (listening, speaking, reading, and writing), as well as other modes of expression, such as art and movement.*

Newcomers are often placed in classrooms where little or no accommodation is made to ensure their understanding of what is going on around them. Sometimes teachers' efforts to address this are based on inaccurate assumptions. For example, when eight-year-old Piedad, a recent arrival from Guatemala, who is a native speaker of Mam, was enrolled in Mr. Kent's second-grade class, he paired her with Raul, a Spanish speaker of Mexican descent, thinking that Raul could explain assignments and classroom routines to Piedad in Spanish. Piedad did not understand Raul's explanations because she did not understand Spanish and, after a few minutes, turned away from him and began to doodle using the pencil that Mr. Kent had given her to complete an assignment.

To ensure meaningful interactions involving newcomer students like Piedad, classrooms should be places where a full range of multi-modal resources can facilitate newcomers' interactions and make language comprehensible for newcomers. In the example from Ms. Tania's third-grade classroom, students launched their study of each social justice leader by studying pictures or photos. Talk was grounded in the images and Ms. Tania charted students' contributions around the pictures to help newcomers track the conversation. This also created a rich bank of print that could support newcomers' language use throughout the unit. In a similar way, fifth-grade teacher, Lisa Arellano, drew a scientific model as she described where falling stars originate in the solar system. She drew the sun and other planets, as well as the asteroid belt, and labeled each component as she narrated her explanation. This use of visual supports helps newcomers both comprehend the language input and make sense of the scientific content. As described in the seventh-grade science example above, newcomers can also communicate a great deal of meaning via scientific models and other visual representations.

In addition to visuals, movement and hands-on activities such as the following support comprehension and language development:

- Science experiments;
- Total physical response activities where students enact or mime different actions described in English (described in Chapter 5: Developing Newcomers' Listening and Speaking);

- Hands-on investigations of historical artifacts;
- Readers' theater (described in Chapter 6: Developing Newcomers' Reading);
- Sensory activities, where students develop descriptive language as they investigate natural materials with different textures, colors, and other qualities; these can be used as a launching point for poetry or activities where students write riddles; and
- Theater activities (described in Chapter 8: Engaging Newcomers in Content Learning).

Teaching Point 6: *Make instructional decisions based on assessing newcomers' language abilities and needs rather than relying on the scope and sequence described in textbooks.*

As we have described in the previous sections newcomers develop language and content while participating in increasingly more complex conversations with the support of others. We stretch and expand newcomers' capabilities by involving them with a rich, meaningful, and challenging curriculum. This requires intentional scaffolding so that newcomers can participate along with their peers, including more intermediate or advanced English learners, as well as native English speakers. Along the way, teachers make countless decisions about how to scaffold and support their newcomers, including the following:

- Whether or how much to modify a text;
- How to pair or group a newcomer with supportive peers;
- How much to rely on the native language;
- How to modify their own use of English or use visuals, gestures, and movement to support comprehension; and
- How to scaffold newcomers' writing (e.g., with sentence frames, model texts, or word banks).

All of these decisions require that we know our students, what they can do, and where and how they need to be guided to go to the next level. Every newcomer's path in learning English will vary depending on their past exposure to the language, native language and literacy abilities, and current exposure to English at school and in the community. We have seen some newcomers who are quickly able to read and write in English but are not yet speaking very much in the language. Other newcomers are quick to speak and engage in English but may take more time with literacy.

Newcomers have a challenging task in front of them: learning grade-level content and developing the oral and written English needed to function successfully in a new country. They have no time to lose or linger in learning situations where they are not supported, encouraged, and even pushed. This means that, as teachers, we need to be constantly observing and assessing newcomer students in order to adapt our scaffolds to their changing needs. This assessment process should be the basis of our instructional decisions rather than an English language development program or sequence of linguistic forms and features. In the next chapter, we will describe and provide multiple examples and strategies for using assessment to inform instructional decisions that support and challenge newcomer students.

CHAPTER 4

Assessing Newcomer Students

WHEN PEOPLE HEAR THE TERM *assessment*, they often think that it refers to testing. For us, however, the most valuable form of assessment for teachers and their students has nothing to do with testing. Instead, it is grounded in careful, ongoing documentation of student learning in order to inform our teaching. This type of assessment guides our instruction and is the basis for how we work with and support newcomers' learning in classrooms.

When teachers use assessment to guide their instruction rather than following a textbook sequence or detailed curriculum or syllabus, they are acting as advocates for their newcomer students. That is, they are grounding their teaching in the needs, understandings, and resources that newcomers bring to the classroom. Textbooks and syllabi or curriculum can be useful guides to teachers, but if they are followed exactly as written, as a script, without regard for what students know and where they are developmentally, there is danger that the needs of students are ignored and the teaching will be ineffective.

The two scenarios that follow involve the same teacher, Ms. Chin, and her newcomer students, and they illustrate two forms of assessment: testing and the approach to assessment that we advocate in this chapter. While reading them, please think about what Ms. Chin can learn about the development and needs of one of her newcomer students, Elham. Which tool or procedure will help Elham's teachers understand what she can do and how they can support her continued English language development and content knowledge? Which of them can give Elham feedback on how she is progressing with her English?

SCENARIO 1

Nine-year-old Elham arrived in the U.S. from Yemen in August, just as the school year was starting. She was placed in a fourth-grade class with a few other newcomers from Africa, the Middle East, and Central America, as well as many children of immigrants and a few native English speakers. Ms. Chin, the school's instructional coach and intervention teacher, pulls Elham four days a week for English language development instruction in a small group. It is now February and the school is required to assess all students designated as English learners on the *English Language Proficiency Assessments for California* (ELPAC), the state's yearly assessment of English language proficiency. The exam includes sections on reading, writing, and listening, which are administered in groups, as well as a one-on-one speaking section. Ms. Chin is given the task of assessing more than 100 students this month, which requires her to put her regular work—coaching new teachers, preparing professional development, and teaching intervention groups like Elham's—on the back burner. This often means that she spends up to six weeks doing the ELPAC assessments, time that she cannot devote to teaching the EL students.

Today, Ms. Chin pulls all the fourth graders who are English learners, including Elham, for the listening portion of the test. Elham is struck by the change in her teacher's demeanor. Ms. Chin is usually patient and kind, always making sure Elham understands what to do and encouraging all her attempts to express herself in English. However, today Ms. Chin sternly instructs the students to sit quietly as she hands out the test booklets, Scantron answer booklets, and number two pencils. Elham looks around confused. Apart from anything else, she has never seen a Scantron booklet.

When all the materials have been distributed, Ms. Chin reads aloud the scripted directions: "Today you will be taking the listening portion of the test. Turn to page 2 in your answer booklet and page 4 in your test booklet . . . ." Elham sees the other students opening their booklets and does the same, trying to look at her neighbors' pages to see if she's doing the right thing and is on the right page. Another student, Yesenia, begins to help her, but Ms. Chin reminds them that it is a test and they must work individually and silently. As they begin the test, Ms. Chin plays several recorded explanations and dialogues from her laptop and then instructs the students to bubble in their answers—students have to listen to the passage, but the possible answers are printed in the test booklet and students record their answers in their Scantron booklets.

At first, Elham tries to match the few words she recognizes in the recordings to the words printed in the A, B, C, and D choices on her paper. For number one, she bubbles both B and C. "Just choose one," Ms. Chin whispers, when she realizes Elham has bubbled in two answers. "Is it this one or this one?" she asks, pointing to the B and C options. Elham gives her a wide-eyed and confused look. "Just do the best you can," Ms. Chin whispers, as she pats Elham on the shoulder. Elham continues coloring in different circles and then, finally, gives up after question 10. She sighs and puts her head down on the desk.

Ms. Chin dismisses the students back to their regular classrooms at the end of the testing period, telling them she'll see them tomorrow for the writing test. She studies the list of one-on-one speaking tests she still needs to complete and maps out how many days it will take her to finish these tests so she can return to teaching her intervention groups. She knows that the school won't receive students' scores for another six months and wonders why she's even doing this. By then, it will be the start of a new school year, and Elham's listening abilities will surely have progressed beyond what they were today.

SCENARIO 2

The next month, Ms. Chin has finally finished the testing and pulls Elham for her regular ELD group, along with other third- and fourth-grade students who have arrived in the U.S. within the last year or so. She has built her ELD curriculum around the theme of environments since it is foundational to the science curriculum that both grade levels are studying in class. Today, they are beginning to explore the creek environment. The school has a local creek that students have briefly visited when they took a walk around the neighborhood; they will be restoring the creek as part of a service-learning project.

Ms. Chin uses a pictorial input chart. Before the class, she has lightly drawn a creek habitat in pencil to introduce key components of the environment. When the lesson starts, she explains to the students that today they will be learning more about the creek they visited (see Figure 4.1). She takes colored markers and traces over the pencil as she describes the creek habitat to her students: "Here is the water in the creek. (*She traces the outline of the creek, shades the water light blue, and labels the creek.*) Many animals live in the water. One animal that lives in the water is the crayfish. (*She traces over the crayfish and labels it.*) It lives under rocks in the creek. (*She traces over the rocks and labels them.*) The crayfish walks on its legs. (*She traces over the legs of the crayfish.*) It has two big pincers, which it uses to grab its food. (*She points to the pincers, makes a pincer gesture with her fingers, and demonstrates how the crayfish brings food to its mouth.*) What do you think it eats?" Students suggest animals and plants, and Ms. Chin affirms their ideas, explaining, "Yes, crayfish eat a lot of different things. They eat plants like algae, small fish, and even other dead crayfish." (*She points to pictures of each of them as she talks about them.*) She continues describing a few other animals in the creek ecosystem, including their body parts, or structures, that help them survive (*while tracing over and labeling them*).

When Ms. Chin finishes, she asks students to write or draw important ideas they

FIGURE 4.1: Pictorial Input Chart

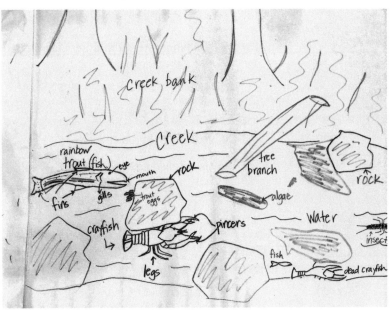

learned about the creek habitat and the animals who live there. Elham writes *water, rocks in creek. Crayfish, fish, insects in creek.* She draws pictures of the animals that Ms. Chin has described and labels them, showing the crayfish eating a plant (see Figure 4.2).

Ms. Chin then asks students to draw a line below what they've drawn or written and share their ideas with a partner; Elham shares with Yesenia. Ms. Chin has deliberately paired the two girls as Yesenia has been in the U.S. for more than a year and is more fluent in English; also, Ms. Chin thought they would work well together and help each other.

After this sharing, Ms. Chin asks the students to add any new ideas that came up in their conversations. Next, the students brainstorm with Ms. Chin

FIGURE 4.2: Elham's Sketch of What She Learned about Creek Life

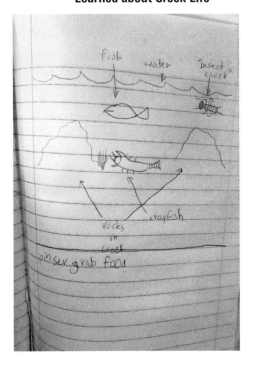

questions they have about creeks and what lives in them, which Ms. Chin writes on chart paper (see Figure 4.3).

FIGURE 4.3: Questions That the Students Generated

* Where does the creek water come from?

* Where does the creek go to?

* Do big fish live in the creek?

* Why is it called a creek and not a river?

* What plants live in or near creeks?

After school, Ms. Chin looks at the students' work to figure how much of her explanation they understood on their own and after speaking with their partners. Ms. Chin notices that, on her own, Elham could label components like water and rocks, as well as the different animals. She is pleased to see that Elham knows how to make use of the environmental print around her (e.g., a chart with pictures of creatures and plants found in creeks, posted near the pictorial input chart) and has grasped the meaning of key terms in Ms. Chin's explanation. Elham also understood one animal-food relationship (crayfish-plant) that Ms. Chin had described. Elham did not label or write about any key body parts on her own, but after speaking with Yesenia, she added *pinser* (pincers) *grab food*. From these data, Ms. Chin decides to have a quick conference with Elham about body parts of creek creatures using a sheet of labeled pictures, a copy of which Elham can keep in her science folder to use as a resource.

When considering these two scenarios, it is clear that the first scenario, the ELPAC test, would provide very dated information and would be of little use, if any, to Ms. Chin or Elham's other teachers. It is a test and does not assess Elham's knowledge and use of English in real-life situations, such as reading, writing, listening, and speaking, inside and outside the classroom. It is intended to assess and track students' development, but it doesn't do this very well either, as it generates a score of 1 to 5 and a student who has actually made tremendous progress can remain in the same score band for more than a year.

In contrast with scenario 1, the second scenario shows how Ms. Chin used assessment in order to find out what Elham had understood about a real phenomenon, creek life, and what she was able to express about this phenomenon in writing and through drawings. This assessment provided Ms. Chin with current, valuable data that helped her plan future instruction.

Testing for Accountability

With the current focus on testing for accountability, students experience increasing amounts of testing in schools and ELs are tested even more than their native English-speaking counterparts. A 2012 report found that, nationwide, states spend $1.7 billion a year on standardized testing (Chingos, 2012). This figure may actually underestimate spending because it was computed before states transitioned to computer-adapted tests, which require schools to purchase hundreds of computers for students to take the tests. In addition, a great deal of staff time is spent administering and managing testing, time which could be better spent working directly with students and teachers, as we saw with Ms. Chin earlier.

Federal Testing Requirements for English Learners

Federal policy requires that districts assess the language proficiency and academic achievement of all ELs annually in order to monitor students' progress and make decisions about reclassification. States have adopted different English language proficiency (ELP) assessments, such as ACCESS for ELLs (WIDA, n.d.), which is used in several states, and the English Language Proficiency Assessments for California (ELPAC) (California Department of Education, n.d.). Although states use different EL assessments, all of them must include sections focused on speaking, listening, reading, and writing. U.S. Department of Education guidance on testing ELs can be found at https://www2.ed.gov/about/offices/list/oela/english-learner -toolkit/chap8.pdf.

If students come from homes where languages other than English are spoken, they are flagged for an initial ELP assessment. If designated as an EL, they are assessed each year until they are reclassified as Fluent English Proficient (FEP). According to the U.S. Department of Education (2016), districts are required to send a yearly report to parents of English learners with information about their child's English language proficiency level and the program options that the district offers. After students have been reclassified, districts must continue to monitor the academic proficiency of former ELs for at least two years to make sure they were not reclassified prematurely and are able to be successful academically without English learner services.

Limitations of Federally Required Assessments

The federally required assessment system focuses on monitoring progress— checking that individual students are making sufficient progress each year— and that programs are doing an adequate job serving students. They are often referred to as *high-stakes tests* because districts, schools, and sometimes teachers are penalized for low scores and/or lack of significant progress on the tests.

One major limitation of these assessments and the way in which they are reported is that they are not fine-grained enough to show growth for students at the beginning stages of language development and they do not help teachers determine what they should focus on in their instruction. Students are typically assigned a numeric proficiency level, such as from 1 (beginning) to 5 (advanced) in speaking, listening, reading, writing, and overall English proficiency. Also, a student may be more advanced in one modality, such as speaking, but this may not be reflected in the score. Newcomers can remain at a level 1 for multiple years, despite the fact that they are making progress. The same is true for English-medium content-subject assessments and English language arts assessments.

An example of this phenomenon is Fermin, who emigrated from El Salvador in the middle of sixth grade with a strong educational foundation in Spanish; however, when he arrived, he was unable to read or write in English. A year later, in February of seventh grade, he was able to read excerpts of grade-level texts in English and explain the main ideas in Spanish. Although he didn't understand every word, he could use his knowledge of context and cognates to figure out key information. For example, he read the graphic novel *Ghosts* by Raina Telgemeier (2016) in a teacher-facilitated literature circle group comprised of other newcomers who had arrived within the last year. At the end of this experience, he wrote the following short essay about the book's theme:

THE THEME IN THE BOOK GHOSTS

Ghosts is about two sisters, Cat the old sister and Maya the little sister. In the beginning the two sisters are moving to Bahia de la Luna because the younger sister is sick to breathe and in the area there is not much smoke. The theme of the book is to remember the people who have died.

Then they meet a boy called Carlos and he wants to take them to a tour of ghosts, but the big sister won't go because she is scared. On page 92, a ghost is playing with Maya and Maya never saw before ghosts. Later on page 197, Cat is hugging a ghost and Cat is not scared with the ghost.

On page 154, Maya is making an altar to her grandma because Carlos told her to. Maya is remembering her grandma because she is making the altar and this shows that Maya is loving her grandma and she is remembering her grandma.

Then on page 58, the mom of Cat said, "so I guess after your abuela died. . . . . A lot of traditions died with her." This shows that Cat mom feels bad because she did not follow the traditions when the grandma died and she is talking of the grandma to her daughters.

In conclusion, the theme of Ghosts is to remembering the people who have died. This evidence shows that the characters are remembering the people who have died because everyone in the book speaks of the ghosts and the ghosts are people who died. This message is important because you have to remember your family because your family is important in your life.

Fermin also played the leading role in a readers' theater rendition of scenes from the book that exemplified how the main character, Cat, had changed through the course of the novel. Despite the significant growth Fermin made in his English reading, writing, speaking, and listening during that year, he was still designated a Level 1 on the ELPAC, the same score he received on the assessment in sixth grade, when he had just arrived and spoke only a few words in English. Clearly, this score did not represent Fermin's growth and was not useful to the school or his teachers in designing instruction that would support his continued growth. In addition, when the test score information was sent home to his family, it did not provide him or his parents with accurate or helpful feedback.

As mentioned earlier, these tests are intended to monitor students' progress and evaluate program effectiveness. As Fermin's example shows, these tests do not achieve either. And, for teachers, they are of limited use for a number of reasons. To begin with, they are administered only once a year and teachers do not receive their students' scores until many months after the test was administered. By the time scores reach the school (and the teachers), they are several months old and are no longer an accurate representation of students' competencies. Also, a common problem with these tests is they assert that they are assessing one modality when one or more additional modalities are required. For example, in the earlier first scenario involving Elham, the listening portion of the test required that she listen to a taped situation, then read the possible responses in a test booklet, and then mark her selection in a Scantron booklet. Clearly, this is not just a listening assessment by virtue of having to read and then mark a response in a booklet, which essentially invalidates the assessment's results. In addition, a very limited number of items are used to assess a student's capabilities in a given modality, which means that if even one item is not answered accurately, it can dramatically affect a score.

English learners who take federally mandated tests should receive appropriate exemptions and accommodations (e.g., reading being assessed in the native language). Newcomers in their first year in the U.S. are exempted from English language arts tests and should receive language accommodations on math and science tests. (More information about test accommodations can be found at https://files.eric.ed.gov/fulltext/ED563044.pdf.) In many states that have computerized tests, these accommodations are pre-programmed into students' tests. For example, on math and science tests, directions and test questions may be translated, or students may be able to hover over certain words to see translations. For students to benefit from such accommodations, however, they will need to be oriented to them and they must be able to read them in their native language, which assumes that they are literate in that language.

Parental Right to Opt Out Their Children from High-Stakes Tests

While the Every Student Succeeds Act (ESSA) mandates that 95% of students in every school take standardized tests, it does not mean that parents must comply with the mandate. Indeed, ESSA authorizes states to allow parents to opt their children out of tests if they wish. Ten states have passed laws that allow parents to opt their children out of standardized tests: Alaska, California, Colorado, Idaho, North Dakota, Minnesota, Oregon, Pennsylvania, Utah, and Wisconsin. No states have laws that prohibit parents from opting their children out of standardized testing. According to FairTest, a non-profit organization that works to end testing practices that it believes adversely affect students (www.fairtest .org), no school has ever lost federal funding because parents opted out of having their children participate in standardized testing. However, many districts provide parents with information that may leave them with the impression that opting their children out of testing is impossible. Because these tests can often be very stressful for newcomers, do not capture a child's progress and needs, and are of little use when making instructional decisions, we urge teachers to let caregivers/parents know that they have certain rights regarding the administration of standardized tests. FairTest's site includes information about the following:

- *Explanations regarding the overuse and misuse of standardized tests*: This includes how testing and test preparation often drive the curriculum in schools and eat up valuable learning time.
- *Suggestions for how caregivers/parents can opt out or refuse to have children take government-mandated standardized tests*: This includes specific information about how caregivers/parents can contact school principals to express their wish to opt their children out of tests.

Assessments That Help Teachers Make Informed Instructional Decisions

In contrast with high-stakes tests, we have found that assessment is beneficial when it helps us target our instruction to the unique strengths, backgrounds, and needs of newcomer students. As described in Chapter 1, newcomer students arrive in U.S. schools with a variety of educational experiences and academic backgrounds. Also, as described in Chapter 3, we know that language does not develop linearly or uniformly for ELs, and newcomers will take different paths and progress at different speeds as they acquire English. As advocates for our students, we must focus on teaching students rather than programs, and assessment tailored to students is, in essence, what enables us to do this. In the remainder of this chapter, we will explore this type of assessment.

How is assessment different from grading, or glancing at student work after a lesson, or simply being a reflective teacher? Here we specify and then discuss four key principles of this type of assessment, as described by Alvarez, Ananda, Walqui, Sato, and Rabinowitz (2014):

1. *It focuses on students' engagement in meaningful tasks.* The focus of assessment should be on obtaining and analyzing evidence about how students make sense of and engage in meaningful academic activity or tasks. When assessing students' language and literacy development, the focus is on their use of oral language, reading, and writing.

2. *It informs learning and teaching:* Unlike standardized assessments, where the goal is to monitor achievement for accountability and/or student progress, assessment is most useful when it has an explicit goal of improving learning and teaching. As a result of this kind of assessment, teachers revise the way they teach and provide targeted feedback and instruction to help enhance student learning.

3. *It elicits evidence about learning and teaching using a variety of data and tools:* Teachers rely on a variety of activities and experiences to assess what students are able to do, what they know, and where they struggle.

4. *It enables students to become self-regulated and autonomous learners:* Students are at the center of the learning and teaching enterprise, and meaningful assessment engages students in self-assessing and using feedback to improve their own learning. By partnering with other students as they self-assess, students understand and sometimes co-construct learning goals and take action. In the process, they develop more efficacy and ownership over their own learning.

Assessment Focuses on Students' Engagement in Meaningful Tasks

Aligned with the principles described in Chapter 2, we advocate assessing students' performance as they engage in the kinds of meaningful activity that is foundational to the way we teach. Thus, instead of having them take a test, we involve them in learning experiences in which they use language, literacy, and content purposively. We use evidence of what students do, including their actions and what they read, wrote, or talked about during those activities to assess what they learned. For example, in Scenario 2 earlier in the chapter, Ms. Chin assessed her students' understanding of what they were learning about creek habitats through looking at the students' drawings and writing about the animals they had observed at the creek. Her analysis of those texts, as well as the notes she took while observing students during the unit, provided her with guidance for subsequent teaching.

When assessing newcomers, it is important to make sure to use assessment-related activities they are able to engage in. Often, newcomers are expected to be able to participate in activities that are tailored to children who are proficient in English. However, newcomers frequently need scaffolds or supports that enable them to participate in a particular activity. For example, Ms. Johnston wanted to find out how much English one of her fourth-grade newcomer students, Francisco, could understand and speak. So, she decided to assess his English through a storytelling activity that used objects as she had noticed that when newcomers used objects and puppets, they appeared to be less self-conscious and more likely to speak. The following scenario describes how this went.

SCENE: A fourth-grade class

PARTICIPANTS: Francisco came from Honduras and has been in the U.S. for two weeks. His teacher is Ms. Johnston.

SCENARIO: Ms. Johnston knows from records that came with Francisco that he went to school for four years and can read in his native language, Spanish. In class, he pays careful attention but does not speak with his peers or teacher. Ms. Johnston has noticed that when it is time to read, he selects books that are about animals. One day, she takes him to a table near the class library and places some miniature, plastic wild animals, trees, and an upside-down bottle lid that is blue on the table in front of them. She surrounds some of the animals with the trees and puts other animals by the bottle lid (*a pond or watering hole*). She begins to tell a story while manipulating the props or objects; she video records Francisco's story using her cell phone and then transcribes their brief storytelling experience for later review.

MS. JOHNSTON: (*Pointing to the trees*) This is a jungle. There are lots of trees (*while pointing to the trees*) and some animals (*while pointing to a tiger and two elephants*). The tiger (*pointing to the tiger*) and the elephants (*pointing to the elephants*) are in the jungle (*gesturing to all the trees*). The tiger is thirsty (*mimes being thirsty*) and goes down to the water (*pointing to the pond and then moving the tiger to the pond*). The other animals are scared (*mimes being afraid*). Two deer run away from the tiger (*moves two deer away in a running motion*).

Ms. Johnston then gestures to Francisco that he can take over telling the story.

FRANCISCO: *El tigre* ("the tiger"). He scare *animales* ("animals"). He want water. *Y comida* ("And food"). He hunger. He run. *Captura* ("capture") animal (*showing the tiger catching a giraffe*). He eat *jirafa* ("giraffe") (*showing the tiger hitting the giraffe and miming eating*).

MS. JOHNSTON: Then what happened?

(*She waits for Francisco to continue, but he doesn't. Instead, he smiles at her.*)

> **MS. JOHNSTON:**   All the animals near the water run away (*moving the four-legged animals away quickly*) or go into the water (*moving a crocodile onto the bottle lid.*)
>
> **FRANCISCO:**   They OK.
>
> **MS. JOHNSTON:**   Yes, they are. They're safe. That was a good story. Thank you, Francisco.

What did Ms. Johnston learn from this brief exchange with Francisco? Quite a bit, including the following:

- He has some understanding of English.
- He understands more than he can say.
- He can tell a story using props.
- He uses his native language to help communicate.
- He knows how to use mime to convey meaning.
- He knows some English verbs and the present tense (e.g., scare, hunger, run, want, eat).
- He knows some English pronouns (*he, they*).

In fact, whereas Ms. Johnston previously thought Francisco didn't understand much in English, she now knows that he actually understands and can speak quite a bit, particularly for someone who has been in an English-speaking environment for such a short time. She also realizes that she needs to make sure that she uses plenty of visuals, props, and mime/gestures when she teaches. It occurs to her that these strategies would probably be useful when teaching some of her other students who aren't strong auditory learners.

Assessment Informs Learning and Teaching

Through using assessments that involve students in meaningful activities, we gain insights into what they know and/or can do, as described above in the scenario involving Francisco and Ms. Johnston. That knowledge is key when it comes to deciding how to support and teach students in ways that are tailored to their needs. For example, in her work with Francisco and other English learners, she learned that they could tell stories with the support of props and miming. Consequently, she decided to build the use of props and dramatic enactments into the way she approached reading stories by enacting scenes in those stories. For example, while reading the beginning excerpt from *Caps for Sale* by Esphyr Slobodkina (1940), she took on the role of the cap vendor. As she pointed to pictures on an enlarged version of the book, she read and acted out the story, as described in the following chart.

What Ms. Johnston Read	What Ms. Johnston Did
Once there was a peddler who sold caps.	Wearing an outfit similar to the one in the illustration, Ms. Johnston held up a cap.
But he was not like an ordinary peddler, carrying wares on his back.	Ms. Johnston wagged her finger and hoisted a large bag full of hats onto her back.
He carried them on top of his head.	Ms. Johnston placed a stack of 10 caps upon her head and followed the reading of the line with an exuberant "Caps for sale!"

Gradually, Ms. Johnston invited students to enact similar scenes. She continued to rely on this approach as she involved children in reading and making sense of increasingly more complex stories. In a few short months, her students were so adept at and delighted with enacting scenes from stories that they asked to put on plays of entire stories for the kindergarteners at their school.

Often, assessment that informs instruction occurs both in the moment (e.g., as teachers make adjustments during a lesson in response to evidence of students' lack of understanding), as well as after a lesson, when teachers examine student work or other data sources. For example, Laura was working with a group of seventh-grade newcomers who had been in the U.S. between six and 18 months. The seven students were all Central American and spoke either Spanish or Mam, an indigenous language. This was their first class and Laura knew very little about their language and literacy abilities. After they read a short chapter in *A Long Walk to Water* by Linda Sue Park (2010), Laura introduced them to a sequencing activity. She had prepared a summary of the chapter and put each sentence on a strip of paper. She asked the students to order all of the events so that they reflected the sequence of events in the text they had just read.

As the students were working, it became clear the task was overwhelming and students were struggling to get started. Although the level of detail in the summary was appropriate for their language levels, there were too many events in the summary for students to sequence. Also, Laura had used different wording from the text, which made it difficult for the students to understand. They had worked hard to make meaning of the text when they first read it, and they needed to see words used in the text. Laura made some adjustments when she realized that the task was poorly planned for most of the students in the group. For example, she took out some of the less important events and guided the group through the task, supporting them to complete it together, instead of individually or in pairs, as she had intended. She also encouraged students to use a strategy that some of them were using—scanning the text for key words in a sentence and placing the corresponding sentence strip next to that event in the text.

Assessment Elicits Evidence Using a Variety of Data and Tools

It is important to collect a variety of assessment data grounded in learning experiences across the curriculum in order to capture as accurately as possible students' strengths, development, and needs. Equally important, for assessment to be feasible for teachers, data must be easy to collect in the midst of a busy day. For example, student work is easy to collect—examples include sketches, writing, diagrams, and exit tickets.

We have also had a lot of success putting a smartphone down to record students' discussions while we circulate or work with a different small group. These brief audio recordings can provide a window into how students use language to negotiate meaning and what they can do without our intervention. Video recording is also relatively easy to do on a smart phone or tablet. Please note, though, that both audio and video recording raise student privacy concerns that are beyond the scope of this book to address. Below we outline some steps to try to address these concerns. But you should always find out—and follow—your school's policy on creating, storing, and using audio and/or video recordings.

- At the beginning of the school year, we let students know we may want to audio and/or video record conversations or presentations in order to help us be better teachers. Each student then has a choice of agreeing or declining to be recorded. We have never had a student refuse to be recorded—they may be a little self-conscious at first, but we have found that they typically enjoy being recorded and later listening to or watching short audio or video clips.
- Also at the beginning of the year, we make a point of informing parents/caregivers, in a language that they understand, that we may wish to audio and/or video record their children, and why. We also give the parents/caregivers a choice of agreeing to this type of recording or

declining on the child's behalf. We recommend that the permission be recorded in writing. Below is a form that we use for this purpose.

Dear Parent/Caregiver,

I am delighted to have your child in my class this year. So that I can better teach children, I sometimes tape-record and/or videotape them. This helps me see what they can do and what I need to teach next. Could you please indicate whether or not you agree to me tape-recording and/or videotaping your child by checking the appropriate boxes below. Thank you very much.

(Name of teacher)

_____ I agree to my child being tape-recorded

_____ I agree to my child being videotaped

_____ I do not agree to my child being tape-recorded

_____ I do not agree to my child being videotaped

Child's Name: _____

Your Name: _____ Your signature _____

Your relationship to the child (e.g., parent, caregiver, legal guardian):

_____

Date: _____

- Ideally, a copy of this form should be prepared both in English and any other language that your students' families speak and sent home with the students for their parent's or caregiver's signature. However, teachers need to be sensitive to the reality that some parents/caregivers may not be literate. (If that is the case for any of your students, you need to find out your school's policy on getting consent from a parent or caregiver who cannot read.)

- We have found that it helps if we explain to students what the release form says and what we are asking of parents/caregivers before it goes home. Back-to-School nights and meetings with parents can provide another way to inform parents/caregivers and answer any questions they may have about recordings.

- Unless both the student and the parent/caregiver agree to the student's being recorded, we take great care not to record that student.

- Once we have confirmed permission to record a student, we keep all recordings that we make throughout the school year in a secure location, but available to show to students to give them the opportunity to hear and see their progress. (Always check your school's policy about how and where you should keep these recordings.)

The following assessment approaches and tools can provide important information about student learning that can inform teaching.

The Role of Careful Observation and Record Keeping

When teachers grade or look at work, they often fail to analyze it for evidence of learning and learning processes, which means that assessment is unlikely to guide future instruction. Observational notes that are focused on what children do during an instructional activity are much more useful. On-the-spot record keeping is the most time efficient (and often the most accurate), but at first, it can sometimes seem overwhelming to take a few moments at the end of an activity to make quick notations on individual students. Teachers we know have different preferred ways of keeping ongoing observational notes or records. Katharine likes to use peel-off labels on which she can write the date, the name of the student, and an observation. See Figure 4.4 below for sample notes on labels that she wrote on Ahmed at the beginning of the school year, soon after Ahmed had arrived at the school. At the end of each day, she peeled off the labels and put them in a binder, one page per student. Elsa prefers to keep ongoing records on a single sheet containing 25 or 30 boxes, with the names of students, one per box; she finds that this helps her make sure to confer with each student at least once every week. Claudia pre-

FIGURE 4.4: Observation Notes on Ahmed Written on Peel-off Labels

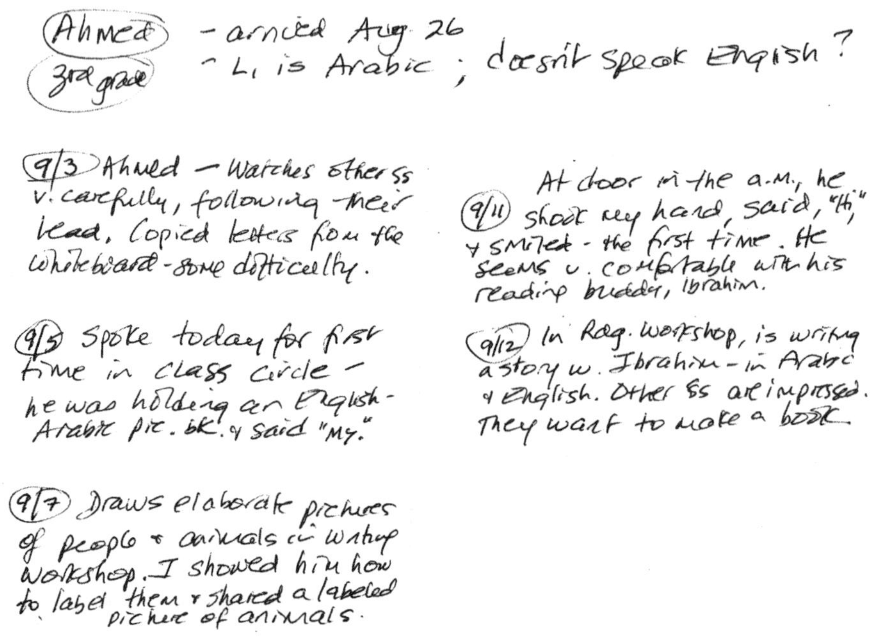
Ahmed 3rd grade - arrived Aug 26 - L1 is Arabic; doesn't speak English?

9/3 Ahmed — watches other Ss v. carefully, following their lead. Copied letters from the whiteboard - some difficulty.

9/5 Spoke today for first time in class circle - he was holding an English-Arabic pic. bk. & said "My."

9/7 Draws elaborate pictures of people & animals in writing workshop. I showed him how to label them & shared a labeled picture of animals.

9/11 At door in the a.m., he shook my hand, said, "Hi," & smiled - the first time. He seems v. comfortable with his reading buddy, Ibrahim.

9/12 In Rdg. workshop, is writing a story w. Ibrahim - in Arabic & English. Other Ss are impressed. They want to make a book.

fers to record her observations in a notebook that has been set up with several pages per student, with tabs for each student for easy access. Jacob prefers to use his cell phone where he records observations for individual students.

Checklists

The checklist is an assessment tool that can facilitate the observation process for teachers. We have found that the most useful checklists are those that focus on a limited number of attributes. For example, fourth-grade teacher Angela Minamoto developed the following English language development checklist with just eight items for her eight newcomer students:

Ms. Minamoto used observation over a three-day period to record what she was able to glean about these students' understanding and use of English. It is deliberately <u>not</u> a comprehensive list. Instead, it focuses on some aspects of language that Ms. Minamoto believed were important at that time and she

	Elsa	Miguel	Hanan	Toni	Tarek	Jakeline	Sonali	Rocío
Can follow single oral directions	√√	√	√	√√	√	√√	√√	√
Can follow complex oral directions	√	--	--	√	--	√	√	--
Uses simple present tense	√ *	√ *	√ *	√ *	√ *	√ *	√ *	√*
Uses present progressive tense	√*	--	--	√*	--	--	--	--
Uses simple past tense	--	--	--	--	--	--	--	--
Participates in choral reading	√√	√	√	√√	--	√√	√√	√
Initiates conversations	√	--	√	√	--	√	√	--
Can ask questions	√ *	--	√ *	√ *	--	√ *	√ *	√ *
√ Does routinely √√ Does some of the time * Non-standard usage -- Does not do most or any of the time								

used it to guide her group ELD instruction. What did Ms. Minamoto learn from this checklist and how did it inform her instruction?

- All of the students could follow single directions at least some of the time (e.g., *Put your paper on my desk.*). However, only half the students could follow multi-step directions (e.g., *Put your paper on my desk, put on your coat, and line up at the door.*). From this, she decided to spend some time focusing on single and multiple directions, including having students give directions to each other.
- All of the students were using the simple present tense some of the time, but only two students were using the present progressive tense. She decided that it would probably be a good idea to teach students when and how to use the simple present and present progressive tenses.
- When referring to the past, the students used the simple present or present progressive tenses (e.g., *Yesterday I play football*, or *Last week we going the store for buy shoe.*). Although none of the students were using the simple past tense, she decided to introduce it as it is such an important tense because so much conversation is around what we thought, did, saw, heard, touched, and/or smelled.
- Miguel, Tarek, and Rocío did not speak as much in English as the other newcomers, but she was not concerned for several reasons. Miguel and Tarek had been in her class for just a couple of weeks and Rocío was very reserved, except on the playground, where Ms. Minamoto had overheard her asking other students "Can I?" and "I go?" when playing ball with them. She decided to introduce some simple scenarios in which students were given a situation and roles and would have to work together in small groups to develop scripts they would then act out. In one situation, students thought the lunch period was too short and they didn't get enough time to play outside; the roles the students had to develop dialogue for were students, the principal, and some teachers.

It is important to note that, in this checklist, although Ms. Minamoto indicated with an asterisk if the students didn't use standard English, she wasn't focused on that. The asterisks referred to grammar, not pronunciation. These were all newcomer students and she was interested in what they were attempting to do in English and whether they were communicating in English. Through her teaching and the learning experiences she offered students, she was confident that, over time, they would become more fluent in English. But, she also knew that it often takes many years to become fluent in a language, and the most important goal is to be able to communicate. Because she wanted to capture growth, she used the asterisks and, over time, the asterisks began to disappear as students became more fluent English speakers.

Ms. Minamoto used checklists frequently, and the items in them changed according to what she was focusing on and the content of instruction. She did not teach English decontextualized from content learning, so checklists often included items related to content units of study (e.g., use of scientific termi-nology in a unit on magnetism; use of dialogue in a memoir-writing unit; and understanding of key events in a unit of study on immigration). She used checklists for individual students (to record individual progress and give her a heads-up on the student's needs), as well as checklists for the whole group, like the one discussed in this section (to inform her instruction and also how and when to group students for instruction).

Oral Samples of Newcomers' Language Use

It can be very helpful to gather samples of newcomers' oral language in a variety of situations (e.g., on the playground; during small-group work in social studies; in pair shares in science or math; during the morning meeting or circle). This is advisable as newcomers' language use can vary consider-ably according to context. We recommend recording short samples in order to accurately capture the students' use of English, using either a recorder or a cell phone, being careful to follow your school's policies for audio and video recording as discussed earlier. For example, Ms. Johnston gained important insights into Francisco's understanding and use of English when they shared a storytelling activity, described earlier, which she recorded on her cell phone.

Children's Texts, Including Writing Samples and Labeled and Unlabeled Pictures

We mention pictures because, for many newcomer students, this is the first step in their development as writers in English. It is important to gather differ-ent kinds of writing (e.g., journal entries, science logs, memoirs, short stories, essays, letters). It is also helpful to gather samples in English and the native language (and other languages in which newcomers are literate), whenever possible. This can be enormously helpful in order to more fully understand what a given newcomer student knows about writing. Writing assessment will be more fully explored in Chapter 7: Developing Newcomers' Writing.

Reading Records

Like writing, it is helpful to gather data on newcomers' reading processes, preferences, strengths, and needs in all languages that they speak, whenever possible, in order to more fully understand their skills, needs, and development as readers. Reading records can include dated lists of books read, including in which language, length, and genre; Clay's concepts of print; and running records. Reading assessments will be more fully explored in Chapter 6: Developing Newcomers' Reading.

Surveys, Questionnaires, and Interviews

It can be very useful to survey students periodically about a range of language, literacy, and content-area issues. For example, a second-grade teacher, Mr. Melo, wanted to know what his students thought about the science unit of study they had just completed on motion, so he designed a brief questionnaire; in the case of two newcomer students, he interviewed them individually and recorded their responses (which also gave him insights into their use of English). The unit had involved doing experiments and writing lab reports, and it lasted six weeks. From the questionnaire results, Mr. Melo learned the children loved the experiments, though they thought the unit went on too long, and hated the tedious lab report writing. In future years, he reduced the length of the unit to four weeks and replaced the laborious lab reports with brief reports about a scientific question each student had, what they did to answer it, what they learned, and new questions they had about motion.

Assessment Enables Students to Become Self-regulated and Autonomous Learners

In order for students to be actively engaged learners, it is important for them to participate in assessing themselves. One key way is to have them set learning goals for themselves every six weeks or so. This can be done for a variety of curricular areas, such as English language development, reading, math, and science. In order to accomplish effective goal setting, we have found it is important to do the following:

- The teacher demonstrates goal setting in a mini-lesson (e.g., in reading workshop, the teacher may say "I want to read books about wild animals"; "I want to spend 30 minutes each night reading"; or "I want to keep a list of words and terms I'm not sure I understand.").
- This is followed by students doing a pair share with a partner, when they talk about their own possible goals.

- This is followed by a whole-group share, when the teacher records on chart paper goals the students generate.
- Students then write or do labeled drawings of their individual goal(s). A prepared sheet can help in this recording process.
- The teacher holds short one-on-one conferences (and small-group conferences with students who have similar needs or are at a similar stage of early English language development). Teachers also contribute their insights to these goal-setting conferences, but ultimately, the goal(s) need to be those that the student wants to work on. These conferences shouldn't last more than about two to three minutes for a one-on-one conference and about five to eight minutes for a small-group conference. However, they may take a little longer with ELs who are very new to English and need more time and support to express their ideas.
- The students and the teacher keep a dated written record of the goal(s) that have been set. (See Figure 4.5 for Alfonso's record.)
- After about six weeks, the students evaluate and record how well they have met their goals in the *Was goal met?* column.

FIGURE 4.5: Alfonso's Goal-setting Record Sheet

Name: Alfonso Grade: 3rd			
Date	Goal	Steps You Need to Take & Support You Need	Was goal met?
Nov. 6	Talk morning circle	Be brayf	Yes
Jan. 8	Know social studies words	Study wid Ibrahim	Most of time
	Read my writing	Read at my tabl	Yes. Now I do.
Feb. 20			
April 2			
May 15			

Alfonso had been in the U.S. for about 6 months but in a U.S. school for a little more than three months when he completed his goal-setting record. His teacher, Mr. Carlos, helped him generate his goal for the fall semester. Mr. Carlos had noticed that Alfonso had begun to talk with peers in pair shares but had always passed in the morning circle. He thought Alfonso needed a little nudge, so he suggested that Alfonso set the goal of speaking up in the morning circle, which Alfonso agreed to.

In January, Alfonso joined two other newcomers for a conference with Mr.

Carlos. Alfonso said he had met his November goal as he had been sharing in the morning circle, which Mr. Carlos concurred with; he congratulated Alfonso on doing this, commenting that what he had shared was very interesting. The group then moved on to setting new goals for themselves. The students talked about not always understanding the science and social studies words (the concepts). Alfonso said that he was OK with most of the science words because he liked science, watched science shows on TV (in English and Spanish), and had studied science in his home country, Costa Rica. However, understanding social studies vocabulary was hard for him, so he put this on his goal-setting sheet. Mr. Carlos made a note to himself that he needed to pay extra attention to making sure that concepts in all subjects, but particularly in science and social studies, were clear to his newcomer and other EL students. Alfonso's second goal for January, re-reading his writing, originated in something that Mr. Carlos had noticed—that the three students rarely re-read their writing. He explained why doing so is important and encouraged them to add that to their list of goals, which Alfonso did. Later that week in writing workshop, Mr. Carlos gave a mini-lesson to the whole class on the importance of re-reading one's writing as he had observed that many students tended to start a new piece rather than re-reading and making revisions to an existing piece.

Student self-assessment can be a very powerful mechanism for students to be aware of their own growth and to help teachers make instructional decisions. Teachers can facilitate this process when using the following tools and approaches.

Students Chart Their Learning

A variety of charts or prompts can be used to help students self-assess, such as *I Know, I Think I Know, and I Don't Know* charts, which help students chart their learning. For example, at the beginning of a unit on the solar system, Mrs. Elliot asked her class of ELD students in grades three through five to each complete a chart of key words related to the unit. The students put a checkmark by each of the words in one of three columns: *I know, I think I know,* and *I don't know.* Before the students worked on their own charts, Mrs. Elliot demonstrated what she wanted them to do by completing a chart on a different topic while talking through and using gestures and sketches to explain why she put checkmarks in each of the columns. At the end of the unit, the students returned to their charts and, using a different colored marker or another symbol, indicated their current knowledge. See Figure 4.6 for the chart Ana María completed at the beginning and end of the unit. The black checkmarks indicate what she thought she knew at the beginning of the unit of study, and the black x's are from the end of the unit of study.

FIGURE 4.6: **Ana María's I Know, I Think I Know, I Don't Know Chart**

Name: Ana María	Solar System Study		
Word or term	I know	I think I know	I don't know
Planet	✓x		
Sun	x	✓	
Rotation	x		✓
Star	x	✓	
Moon	x	✓	
Asteroid		x	✓
Gravitation	x		✓
Orbit		x	✓
Telescope	x		✓

As this chart shows, Ana María thought she had learned a lot. Mrs. Elliot was aware that many scientific words have a Latin base and are cognates in English and Spanish. That is, they look similar, mean the same thing, and often sound similar. Because she had several students who spoke Spanish with family members and friends, including Ana María, Mrs. Elliot spent some time during the unit exploring with students words that are cognates. For homework, she asked the students to check with people they lived with to decide if any of the words were cognates in their home languages. In Ana María's chart, the following pairs are cognates in English and Spanish: planet/ *planeta*, rotation/*rotación*, asteroid/*asteroide*, gravitation/*gravitación*, orbit/*orbita*, and telescope/*telescopio*. Cognates, partial cognates, and false cognates are addressed in Chapter 6: Developing Newcomers' Reading.

Students Assess Their Work

It is a good idea for students to store samples of their work in a portfolio so they can periodically assess their progress in a very concrete way. For example, at the end of a semester, they can analyze their progress, accomplishments, and goals through reviewing their literacy portfolios containing samples of their writing with accompanying letters to readers; their reading records; and their reading response journals. They can then reflect on and write or talk about the following:

- What they were able to do when they first came to this class (e.g., *I do not write English in September.*).
- Here is what I can do now (e.g., *Now I write storys.*).
- Here's what I'd like to be able to do by the end of the next semester (e.g., *I want write poetrys.*).

Until students are familiar with this kind of reflective work, the teacher will need to model the process, followed by students going through their portfolios and then sharing what they find with a peer or peers.

Assessing Newcomers Who May Have Special Needs

The U.S. Department of Education's ED*Facts* data collection sheds light on the number of EL students who have disabilities. In fall 2015, about 713,000 ELL students were identified as students with disabilities, representing 14.7% of the total EL population enrolled in U.S. public elementary and secondary schools (Abedi, n.d.).

Federal law requires districts to identify and provide appropriate services for English learners with learning disabilities. (See Chapter 6 in the U.S. Department of Education Toolkit [2016, 2017] at https://www2.ed.gov/about/offices/list/oela/english-learner-toolkit/chap6.pdf for more detailed information on working with ELs who have or are thought to have a learning disability.) However, it is essential for teachers to understand that being an English learner is not a learning disability. And, if you think there may be a learning disability, newcomers and all ELs need to be evaluated in their native language, whenever feasible, in order to identify whether there is actually a learning disability.

It can be hard to identify learning disabilities in newcomers because they are often grappling with a lot of challenges and transitions (e.g., trauma from family separation and their immigration journeys, adapting to a new culture and community, adjusting to new expectations compared to schools in their home countries, and negotiating everything in a new language). Also, if students have experienced interrupted schooling, they may be just beginning to develop literacy and math skills that are typically associated with younger students. These students are considered SIFE (students with interrupted formal education) or SLIFE (students with limited or interrupted formal education). They do not necessarily have a learning disability and need targeted and age-appropriate instruction.

Learning about a child's educational history through an intake interview can help schools distinguish between SIFE or SLIFE students and students who have struggled with early literacy or math in their home countries because of undiagnosed learning disabilities. Are they just learning to read because they haven't attended much school? Or, did they go to school but were in large classrooms or didn't have consistent teachers each day? Such experiences may lead to students appearing to have learning difficulties, when they simply haven't had adequate educational opportunities. Once they receive appropriate instruction, these newcomer students can make rapid growth.

In other cases, students may have been identified as having learning difficulties or disabilities in their home country—this is essential to know, so that they can get assessed in the U.S. (in their native language) and receive appropriate special education services. Or, children may have attended school in their home countries but struggled because of learning disabilities that were not diagnosed or addressed. They may have been retained and spent multiple years in first or second grade, or they may have been passed through the grades and continued to experience difficulties in school. For example, Katharine was visiting a fourth-grade class and noticed that Angelica had a hard time writing anything, including her name. She was not a reluctant writer, but didn't really know how to write. At the end of the day, the teacher told Katharine that Angelica had attended the school since kindergarten. This led to a conversation about Angelica possibly having a learning disability. The teacher said the district was very slow to respond to requests for assessing students with possible learning disabilities, which led to Angelica never having been referred. Katharine urged the teacher to request an assessment. A few weeks later, when Katharine saw the teacher again, they talked about Angelica. She had been assessed, had been found to have a learning disability, and was now receiving appropriate support.

The following account of an experience that Laura had further illustrates the importance of assessing students who might have special needs. Camila emigrated from Honduras in fifth grade. She had attended school regularly in Honduras but had struggled with literacy and math. Her mother had left for the United States years before, to seek out better economic opportunities and send home much-needed money. During this time, Camila lived with her grandmother. By the time Camila's mother had saved enough money to send for her daughter, she had a new husband and son. Camila had to adjust not only to a new country, language, and culture, but also to a step-father and new sibling. She attended three schools in two years and was pushed out of a charter school for academic and behavioral challenges before arriving in Laura's seventh-grade class. By this time, Camila was well-versed at hiding her academic difficulties by averting eye contact, looking busy, and relying on her tablemates. However, Laura suspected that she may have special learning needs and recommended she be assessed. After she was evaluated in Spanish, Camila was diagnosed with a specific processing disability that had impacted her literacy development in Spanish and English. She was able to get support from the school's special education teacher, as well as from her other teachers. Soon, Camila started participating in class, asking for help, and completing her classwork.

The U.S. Department of Education provides some guidance on identifying and working with ELs with disabilities. For example, their *Resources for Addressing English Learners with Disabilities* (U.S. Department of Education, 2016) includes a comparison of behaviors that are probably related to being an EL rather than a learning disability. This document also offers guidance on developing an IEP for an EL student. We would like to stress again that being an English learner is not the same as having a learning disability.

The Role of Professional Development (PD) in Supporting Assessment

The assessment practices described earlier in the chapter can be taken by individual teachers. But, it can be particularly valuable when schools and districts provide structural supports for this kind of assessment-informed teaching, which is at the heart of all good teaching. All of the practices we've described above take time. Teachers need time to thoughtfully plan activities that are aligned with targeted learning goals and the needs of students and that engage and support a heterogeneous group of students. And, teachers need time to look carefully at evidence of student learning—their processes and their work—not simply to check for completion or to quickly grade, but to identify what students can do and where they need to go next. These practices are key to individualizing and differentiating instruction for newcomers.

It is possible to create time in teachers' workdays to do this vital activity by putting the kind of assessment that we have described in this chapter at the center of professional development (PD) time. For example, at Laura's school, students are dismissed early each Wednesday so that teachers can participate in inquiry-based professional development that she facilitates. She has created an inquiry cycle approach (see Figure 4.7 below), which is built on work she has done with Mills Teacher Scholars, a professional development program at Mills College (https://www.teacherscholars.org).

At the beginning of the inquiry cycle, teachers articulate a long-term learning goal for students that they will be working on with their students for the next six weeks, such as *I can clarify unfamiliar words when I read* or *I can write arguments using evidence from science experiments and readings*. Teachers identify

FIGURE 4.7: Inquiry Cycle Approach

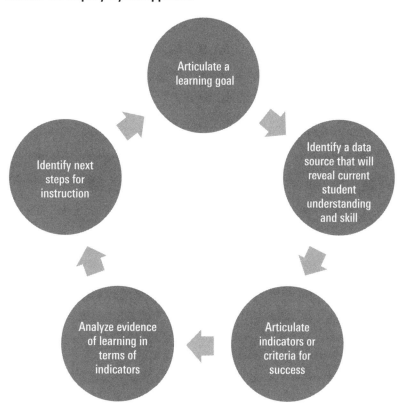

data they can bring to understand where their students are relative to the learning goal, including student work, self-assessments, observation notes or checklists, or audio recordings. They also select a small number of focal students (often three to six) so they can look closely at their data. Sometimes, teachers focus on a particular subgroup of students in their class, such as newcomers or ELs, and other times, they choose a variety of focal students who represent different subgroups in their class. Each week, teachers bring and analyze their students' data and have time during PD to collaborate and plan their next steps for instruction. At the end of the six-week cycle, teachers share what they have learned and their students' progress with colleagues; this is designed to build alignment of practices across classrooms and to celebrate and honor both student and teacher learning. We believe that structures such as these, which provide time and support for teachers to thoughtfully look at formative assessment data, collaborate, and plan, is key to improving teaching and learning in schools. It is essential that schools use their PD time wisely so that it is of maximum use to teachers and of the greatest help to students.

CHAPTER 5

Developing Newcomers' Listening and Speaking

TEACHERS SOMETIMES FEEL at a loss when their newcomer students do not speak English (or a language that they, the teacher, speaks). We like to be able to communicate with our students, to make them feel welcome and special, and when we aren't able to do that in ways that we normally use, it can be a little stressful or discouraging. In the following scenario, a classroom teacher has encountered this experience and, when she meets the school's Title 1 teacher in the hallway, they explore ways they can work with some new students who do not speak English.

SCENE: The hallway in an elementary school

PARTICIPANTS: A third-grade teacher, Allison, and the school's Title 1 teacher, Frida. Alex is the principal.

SCENARIO: It is morning recess and Allison has run into Frida on her way to the staff room.

ALLISON: I'm so glad to see you, Frida. I just got two students. From Yemen, I think it is. That's in the Middle East, near Egypt, isn't it? Isn't Yemen where there's that civil war?

FRIDA: I'd heard that we'd be getting some Yemeni students, but I didn't realize they'd arrived yet. You're right, Yemen *is* in the Middle East and there's a civil war that's been ripping the country apart. I remember seeing a map of the region and Saudi Arabia borders Yemen to the north and Egypt is further away, to the northwest, in North Africa. So, how did it go with your new students?

ALLISON: To be honest, not so great. In the past, when I've had Spanish-speaking kids, it wasn't bad because I could communicate a bit with them in Spanish and help them feel welcome. But neither of these kids from Yemen speaks any English and they look so scared. I tried talking with them, slowing down what I was saying and trying to make sure my sentences weren't too complicated, but that didn't seem to help. Alex brought them to my classroom and she gave me folders on them. I haven't had a chance to read them carefully, but I saw that they had attended some school. Do you have any suggestions for what I can do to communicate with them and make them feel welcome?

FRIDA: Well, what you're doing, speaking more slowly and keeping your sentences short, is going to be a help as they learn English. I know you've used buddies in the past, so I'd get that going as soon as possible, if you haven't done that already.

ALLISON: I don't know why I didn't think about that myself because you're right, I've used peer buddies in the past and it's been really successful. I wish I'd known these two girls were going to be in my class a few days ago so I could have prepared the class. And myself. Like finding out more about them and their country, their culture, and how they came to the U.S. Do you think they speak Arabic?

FRIDA: Yeah, probably, from what I know of Yemen. But it's possible they may speak another language at home. We need to find out. We haven't had other children from Yemen or Arabic-speaking children in the past, so I'm going to check with the district office and the county office to see what resources they might have.

ALLISON: Thanks, Frida. Just talking with you makes me feel like I'm not alone. But how alone do you think those two little girls must feel in school right now?

FRIDA: I agree. It must be pretty scary. By the way, I've seen you using a lot of visuals and gestures when talking with English language learners, and that will be hugely helpful to these two girls. I'll check into resources and we can then come up with a plan. There may be other teachers who have Yemeni students or have ELs they can't yet communicate with very well, so maybe we can work on this together. I bet Alex would let us use the staff meetings to work on this.

ALLISON: Thanks, Frida. I think working on it together would be really helpful. So, buddies, visuals, gestures . . . and lots of encouraging smiles, right!?

FRIDA: That's a very good start.

As this short conversation between these two teachers illustrates, there are some fairly straightforward ways that we can support newcomers, to help them feel welcome and understand the new language and culture that they are now immersed in, and to help them to acquire English when first exposed to the language—not speaking rapidly, using less complex sentence structures, and using visuals and gestures—all of which help make English more comprehensible to newcomers. Also, a welcoming, kind smile can go a long way in helping to relax a newcomer student. Once relaxed, students are better able to concentrate on the task at hand. However, keep in mind that not all cultures may share the same tendency to smile when welcoming others, such as many communities in Japan and Russia (Bhana, 2015).

Where to Start when Teaching Newcomers

When working with newcomers, teachers may wonder, "Where do I start?" or "What should I focus on instructionally?" As mentioned in Chapter 3, all four language modalities (listening, speaking, reading, and writing) work together to support English language development. However, it has been estimated that listening occupies about 45% of the time that adults spend communicating with others, in contrast with 30% spent on speaking, 16% on reading, and 9% on writing (Ahmed, 2015). For children, the percentages are likely to be even higher in listening and speaking. It is often very difficult for newcomers to understand what others are saying due to a variety of factors, including people speaking too quickly or too softly, a lack of visual supports, and not being familiar with the content of the verbal interaction. Therefore, it is to be expected that listening and speaking gain prominence with newcomers who do not speak much, if any, English. Although listening and speaking are often the two modalities that are the focus of instruction for newcomers to English, we would like to emphasize that, even when focusing instruction on listening and speaking, reading and writing are often involved, as many of the strategies that follow illustrate.

Strategies to Support Newcomers' Listening and Speaking Development

There are many strategies we can use to support newcomers who understand and speak no or very little English. Keep in mind that it is very common for newcomers to understand more than they speak. What follows are some strategies to support newcomers' listening and speaking development, which are organized under the following headings:

- Talking with newcomers;
- Providing physical supports;
- Integrating the arts;
- Classroom experiences and routines;
- Conversation starters and storytelling; and
- Practicing English.

Additional strategies focused on listening and speaking development in the context of literacy or content learning can be found in later chapters. For example, in Chapter 6: Developing Newcomers' Reading, ways of making read-alouds more accessible to newcomers, illustrated books on tape, and cross-age tutoring are all addressed.

Talking with Newcomers

Some strategies that can be really helpful when talking with newcomers follow. You will see they often rely on non-verbal communication.

Use Gestures and Mime to Convey Meaning

Using gestures and mime can help newcomers better understand a message. For example, in the following scenario, the second-grade teacher, Mr. Berg, is explaining to his class that they'll be going outside and running.

PARTICIPANTS: A second-grade class that has a few English learners and two recently-arrived ELs.

SCENARIO: The teacher is preparing his class for gym, which will be held outside.

"Today in gym, we're going outside" (*Points through the window to the playground*).

"We're going to run laps" (*Demonstrates running in place and puffs his cheeks in and out, as if running hard*).

"You won't need your jackets or sweatshirts" (*Points to his sweatshirt, shakes his head, takes off his sweatshirt and puts it on the back of his chair, then motions with his hands for students to do the same*).

"Make sure your laces are tied" *(Bends down and mimes tying his shoelaces)*.
"Let's go" *(Uses hand gestures to lead students to the door; glances over to two newcomer students, Dalisay and Joselito, to make sure they've understood)*.

In this situation, Mr. Berg used both gestures and mime to help make his directions clear to his two newcomer students.

Keep Talk Concrete

Like all languages, English is full of informal language, particularly in speech, and can be very difficult for newcomers to understand. This includes the following categories of language:

- Colloquial words and phrases, such as *ain't, bamboozle* (to confuse), and *fire* (to dismiss);
- Aphorisms, which are statements of wisdom that have some bearing in truth (e.g., *Actions speak louder than words*);
- Figurative language, including metaphors and similes (e.g., *I was happy as a clam*);
- Jargon, which is like a shorthand used by members of a specific group (e.g., *P.E.* for *physical education*);
- Slang, which is informal language that is often restricted to a specific group (e.g., *LOL*, meaning *laugh out loud* or *dead* when referring to being very tired); i t's entirely possible that your newcomer students will acquire age-based slang used by their peers more quickly than you; and
- Idioms, which are words or phrases that aren't taken literally (e.g., *jump the gun*, meaning to do something early; *pass the buck*, meaning to shift the blame from oneself to another person).

While becoming fluent in a language means also having a handle on these aspects of language, it is important for us to monitor our language with newcomers so that it is as comprehensible as possible. In time, newcomers will be ready to take on these uses of language; in fact, some of their earliest utterances may be informal language that they have heard their peers using (e.g., *real good; Dude, do you wanna come?*).

Here is an example of a teacher using very informal language first and then revising it to be more understandable to newcomer students:

Informal Language	More Understandable Language
Yesterday evening, I read your essays and I was on cloud nine! They were awesome. Unbelievably awesome!	Yesterday evening, I read your essays and I was very happy. They were very, very good.

It can be helpful to keep charts of frequently used, informal, colloquial language with explanations and sketches to illustrate meaning. This can be particularly helpful for newcomers who may have learned some English prior to coming to your class and may read more than they speak, as well as newcomers as they progress. It is also an example of how to develop students' vocabulary through word consciousness. (Word consciousness will be addressed in depth in Chapter 6: Developing Newcomers' Reading.) An example of such a chart follows.

Informal Language	Meaning	Examples and (Possible Visuals)
I was happy as a clam.	I was very <u>happy.</u>	(Picture of a smiling face)
When I got home, I was dead.	When I got home, I was very <u>tired.</u>	(Picture of a tired face)
I bombed that test.	I did not do well on the test.	(Picture of a test paper with a big X through it)
FYI	For your information	(FYI, the project is due on Tuesday)
See ya!	Goodbye!	(Picture of a person waving goodbye to another person)
Who got up on the wrong side of the bed?	Who is in a bad mood?	(Picture of a bad-tempered face)
My bad.	My mistake.	(It was my mistake that . . . .)

Keep Language as Accessible as Possible

When we are fluent in a language, we often use very complex sentence structures, which can be very hard for ELs, particularly newcomers, to process and understand. It is wise to monitor our language when speaking with newcomers, limiting, for example, how complex our oral (and written) directions are. The following example shows how second-grade teacher, Ms. Davis, used a complex sentence when reviewing homework and then adjusted it to make it more easily understood by breaking it up into shorter sentences and using vocabulary she thought her newcomer students could understand.

Complex Language	More Comprehensible Language
"This evening for homework, you need to read for half an hour. You choose what you read, but it has to be challenging for you. And also draft your interview protocol for social studies."	"Here's your homework for this evening. 1. Read for 30 minutes. You choose your book. 2. Write down some questions for your social studies interview."

In the second example, Ms. Davis used gestures and mime while speaking to illustrate selecting a book and reading it and writing questions. She also pointed to a chart that the class had collaboratively generated of questions they could ask family members and neighbors for a social studies unit on their neighborhoods—questions included *Where can people play sports and games?* and *What do you like most about your neighborhood?* In addition, Ms. Davis wrote the homework from the second column (*More Comprehensible Language*) on the whiteboard. This example also shows how language development and teaching isn't limited to one modality as Ms. Davis's instructions (and the homework assignment) asked students to listen to the directions, read the directions and the chart, and write interview questions. Also, she did not penalize any students for not writing grammatically or semantically accurate questions as she knew that it was more important for her students to focus on the content and to communicate.

We sometimes use words and phrases that capture a concept quickly and completely, but they aren't necessarily accessible to newcomers. In these cases, it can help to add an explanatory example, as Ms. Davis had done earlier in the class discussion. For example, when she asked "How diverse is your neighborhood?" she realized that *diverse* and *neighborhood* may not have been familiar to newcomers (and *diverse* may not have been familiar to many of her English-speaking students). She clarified the meaning of *diverse* when she said, "How diverse is your neighborhood? Are there people who come from different countries? Or who speak different languages? Or come from different ethnic or religious backgrounds (*while gesturing around the classroom to illustrate how the children come from a variety of ethnic and religious backgrounds*). I live in a diverse neighborhood (*emphasizing "I" while pointing to herself*). On my street, my neighbors are from Ethiopia, New Zealand, Peru, El Salvador, and the U.S." (*while pointing to each of these countries in turn on a map of the world hanging on the wall on which students had previously posted small sticky circles identifying where their families had originally come from*). She then quickly sketched a map of her street on the whiteboard and labeled the houses with where people came from (in some cases, more than one country) and languages spoken (often multiple languages, such as Amharic, English, and Italian in the home of a family from Ethiopia) (See Figure 5.1).

FIGURE 5.1: Ms. Davis's Street with Countries of Origin of and Languages Spoken by Her Neighbors

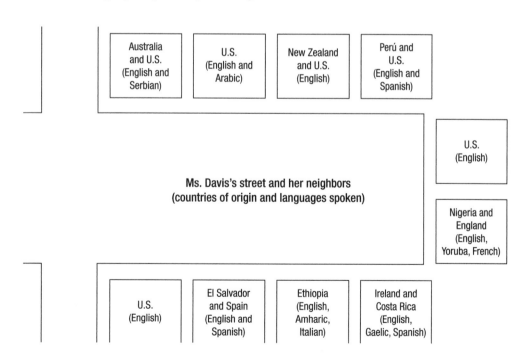

Say Things in More Than One Way

It is a good idea to use a variety of words that capture a concept as newcomers may know a particular word (e.g., *river*), but not another (e.g., *stream*). In these situations, it is also important to briefly explain any slight differences in meaning, accompanied by sketches or pantomime (e.g., "The stream starts at the top of the hill. A stream is a small river" while sketching a hill, with a narrow stream coming down it, and while using gestures to emphasize the narrowness of a stream).

Use Repetition or Redundancy to Amplify Meaning

As the example above about saying things in more than one way illustrates, this type of redundancy can be very helpful when conveying or amplifying meaning of unfamiliar words or terms. When giving directions, it is also important to repeat key information, along with written directions and gestures, as appropriate. For example, Ms. Chang's third-grade class is going on a field trip the following day and she wants to remind students to bring a packed lunch. She says, "Tomorrow, we're going to the science center. We're taking the bus. You need to bring a packed lunch. So, the field trip is tomorrow (*gesturing with a hand movement moving away from her body to signify the future*). Bring your lunch. Some food and a drink" (*and mimes putting food in a bag and eating and drinking*). While repeating the directions, she writes them on the whiteboard; she prints the directions as she has learned that newcomers often have difficulty reading cursive.

- Field trip to Science Center
- Tomorrow
- On bus
- Bring lunch (food and a drink)

It is also helpful to highlight key words or terms. This can be accomplished through using capital letters, a different colored pen or marker, or a highlighter.

Use Newcomers' Native Language when Needed

There are times when it is clear that newcomers are completely confused about the meaning of a key concept or a direction, even after we have used a variety of strategies to try to make meaning clear. In these situations, it can be very helpful to translate the word or term into the newcomer student's native language, if you are able to do so. Sometimes Google Translate can help with this, if you do not speak the language of your student, but use with care as Google Translate is not always accurate. Also, we would like to stress that this is not a strategy that we recommend relying on as it can lead to a dependence on translation rather than encouraging students to actively figure out meaning and build their English proficiency. And, it can lead to a reliance on translation on the part of teachers rather than using multiple strategies to convey meaning.

Provide Visual and Physical Supports

When learning a new language, having visual and physical supports can be very helpful and the following strategies rely on them.

Use Lots of Visuals, Including Videos

School often requires a lot of auditory learning, which is hard for many students, but particularly hard for newcomers, whose understanding of English may be very limited to begin with. We cannot emphasize how important it is to use charts, maps, pictures, sketches, photographs, and videos to help convey meaning, whether teaching one on one, in small groups, or the entire class. They are also beneficial when introducing a topic or unit of study by providing key background information before embarking on the unit or topic.

Sketching while speaking is also a very useful strategy. For example, pictorial input charts, made popular by GLAD (Guided Language Acquisition Design), can be very helpful when introducing a new topic to students and whenever introducing new concepts and vocabulary. The following example shows how Ms. Anders, a pull-out fourth- and fifth-grade ELD teacher in a large urban school, used a pictorial input chart to introduce her students to a science topic. First, we show the completed chart (Figure 5.2), followed by steps in preparing a pictorial input chart (Figure 5.3), and then a scenario illustrating how she developed and used the chart to introduce her students to a study of what plants need _most_ to grow.

FIGURE 5.2: Completed Pictorial Input Chart

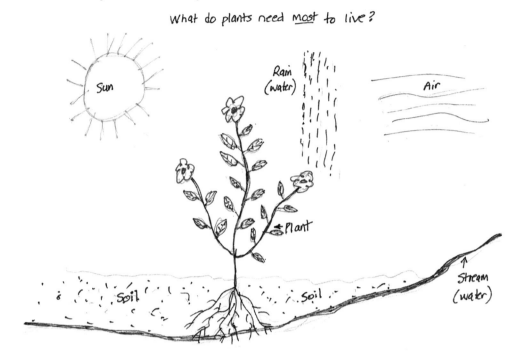

What do plants need most to live?

FIGURE 5.3: Steps in Preparing and Using a Pictorial Input Chart

Before the lesson:
• Find a picture (or make your own) that captures the focus of the lesson.   • Project the picture onto large chart paper. (Alternatively, sketch on a smaller piece of paper and project it later on a document projector.)   • With a pencil, lightly trace over the most salient parts of the picture and label key items.
When teaching:
• In front of the class, trace over the picture with colored markers while talking through and labeling the picture.   • After a few minutes of tracing and talking, allow students two minutes to talk with a partner to answer a question you have given them.   • Continue tracing and talking and, at regular intervals, give students opportunities to talk with their partners.

SCENE: Ms. Anders' ELD class for fourth and fifth graders

PARTICIPANTS: A class of 18 students. All the students are ELs who speak multiple native languages. Four students are newcomers—Angel and Adriana speak Spanish, Nabeel speaks Arabic, and Nima speaks K'iche', an indigenous Guatemalan language; they arrived in the U.S. a few weeks earlier.

SCENARIO: Ms. Anders is introducing the students to a science unit on where plants get the materials they most need to grow. In preparation for this unit, she has lightly sketched a pictorial input chart in pencil on a large piece of chart paper and labeled key items (e.g., plants, sun, air, water, and soil). This chart now hangs on the whiteboard.

MS. ANDERS: Today, we're going to learn about where plants get the materials they need <u>most</u> to live. (*She emphasizes* most; *using a colored marker, she traces over the picture of the plants and labels them* plants.). We already know that they need air, water, sunlight, and soil. But, do plants rely mostly on the sun? (*Traces over the sun with a marker and labels it* sun.) Or do plants rely mostly on the air? (*Waves her hands in the air and traces over lines in the sky on the chart and labels them* air.) What about soil? Do they rely mostly on the soil? (*Puts her finger in a flower pot holding soil, shows some soil, and then traces over the soil on the chart with a marker and labels it* soil.) And how about water? Do plants rely mostly on water? (*Traces over the pictures of rain and a stream and labels them* water.) In the next few weeks, we're going to do some experiments to find out what plants <u>most</u> need to grow. (*She writes* What do plants most need to grow? *on the top of the chart and emphasizes* most.) Right now, I want you to talk with your partners about your hypotheses. What do you think plants <u>most</u> need to grow? Water, soil, air, or sun? (*Pointing to each labeled sketch while saying the words.*)

The students move to their tables and gather in their partner groups of two or three students. Nima and Adriana meet with Bobby, who speaks Spanish and has been trained to be a peer buddy. Adriana has been in the U.S. for about 11 months and her English has been developing well. Although Ms. Anders knows that Nima speaks an indigenous language at home, she has heard her speak some Spanish with Adriana and she hopes that Adriana can help Nima contribute to the conversation by translating for her into and from English. Angel is in a group of three that includes Javier, who speaks Spanish, and Nadine, who speaks Arabic, has been in the U.S. for about a year, and has been trained to be a peer buddy. Nabeel is paired with Oscar, who speaks Spanish, is a trained peer buddy, and has said he loves different languages. Adriana,

Bobby, and Nima use both Spanish and English to discuss the options and eventually decide that all four elements are equally important for plants to grow. Angel, Javier, and Nadine decide that sunshine is most important because they have all seen deserts and know that cacti don't need a lot of water and they think the soil they grow in isn't very rich. Nabeel and Oscar can't decide between soil and water.

Use Lots of Realia/Objects to Support Understanding

Using physical supports, such as objects from real life (often called *realia*), is an important strategy for helping newcomers understand concepts. Too often, students in the U.S. are taught about very complex concepts through reading textbooks and/or listening to a teacher talking rather than through activities that include seeing, touching, and working with objects.

As the following scenarios will show, two fifth-grade teachers in the same school approached teaching about archaeology in quite different ways. Read the following scenarios and decide which approach is likely to be more effective with newcomers (and possibly all students) when introducing them to archaeology.

SCENARIO 1

The students open their social studies textbooks to a new chapter, which is labeled "Archaeology." The teacher asks students what they know about the topic. As students offer their insights, the teacher writes their comments on chart paper (e.g., "It's about history," "Is it about archery?," "It's about old places."). None of the newcomer students speak. The teacher then explains a little about archaeology: "Yes, archaeology is about history and it involves digging into the ground to find evidence of

SCENARIO 2

The teacher begins the period by asking students what they know about archaeology while pointing to the word on the whiteboard. The students are silent for a while and eventually one student raises her hand and offers, "It's like a science." Other students add, "Is it about arches?," "I think it has something to do with history," and "I read a book once and it's about old places." The teacher jots down these ideas on chart paper. He then starts reading a picture book about archeology that is projected onto the how people before us lived. Often, a long time ago. Archaeologists have to hypothesize from what they find under the ground how people may have lived and what they did for a living." The teacher then asks students to silently read the first two paragraphs in the textbook and write down words or terms they are unfamiliar with. The newcomer students look around them and appear to be looking at the pictures. This is followed by students calling out terms they are unfamiliar with, which the teacher writes on a second piece of chart paper. Again, newcomer students do not speak.

The process continues like this for most of the rest of the class period. Toward the end of the period, the teacher puts a star next to six of these words/terms and tells students to write them down in their notebooks. For homework, they are to refer to their textbooks and write definitions for each word. The unit continues like this for several days and involves primarily reading from the textbook, writing down key terms, and finding their definitions. During one period, students watch a video of archaeologists at work, which they find interesting and enjoy talking about. At the end of the unit, students are tested on their knowledge of archaeology by taking a multiple-choice test. The newcomer students all get 0 on their tests.

whiteboard so that students can follow along and see the illustrations. The teacher points to each illustration when the text refers to it, and the class talks about it briefly. The newcomer students do not speak at this point. Every two to three minutes, students are asked to pair share on a question the teacher has asked (e.g., "What tools do archaeologists use?"). One newcomer student is placed with a student who speaks her home language, and the second newcomer student is paired with a student who has been trained as a peer buddy. In both partnerships, the newcomer students offer suggestions, sometimes pointing to the picture and sometimes speaking and using gestures (e.g., "A . . . .?" and using hand motions to suggest a brush).

This process continues until the book has been read in its entirety. At the end, the teacher asks students to pair share about what they now know about archaeology. This is followed by a class share-out, which the teacher records on another chart. The teacher then explains that they are about to embark on a short study of archaeology. He has brought in lots of picture books about archaeology, which students select from to read for homework and then talk about in the following class in small groups. In a later class, the teacher brings in gallon milk jugs, which are filled with layers of plaster of Paris and miniature plastic objects; students work in small groups to unearth the layers with small brushes and hypothesize about the cultures represented by these artifacts. This exercise is in preparation for an actual dig in a corner of the schoolyard. As a final activity, students are asked to each make a labeled drawing of what they know about archaeology. Although the newcomer students do not verbally participate in whole-class discussions, they are active participants in the pair shares and small-group conversations, which the teacher has carefully organized to ensure that newcomer students will have opportunities to speak with their peers.

Which scenario do you think would have been more accessible to newcomers? In the first scenario, the following strategies could have been helpful to newcomers:

- Writing what students said on chart paper and
- Showing a video about archeology.

The teacher in the second scenario used many more strategies that could have been helpful, including the following:

- Writing what students said on chart paper;
- Projecting a picture book so the text and illustrations could be seen by students;
- Pointing to illustrations while reading aloud to help clarify meaning;
- Stopping periodically so students could process the content in pair shares;
- Providing accessible and engaging texts about archaeology (picture books) for students to read and browse through;
- Giving students a hands-on experience resembling the work of an archaeologist (with the jugs of layered plaster and objects);
- Taking students on an archeological dig; and
- Carefully placing newcomer students in pairs and small groups with

students with whom they could talk in English and/or their native language.

Although newcomers in the second scenario may well have been confused at times, it is very likely that they would have left with a greater understanding of archaeology than from reading a textbook and matching words with definitions.

Integrate the Arts

Many children who are very quiet or are new to English respond well to activities that integrate the arts, such as drawing and painting, singing, and play acting. For example, they can convey understanding through drawing key events in a story or drawing charts of science concepts. We suggest a few additional strategies here.

Craft Activities

It can be very helpful to incorporate craft or construction activities for newcomers as following the directions is integral to such activities and, when combined with step-by-step directions, these activities can assist students in understanding concepts and language. If newcomers are already literate in their native language, straightforward, illustrated written directions can also help. In one class, third-grade students were studying westward movement in the U.S. They read a variety of books about this era, including *Patty Reed's Doll* by Rachel Kelley Laurgaard (1956), a descendent of the Reed family. Some students, including newcomers, elected to make tiny dolls and dress them in clothing typical of the era, similar to the doll that eight-year-old Patty Reed took with her when her family moved west as part of the Donner Party. In another class, students were studying about slavery and the Underground Railroad, and some newcomers elected to make Underground Railroad lanterns to accompany a three-dimensional class display illustrating the Underground Railroad.

Use Songs, Chants, Raps, and Poems

Songs, rhythmic chants, raps, and poetry are often very effective ways to introduce students to English and reinforce content vocabulary, concepts, grammar, pronunciation, and prosody (the rhythm of a language). Popular chants include "We're Going on A Bear Hunt," "Mashed Potatoes," and "Colors." Many years ago, ESL teacher and jazz pianist Carolyn Graham (n.d.) published books of jazz chants that were developed for EL adults and, later, for children. These jazz chants integrate authentic, English language with jazz beats. Graham can be seen explaining jazz chants at https://www.youtube.com/watch?v=R_nPUuPryCs.

Even when newcomers have lived in very remote places, it is not uncommon for them to be familiar with popular raps and songs in English. This is often the consequence of having access to a TV and the Internet. It is a good idea to use some of these songs and raps to teach about English—your students will be able to help you select them.

Classroom Experiences and Routines

Newcomers benefit enormously from some specific classroom experiences, such as the following:

- Consistent established classroom routines;
- Opportunities to listen to and talk with others;
- Hearing normal conversational speech;
- Being given physically active tasks; and
- Being partnered carefully for pair and small-group work.

We describe these experiences in the following pages.

Consistent Established Classroom Routines

It is important for all students, but especially newcomers, to have clear, predictable daily and weekly schedules that are posted, along with times and sketches that support ELs and other students who need this kind of support. For example, the day in a first-grade class may start with a morning circle, followed by a reading block. The reading block may begin with shared reading with the entire class, followed by independent reading and guided reading groups with the teacher, and end with an interactive read-aloud. When ELs realize that there are classroom routines that are regularly scheduled, it helps them to understand what is going on in class and prepare for these events.

Opportunities to Listen to and Talk with Others

In many classrooms, silence is often prized, and this can hinder the language and literacy development of newcomer students (as well as many other students). We are talking here about the kind of talk that students engage in to clarify expectations and directions, share and discuss ideas, and understand content. In many cases, teachers are well-intended when they seek a very quiet classroom. For example, in some writing workshops we have visited, students are urged to work quietly (i.e., silently) while writing independently, and the rationale is that "real" writers (i.e., adult, often professional writers) often work best in a very quiet environment. However, students in grades K-8 are not adults and even many older writers find a collegial environment to be helpful to them—a place where they can wander over and get some feedback from another writer or confer with a neighbor. We are not advocating for a chaotic, noisy classroom—far from it. The following two scenarios show how one fourth-grade teacher altered her writing workshop to accommodate talk after she had been shown data on how confused her ELs were before talk was allowed in the writing workshop and how they benefitted from being allowed to talk when she stopped insisting that the independent writing part of writing workshop be quiet.

SCENARIO 1

Early Fall Writing Workshop

After a mini-lesson on writing different kinds of leads, in which Ms. Tennison did almost all of the talking, the students are directed to write three different leads for their nonfiction books about people who made a difference in the United States. The students are sitting at table clusters and they take out their folders. Newcomer student, Mauricio, looks around, with a puzzled look on his face. He leans over and whispers to Marina "¿Qué tenemos que hacer?/*What do we have to do?*"). Marina begins to respond, but Ms. Tennison is walking by and says "Mauricio and Marina, no talking now. Remember, it's time to write." As Ms. Tennison moves on, Marina shrugs and starts writing a new lead for her biography on César Chavez. Mauricio opens his writing folder and flips through the pieces of paper, which have lots of labeled drawings. He looks around from time to time, but he doesn't write. Eventually, he puts his head on the table and closes his eyes. The room is so quiet that the only sounds are children coughing, pencils scratching on paper, and the muffled sounds of traffic outside.

SCENARIO 2

Writing Workshop Four Months Later

A mini-lesson on including authentic-sounding dialogue in their stories has just ended. The students have been instructed to check on any dialogue in their stories and, if they don't have any, consider where it could go, and then share what they generate with their table partners. The classroom is quiet, except for students occasionally calling out to table partners, such as, "What do you think with this one?" and "I like that one. It good." Jian, Jakeline, and Salma are all newcomers and they sit at tables with students who are more fluent in English; there are students at their tables who speak their native languages. "What we do?" asks Jakeline of the students at her table. Luisa speaks Spanish and explains in both Spanish and English what they have to do. Ms. Tennison overhears their conversation and suggests that the two of them work together to generate dialogue, using both English and Spanish. After about 10 minutes, a hum can be heard in the class as students share their dialogue samples with each other, critique them, laugh when they are funny, and ask questions of each other.

Another type of talk that we often hear in classrooms where there are young students or older students who are less fluent in English is subvocalizing when they are reading and writing. That is, they talk to themselves in very low voices as they write and/or read. An example of this follows:

SCENE: A dual language, second-grade bilingual classroom

PARTICIPANTS: Mr. Castro and his 26 students. Fourteen of the students are native speakers of Spanish and 12 are native speakers of English. Three of the students are newcomers from Honduras and El Salvador. Marco is a newcomer who has been in the class for about seven months.

SCENARIO: As part of their English medium instruction, the students have spent four weeks in a science unit of study and they are about to publish their science reports. The teacher has just finished a mini-lesson on editing, with a focus on when to use capital letters. The students are at their table clusters, going through their writing. Marco has taken his writing from his folder and is softly singing to himself in Spanish, "Ciencia, ciencia, ciencia (*Science, science, science*)," as if to prepare himself for the task at hand. He begins reading his writing and as he edits it, he subvocalizes. He crosses out several beginning letters of words with slash marks and adds capital letters (e.g., *P* in *Put*, *D* in *Den* [for *Then*]). As he does this, he sometimes says the letter aloud in a soft voice. He continues, saying words and what he has to do or is doing (e.g., "Found. Capital F. A, capital A. T, capital T. I got that. I almost done."). He begins reading his piece from the beginning, continuing to subvocalize.

It is worth remembering that reading one's writing aloud is a very useful tool for writers of all ages and levels of proficiency, not just young children, inexperienced writers, or ELs.

Hearing Normal Conversational Speech

When we interact with each other and are asked a question, it is not required that we respond with a complete sentence, as teachers sometimes require of students. In fact, normal speech is full of stops and starts and sentence fragments, as the following example of two teachers in the staff room illustrates:

JANICE:	So, how did it go yesterday?
DELIA:	Fine.
JANICE:	Just fine?
DELIA:	Sort of. Not as I expected, I suppose.
JANICE:	How so?
DELIA:	Hard to say. A lot of talking. At us. Not much time for questions. You know how it often is at those meetings.
JANICE:	Uh huh. I'm sorry, though, as it sounded like it could be interesting.
DELIA:	Me, too!

When teachers require that students respond in complete sentences, it isn't helpful and can make talking more stressful than it needs to be. There are, of course, occasions when more formal speech with complete sentences is appropriate, such as when making speeches or presentations, often grounded in writing, which is often more formal than oral language. However, even in these kinds of circumstances, incomplete sentences are often heard. We recommend that teachers focus on supporting newcomers in communicating ideas rather than on producing "perfect sentences." The following two scenarios illustrate this point:

SCENARIO 1

PARTICIPANTS: Ms. Larkin, third-grade teacher, and José Antonio, who came from Honduras six months earlier

SCENARIO: They are having a writing conference.

MS. LARKIN: So, what did you write?

JOSÉ ANTONIO: This (*pointing to an illustrated story he has written about playing soccer*).

MS. LARKIN: What's it about?

JOSÉ ANTONIO: *Fútbol* (Football).

MS. LARKIN: Say it in a complete sentence. It is about football.

JOSÉ ANTONIO: Is about *fútbol.*

SCENARIO 2

PARTICIPANTS: Ms. Fouda, second-grade teacher, and Amima, who speaks Arabic at home, and Claudia, who speaks Chinese. Amima is a newcomer, but Claudia has been in the U.S. for almost two years.

SCENARIO: They are having a small-group writing conference at a small table. The two girls have their writing folders open and are holding their drafts of their biographies of famous people. Amima's is about Malala, the young Pakistani woman who was shot and almost killed when she advocated on behalf of girls getting an education. Claudia's is about the figure skater, Michelle Kwan.

MS. FOUDA: So, I remember that you both had lots of questions that you wanted to answer in your writing. (*She points to a list of questions on a sheet of paper in Amima's folder.*) How are you doing? Are you finding your answers? (*She looks quizzical while pointing to Amima's questions, to indicate that she's referring to their questions.*)

CLAUDIA: Sort of. Most of them.

MS. FOUDA: What's one of the questions you haven't been able to answer?

CLAUDIA:	I don't know how many wins she had. Not wins. You know, like trophies.
MS. FOUDA:	You mean how many championships she won? Like the Olympics?
CLAUDIA:	Yeah.
MS. FOUDA:	Well, you might find it in the list at the back of this book you've been reading. (*She opens a book about Michelle Kwan that Claudia has been using as a mentor text and pointing to a page that lists Kwan's accomplishments.*) OK?
CLAUDIA:	Uh huh (*nodding her head*).
MS. FOUDA:	How about you, Amima?
AMIMA:	No much.
MS. FOUDA:	What's one of your questions?
AMIMA:	Where she live?
CLAUDIA:	I know. I saw it on TV. She in England, I think.
MS. FOUDA:	(*Pointing to Claudia*) So, Claudia can help you. OK, Amima?
AMIMA:	OK.

The conference continues for about two more minutes, with Ms. Fouda focusing on the questions the girls are having difficulty finding answers to and helping them generate ways to locate answers.

As can be seen in the first scenario, Ms. Larkin focused on whether the newcomer, José Antonio, was using a complete sentence, even though in normal speech it wasn't necessary; she also modeled the formal *It is* instead of the much more natural, contracted form, *It's*. In the second scenario, Ms. Fouda focused on the girls' writing and what they were doing to research their topics.

Being Given Physically Active Tasks

Newcomers who are recent arrivals can really benefit from being given meaningful tasks. For example, being asked to pass out paper, collect books, hand out playground equipment at recess, and open and close the door before and after lunch enable newcomers to learn vocabulary and also feel they have a meaningful presence in the class.

Being Partnered Carefully for Pair and Small-group Work

Small-group work, including triads of students, can be very helpful for new-comers because it gives them opportunities to interact with others, often including native or fluent speakers of English. However, we have learned that it is very important to make sure that students are partnered care-fully. For example, fourth-grade teacher, Marcia Obregón, had placed new-comer student, Javier Luis, in a group of four students for a social studies unit of study. She had prepared the class for how to work together, includ-ing how to incorporate newcomers in group work. However, after a week, she realized that Javier Luis was completely excluded from group work, so she moved him to another group. In this group, he became a key member as he took on the role of illustrator. In the process, she heard him using both Spanish and English to clarify what the group was doing and to make suggestions.

Conversation Starters and Storytelling

Storytelling, whether telling an anecdote or making up a story, is a key com-ponent of human interaction. We tell stories throughout the day (e.g., about what happened at the store or work; recalling a memory from childhood). There are several strategies that help newcomers do this. As can be seen from a couple of the strategies that follow, many of them involve using props to help in the storytelling, which helps convey meaning, but also directs the attention of the listener away from the speaker, which many newcomers appreciate.

Use Puppets for Storytelling

Shy students, in particular, are often more likely to speak when they have objects to use as props or a puppet on their hand or finger. This is often particularly true for primary-grade students, but we have found that it is also true for many newcomer students in the intermediate grades and mid-dle school.

Use Photos, Posters, and Pictures as Conversation Starters

Posters, pictures, and photos (a single photo or a group of photos that lend themselves to telling a story) can be very successful at encouraging newcomers to tell stories. Students or the teacher can bring in these visuals. They can be collected from newspapers, magazines, and the Internet. They can be purchased. They can be family treasures. There are some series of pictures that are intended to assess and teach children sequencing; if you have access to these picture sequence cards, keep in mind that, with newcomers, the oral language development purpose is to facilitate them speaking and telling a story.

Use Wordless Picture Books to Tell Stories

When wordless picture books (books with only pictures and a title) became available many years ago, they were intended primarily for young children. However, over the years, more complex and sophisticated wordless books that appeal to older students have become available. Wordless picture books are a good resource for encouraging newcomers to tell stories. Some strategies that we have found work well include the following:

- Select books that are likely to appeal to the age and background of the newcomer. However, even some books intended originally for young children can be very appealing to older ELs, particularly if they include humor. If you have instituted a cross-age buddy reading program and your students are the "tutors," they can use wordless picture books when working with their younger tutees.
- At first, select books that have a limited number of pages so that the task isn't overwhelming for the student(s).
- Demonstrate leafing through a book first and then telling a story.
- Be prepared to wait while students process what they are going to say. Sometimes, their utterances may be single words.
- Students can work in pairs, either taking turns to tell the story or going page by page or double spread by double spread.

Use Cuisenaire Rods to Tell Stories

Although Cuisenaire rods were designed to teach math concepts, these rods, which come in 10 sizes and colors, are excellent for storytelling purposes. This is because they direct attention away from the speaker, but also because they allow for imagination to take the place of real-life objects, animals, and people that may not be available in, for example, pictures. A short scenario illustrating how one teacher uses them follows.

SCENE: Mr. Fagan's second-grade class

PARTICIPANTS: Second-grade teacher, Mr. Fagan, and two newcomer students, Fatima and Esmerelda

SCENARIO: A storytelling literacy center in which Mr. Fagan and the two newcomer students are working together.

Second-grade teacher, Mr. Fagan, works in a public school in a university town. Many of his students are children of graduate students and professors who come from abroad, and many of the children are newcomers to English. Each morning, there is a literacy centers' half-hour. One of the centers is designed with the needs of newcomer students, Fatima and Esmeralda, in mind; however, other students love to work in that center. It is a storytelling center using Cuisenaire rods. On this day, Mr. Fagan and the two girls are setting up their rods to approximate the streets where they live. The tallest, orange rods act as apartment buildings; the medium sized green rods are houses; and the remaining smaller rods act as adults and children. Mr. Fagan, Fatima, and Esmeralda take turns describing their block and its residents. For example, on Fatima's block, there are two apartment buildings and several houses. When she describes her block and its residents, she begins by saying, "Here my house (*while pointing to a green rod*). I live (*while moving a purple rod next to the house*). My two brother live (*while moving a small white and a small red rod toward the green house rod*). They little."

The rods can be used to retell personal experiences or familiar stories, such as Cinderella, which has many versions around the world. They can also be used to retell an event in history or describe a scientific event or experiment.

Use Magnetic or Felt Boards to Tell Stories

There are many objects that can be stuck to magnetic and felt boards, which makes them very versatile storytelling tools. They also provide opportunities for students to practice newly acquired vocabulary. In addition, they can be used to introduce students to new vocabulary.

Tell and Then Repeat a Story

We were introduced to this strategy in a kindergarten classroom, where the teacher had noticed that her students tended not to listen to each other. We have found that it works well with newcomers of all ages. Students work in pairs and sometimes triads; they can be just ELs or ELs with fluent speakers of English. One student tells a brief story or anecdote. The other student(s) listen and then have to repeat it back to the storyteller, who verifies if the retelling was accurate. An example follows:

SCENE: A third-grade class in which students are practicing telling stories to each other.

PARTICIPANTS: Zahara is a native speaker of English and Ha is a native speaker of Vietnamese and has been in the U.S. for about six months.

SCENARIO: The two girls are sitting opposite each other. Zahara is the first to tell her story:

ZAHARA:	At church on Sunday, there was a big party. My cousin got married and we had lots of good food and dancing. (*She demonstrates eating and dancing while saying this.*)
HA:	Ch, ch, chur?
ZAHARA:	Church. You know, where you go to pray. (*She bows her head, closes her eyes, and puts her hands together, as if praying.*)

(Ha nods her head.)

HA:	You go to place to (*and puts her hands together as if praying*).
ZAHARA:	Yeah. To pray. To church.
HA:	To pay (*pray*). And you get lot food and dancing.
ZAHARA:	Yeah. You got it. Now your turn.
HA:	I go zoo Sunday. Many animal. Elephant. Lion. Big monkey.

> **ZAHARA:**   So, on Sunday, you went to the zoo and you saw lots of animals. Like, elephants and lions and . . . Was the big monkey like a gorilla? (*She imitates a gorilla scratching its chest.*)
>
> *(Ha laughs and Zahara joins in)*
>
> **HA:**   Yeah. Like gorilla.

Practicing English

Although newcomers are essentially practicing language whenever they engage in any of the activities and strategies described earlier, there are occasions when it is helpful for ELs to practice listening to or using a particular grammar point or newly introduced vocabulary. The following activities support these types of goals.

Information Gap Tasks

In this activity, the focus is on giving oral directions and following them through sketching. The procedure is as follows:

- Two people sit opposite each other at a table. One or both of them are newcomers, but the second person can be a student who isn't a newcomer or a teacher, instructional aide, volunteer, or older student.
- One person has a simple drawing on a piece of paper and gives directions for how to reproduce the drawing to the newcomer, who cannot see the drawing.
  - An upended folder works well as a barrier.
  - The picture can be as simple as a square above a circle in the center of the paper; a person standing next to a tree; a house with four windows; a classroom with six tables, eight children, and a teacher; or a circle with a dog inside it. It is best to keep the drawing simple.
- The newcomer draws what s/he hears in the directions—at this point, this is a listening activity for the newcomer. It is helpful to

have labeled pictures of shapes and objects at hand in case the newcomer needs support.

- The newcomer can then give directions, which become a speaking activity.

The following is an example of two boys working together:

SCENE: A pull-out ELD class for ELs, including newcomer students, in grades 3–5.

PARTICIPANTS: Oscar, a third-grader, and Jorge, a fourth-grader. They both speak Spanish at home. Other students are working with partners, too.

SCENARIO: Oscar is holding a picture of a man and two dogs that are standing to the right of the man. There is a folder acting as a barrier so that his partner, Jorge, a newcomer, cannot see the picture that Oscar then describes, stage by stage:

OSCAR: Draw a man.

(Jorge draws a stick figure in the middle of the page.)

OSCAR: Draw a big dog.

(Jorge draws a sketch of a big dog standing under the man.)

OSCAR: Draw one more dog. A little dog.

(Jorge draws another dog about the same size as the first dog. The two dogs are standing next to each other.)

Once the boys are finished, they compare their pictures and talk about what is different. Jorge uses a lot of pointing and one or two words to indicate what he sees (e.g., pointing to the two dogs in Oscar's picture, while saying, "*Dog, dog, one big. One* pequeño (*small*)." He then laughs and shakes his head while pointing to the two dogs in his picture. The boys then switch roles and Jorge gives directions for a picture with shapes, which his teacher selected for him as she has observed that he knows several shape words in English and is ready to use more of them.

Similar listening activities can be done with pattern blocks, Cuisenaire rods, and miniature figures. In each case, the original pattern or design is shielded from view. However, when introducing students to this activity, it is important to first demonstrate without a barrier in place. Also, students often need practice without the barrier in place (i.e., a listening and seeing activity) before moving to a strictly listening activity. In these situations, one student makes a design, builds a tower, or locates objects (e.g., plastic farm animals and implements) in relation to each other, and the other student follows the directions and does the same. Additional information gap activities can be found in Appendix 3.

Use TPR (Total Physical Response)

TPR is a language teaching method developed by James Asher (1996) that integrates language and physical movement. Initially, it is a listening and response activity in which the teacher gives directions that involve physical actions (e.g., *Stand up*; *Pick up a pencil*), which become increasingly more complex (e.g., *Stand up, turn around, pick up a book, and sit down*). When introducing new vocabulary and phrases, the teacher demonstrates while giving the commands. Once students are familiar with the language, only the commands can be given. Then students can take on the role of teacher and give commands that involve action. Also, content-area studies can be incorporated (e.g., *Walk over to the map; Touch the globe; Point to the chart of planets*).

Toss and Talk Activity

The toss and talk activity can be used to reinforce recently taught features of English (e.g., a verb tense or pronouns), key vocabulary in all subject areas, and storytelling in a relaxed atmosphere. The directions follow:

- Cover an empty shoebox or tissue box with material.
- Place six pictures corresponding with the target teaching/learning point on each side of the box, using rubber bands to keep them in place. For example, in a study of the internment of Japanese Americans in World War II, there may be pictures of the following:
  - Families packing their bags with as much as they can take;
  - Children carrying soft toys onto a train that will take them to a detention center;
  - A written government detention order;
  - Families staying in Tanforan, a former racetrack that was turned into a detention center;

- A Japanese American family saying goodbye to neighbors;
  - One of the detention centers, such as Manzanar, in California;
  - Yoshiko Uchida's novel for children, *Journey to Topaz*; and
  - Japanese American young men going off to war in Europe.
- Students sit in a circle and take turns tossing the box from one person to another.
- The receiver of the box has to say something corresponding with the picture. For example, a student catches the box with a picture of children carrying soft toys onto the train that will take them to the detention center and may say, "Boy and girl have toy bear. They sad."

What Does Not Help Newcomers?

There are some strategies that people sometimes use that are <u>not</u> helpful when speaking with ELs, including the following:

Avoiding Speaking with Newcomers Does Not Help

There are times when teachers are reluctant to put any more pressure on newcomers, particularly if the student has experienced great trauma in coming to the U.S. This is sometimes manifested in a reluctance to talk with newcomers, perhaps relying on peer buddies to do the talking for them. While setting up a peer buddy system is a <u>very</u> important and useful strategy, teachers should <u>not</u> avoid speaking with newcomers. Instead, it is helpful to progress from short, comprehensible sentences to increasingly more complex sentences as students become more comfortable with English. Here are some strategies teachers have used to interact verbally with their newcomer students:

- Greeting students in the morning at the door as they come into the classroom with a "Good morning," a "Hello," or another greeting, such as "How was your soccer game/recital/visit to the library/party at your aunt's house?" with the option of a fist bump, high five, or hug—each student gets to choose the option. Newcomers typically learn quickly what is going on and participate. (See Chapter 2 for an example of how Mr. Navarro uses greetings in his classroom.)
- The teacher asks a question that requires just a nod or shake of the head or a "yes/no." For an example, see the following scenario.

SCENE: Ms. Martinez's first-grade class

PARTICIPANTS: A class of 22 students. Three students are English learners and Ismael is a newcomer student. The rest of the students are native English speakers.

SCENARIO: The class is engaged in a study of pets and how to take care of them. On previous days, they have brainstormed all the animals that the children have had as pets and have created a class frequency chart of pets (dogs and birds were the most frequently occurring). They have also discussed some differences around the world with regard to having pets (e.g., although children around the world come in contact with animals, they don't always think of them as pets and may not be allowed to touch some animals). On this day, the children are sitting on the rug. Ms. Martinez hands out pictures of animals, both animals often kept as pets (e.g., dog, cat, lizard, snake) and animals that aren't typically pets (e.g., lion, elephant, tarantula, bat, scorpion). The students are directed to think about whether the animal in their picture is one they would like to have as a pet and say why or why not. Ms. Martinez has been careful to give Ismael a picture of a bird; she had seen a songbird in a cage when she visited the family the week before. When it comes to Ismael's turn, this is how the conversation proceeds:

MS. MARTINEZ: Ismael, would you like a bird for a pet? Yes? (*accompanied by a vigorous nod of her head and smile*) or no? (*accompanied by a vigorous shake of her head and an exaggerated frown.*)

ISMAEL: (*Nods his head.*)

(*Ms. Martinez waits quietly for a couple of seconds.*)

MS. MARTINEZ: Why? (*and lifts up her hands in an inviting, questioning gesture*)

ISMAEL: I like (*and points to his mouth*).

MS. MARTINEZ: You like the song the bird makes? (*points to her mouth and makes a singing sound and nods her head*)

ISMAEL: Yes.

MS. MARTINEZ: Thanks, Ismael.

Ms. Martinez knows that in some cultures nodding and shaking the head do not mean *yes* and *no*, respectively, but when working with Ismael one on one in past days, she knows that he understands the difference.

Speaking More Loudly Does Not Help

If a person does not understand a new language, speaking more loudly does not help. In fact, it can be very off-putting or insulting. Instead, a clear, normal voice is all that's needed, along with gestures and mime.

Speaking in an Exaggeratedly Slow Way Does Not Help

While it <u>does</u> help to slow down a little and enunciate clearly, slowing down in an exaggerated way does <u>not</u> help a newcomer who does not have access to the language that is being used. For example, slowing down and drawing out "W-e-l-c-o-m-e t-o o-u-r c-l-a-s-s. C-o-m-e a-n-d s-i-t d-o-w-n o-n t-h-e r-u-g" doesn't make the message more comprehensible. It can also be viewed as insulting.

Using Truncated English Does Not Help

When speaking with ELs, particularly newcomers, people sometimes think that using a truncated form of the language helps in communication (e.g., "School not open" or "No go"). It doesn't. "The school's not open" and "Don't go" provide natural, fairly simple language that is preferable to the signal forms of "School not open" and "No go." It is best to <u>not</u> use an inaccurate form of the language, even if the newcomer uses that form of the language initially. Apart from anything else, it can be insulting.

Discouraging Students from Using Their Native Language Does Not Help

It can be extremely stressful to be in a classroom where one is unable to understand much and possibly unable to say anything, so having occasions when one <u>can</u> communicate is a way to reduce the stress that can be associated with being a newcomer. Teachers are sometimes concerned that, if students speak their native language, they will not learn English and/or they are talking off topic. In fact, research shows the following:

- Speaking the native language doesn't inhibit the development of English (Byers-Heinlein & Lew-Williams, 2013; Ramirez, Yuen, Ramey, Pasta, & Billings, 1991).
- When ELs are speaking in their native language with another

student in class, they are typically clarifying such things as expectations and directions and working on the task at hand (Schinke-Llano, 1983; Swain & Lapkin, 2000).

- Using the native language can often help newcomer students understand important directions (e.g., Samway & McKeon, 2007; Storch & Wigglesworth, 2003).

We believe that it is important to encourage newcomer students to use their native language whenever they have the opportunity to speak with another person who shares that language.

Correcting Pronunciation Does Not Help

Newcomers' pronunciation of English words is often in a very early stage of development, and teachers are sometimes tempted to correct it, in part because it is so obvious. This is not advisable. Instead, pay attention only to pronunciation that may cause embarrassment or complete confusion (e.g. when "ship" is pronounced like "sheep"). However, correcting these pronunciations is unlikely to help. Instead, ELs need to be shown how the mouth, tongue, and teeth are involved in making sounds that may be unfamiliar to them. For example, in the case of "ship," the lips are pursed together and pushed out, whereas with "sheep," the corners of the mouth are pushed up toward the cheeks. We have found that most younger newcomer students have very little need for pronunciation instruction.

CHAPTER 6

Developing Newcomers' Reading

WHAT DO WE MEAN by the term *reading*? In many schools, reading instruction, particularly in the lower grades, focuses on phonemic awareness and phonics. Although both have a role to play in decoding words (i.e., making letter-sound connections/phonics), reading is much more than that—it is a meaning-making process. When working with a group of struggling third-grade readers, Katharine found that all of them were able to decode quite effectively, which was no surprise as their previous reading instruction had focused heavily on phonics. However, none of these children realized that the whole point of reading is to make meaning. They often guessed at (predicted) unfamiliar words using graphophonic cues but did not re-read or self-correct when it didn't make sense. It took a while for the youngsters to internalize that they needed to be making sense of the text rather than relying exclusively on decoding, but when they did, they became much more successful readers and enjoyed reading more.

In order to illustrate how central making meaning is when reading, please read the following passage and, in your mind or on paper, paraphrase it.

TODAY'S CRICKET

The batsmen were merciless against the bowlers. The bowlers placed their men in slips and covers. But to no avail. The batsmen hit one four after another with an occasional six. Not once did a ball look like it would hit their stumps or be caught.

(Source: Tierney & Pearson, 1981)

It is possible that this passage made very little sense to you, although you had no difficulty decoding it and probably figured out that it is about some kind of sport involving bats and balls. You may also have heard about the game of cricket, though at first, when you saw the title, you may have predicted that the text would be about the insect cricket.

Next, read and paraphrase the following version, which has simplified vocabulary and sentence structures, something that texts designed for ELs often incorporate.

(LOWER READABILITY VERSION)

The men were at bat against the bowlers. They did not show any pity. The bowlers placed their men in slips. They placed their men in covers. It did not help. The batsmen hit a lot of fours. They hit some sixes. No ball hit the stumps. No ball was caught.

(Source: Tierney & Pearson, 1981)

Were you able to make any more sense of this simplified text? Probably not, if you didn't have the *schema* (background knowledge) for the game of cricket, which is played primarily in England and several former British colonies. Katharine, who is from England and grew up watching a lot of cricket (and playing a little), is able to read (understand) the passage, "Today's Cricket," because she knows the following:

- *Bowlers* are like the pitchers in baseball.
- *Slips* refers to the fielder's positions behind the batter, not a piece of underwear.
- *Covers* refers to another fielder's position that is further away from the batsman (not a cover for a bed or couch).
- *Fours* refers to balls that touch the field before crossing the boundary line (the outer limit of the playing field) and score four runs.
- *Sixes* refers to balls that cross the boundary line before touching the ground, like a home run in baseball, and score six runs.
- *Stumps* refers to three vertical posts that are topped with two smaller pieces of wood called *bails*, and these together are called the *wicket* (see photo on next page).
- One way for a batter to be out is if the bowled ball hits the wicket and knocks off the bails.

FIGURE 6.1: Wicket

Source: https://en.wikipedia.org/wiki/Wicket

Katharine can read (i.e., understand) this text because she has the schema to do so, which many readers may not have. The photo of a cricket wicket and, on the next page, a labeled drawing of fielder positions on a cricket pitch may help you better understand the passage.

What does this example about cricket have to say about teaching reading to newcomers? Although you may still not be sure what was going on in "Today's Cricket," we think that the sketch and photo may have helped—strategies that help ELs, too. It is also important to build on and extend the repertoire of experiences newcomers can draw on (i.e., build their schemas). This can be accomplished many ways, including through giving them many opportunities to interact with books, go on field trips, and have access to digital resources, such as content-area videos. In many cases, newcomers may come with the schema but not have access to the vocabulary in English or know how English print looks and works. Returning to the cricket example, in the case of newcomers who come from regions in the world where cricket is popular, such as India, Pakistan, and Sri Lanka, they will likely have the schema, but they may not know the English vocabulary or how English print looks and works.

Newcomers who are already literate in their native language have a distinct advantage over newcomers who are not. For example, they already come to English reading knowing about print and how it works, even if their native language's script is quite different from English (e.g., Arabic, Farsi, or Japanese) and is read from right to left (e.g., Arabic, Hebrew) rather than left to right. If their native language is grounded in a Latin script, such as Spanish, French, Portuguese, or Italian, they will already be familiar with many of the same letters that are found in English, even when their lan-

FIGURE 6.2: **A Guide to Some Fielding Positions in Cricket**

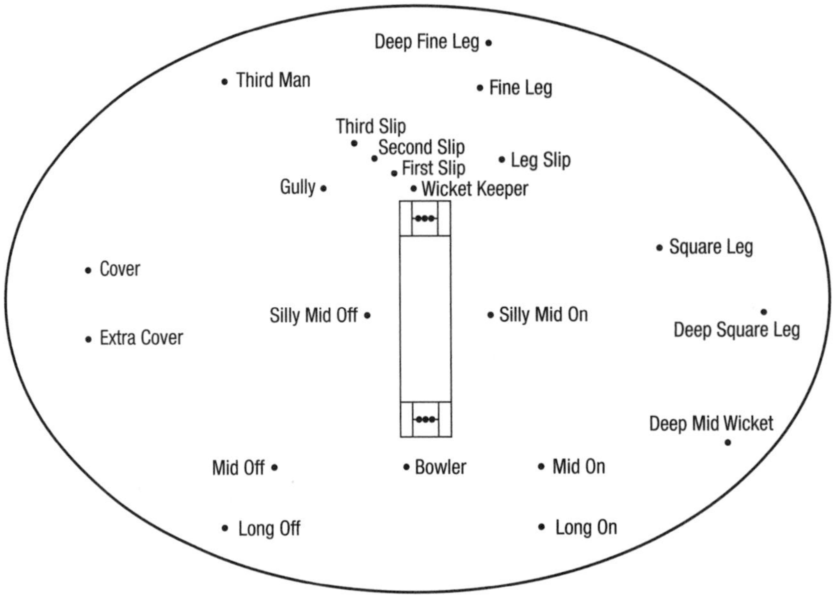

Deep Fine Leg •

• Third Man   • Fine Leg

Third Slip
• Second Slip
• First Slip   • Leg Slip
Gully •   • Wicket Keeper

• Cover   • Square Leg

• Extra Cover   Silly Mid Off •   • Silly Mid On   Deep Square Leg •

Deep Mid Wicket •

Mid Off •   • Bowler   • Mid On

• Long Off   • Long On

guage has additional letters (e.g., the *ñ* and *ll* in Spanish) or when letters are pronounced differently in English and their language (e.g., in Spanish, the *h* is silent, the *j* is pronounced like an *h* in English, and the *th* does not exist).

In Chapter 8: Engaging Newcomers in Content Learning, you will find information about teaching reading in content areas such as science, history, and math. In this chapter, we address teaching reading to newcomers in the context of language arts instruction. Many of the strategies that we explore may be familiar to readers, but we emphasize how to use them with newcomers for whom English is a new language and who may/may not be able to read in another language. This chapter will address the following:

- Assessing reading;
- Familiar classroom reading experiences;
- Choosing texts for newcomers; and
- Vocabulary development.

Assessing Reading

In Chapter 4: Assessing Newcomer Students, we explored some general assessment strategies that are meaningful and helpful to teachers. In this chapter, we discuss the following assessment strategies that focus specifically on reading: observation surveys, running records, and anecdotal student records. We focus on these tools as they assess newcomer students in the act of reading complete texts rather than fragments of texts and provide teachers with important information on students' reading strategies, strengths, and needs, which then provide guidance to teachers on what to teach next. When assessing reading, it is important to focus on more than accuracy—that is, whether a student pronounces words correctly (known as *decoding*) or reads quickly. The following reading assessments do not ignore decoding, but they consider it as just one part of the reading process.

Clay's Observation Survey

Although Marie Clay's *An Observation Survey of Early Literacy Achievement* (1993, 2002, 2005, 2013) was not designed for newcomers to English, it can be a very useful tool for assessing newcomers' knowledge of print (referred to as concepts about print), as well as the strategies they use when reading. The Observation Survey has been reconstructed (not simply translated) into various other languages, including Spanish—educators in Arizona collaborated with Clay to produce *Instrumento de Observación de Los Logros de La Lecto-Escritura Inicial* (Escamilla, Andrade, Basurto, & Ruiz, 1996). In this section, we will focus on two of the components in the Observation Survey that we have found to be most useful with newcomers: a) the concepts about print observation task, and b) running records of a student's reading of a continuous text.

Concepts about Print Observation Task

This tool is intended for young children upon entering kindergarten but can also be used effectively with newcomers whose intake assessments suggest they may not have received much, if any, formal schooling in any language. It is a way to determine what children have learned from their experiences with print (including books). Some of the concepts assessed include the following: In what direction does print move? How does one move through a word? How does one move through a series of words in continuous print? With this assessment, the teacher reads one of a collection of stories designed for this task while also asking questions to elicit the child's knowledge of, for example, where the front of the book is, directionality, letter order, and punctuation. The teacher unobtrusively records the child's responses on a record sheet.

Some words of caution are needed when using this assessment with newcomers:

- If newcomers have been exposed to print that does not move from left to right (e.g., Arabic), their response to the direction, "Show me where to start" may suggest they do not have any knowledge of this aspect of print, when in fact they may, albeit not in English.
- If newcomers have been exposed to books that are opened and read from what, in the English language, is the back of the book (e.g., Arabic), their response to the direction, "Show me the front of this book" may suggest they do not have any knowledge of this aspect of print, when in fact they may, albeit not in English.
- As mentioned in Chapter 4: Assessing Newcomer Students, in order to get a more complete sense of newcomers' familiarity with print, it is important to assess them in their native language, which should be done as soon after the child enters the English-medium school as possible.

Running Records of a Student's Reading of a Continuous Text

In contrast with the many reading assessments that test reading ability by counting the number of letters, sounds, or words a youngster knows, a running record is an assessment of text reading that supports teachers in making instructional decisions. It is taken while a student reads orally from a continuous text, such as a storybook, a nonfiction book, or a student's published piece of writing that has been edited. In this way, miscues (errors) occur and the teacher can determine which reading strategies the reader used when confronted by unfamiliar text. The record reveals reading behaviors, including errors, self-corrections, repetitions, all the tries the reader makes on a given word, and how fluid the reading was. After the reading, the teacher analyzes the record by counting how many errors and self-corrections the reader made. Self-corrections are very desirable behaviors as they suggest that the reader is self-monitoring his/her reading and paying attention to meaning. For each error and self-correction, the teacher also marks which of the following three cueing systems the student used:

- Visual (i.e., letter-sound correspondence, such as substituting *hand* for *hang*);
- Meaning (i.e., substituting a word that is similar in meaning, such as *woman* for *lady*); or
- Structure (i.e., grammar, such as substituting *walking* for *getting*)

When working with ELs, especially newcomers, we need to ensure that we aren't marking as errors words that are actually related to emerging English pronunciation. The following scenario illustrates this.

SCENE: A third-grade class

PARTICIPANTS: The classroom teacher, Mr. Pérez, and Ana María, a newcomer from Ecuador whose native language is Spanish and who attended school in her home country and has been in the U.S. for four months.

SCENARIO: Mr. Pérez is assessing Ana María's reading in English using a running record. After she finishes reading the text, he asks her some clarification questions based on some of her errors that may be related to pronunciation rather than meaning. For example, she read *The children are getting cold* as *The chilren are gerring coal*.

MR. PÉREZ: Thank you, Ana María. I noticed here that you said, "The chilren are gerring cole" (*while pointing to the sentence in the book*). What are "chilren"? (*while pointing to* children*)*

ANA MARÍA: Like here (*and she points to a picture of three children*). Like me. And Marco. And Sam.

MR. PÉREZ: OK. Children. And, when you said, "The chilren are gerring cole," what do you mean by they're "gerring cole" (*while pointing to* getting cold)?

ANA MARÍA: Like they coal. Coal. *(while hugging herself as if she's very cold).*

MR. PÉREZ: Right. They're cold. Thanks very much, Ana María.

Based on this short conversation, Mr. Pérez decides that these three apparent errors are not really reading errors as all three cueing systems are in place (visual, meaning, and structure), and they are most likely related to the fact that Ana María is new to English and her pronunciation reflects this. He makes a note to himself to pay attention to and address any pronunciation issues that may cause confusion or embarrassment, but he knows that he needn't spend much time on pronunciation because young children like Ana María typically develop native-like pronunciation over time.

It often happens that errors and self-corrections reflect more than one cueing system. For example, in the sentence *The ball got squashed,* Arnaldo read, *The ball get flat.* In his reading, there are two errors (*get* for *got* and *flat* for *squashed*). In the case of *get* for *got*, he used the visual and meaning cueing systems. In the case of *flat* for *squashed*, he used the meaning and structure cueing systems.

After students have read a text and the miscues and self-corrections have been analyzed, a running record also provides a system for determining whether a text is at an appropriate level for that student. It is important to have students read a variety of texts and genres, to get a more complete picture of their reading processes and needs as familiar content is likely to generate fewer errors than unfamiliar content, even when the books are determined to be at a similar reading level. Succinct guidance on how to take, interpret, and use running records can be found in *Running Records for Classroom Teachers* (Clay, 2017).

The analyzed running record provides valuable information for a teacher as it points to the reading processes that the student relies on when confronted by unfamiliar text and those that would be beneficial to develop. In order to arrive at these insights, it is important to carefully analyze every type of miscue and observed reading behavior (e.g., errors, self-corrections, repetitions) rather than relying on one or two instances that look interesting. The completed running record of Guillermo's reading reflects this. (See Figure 6.3 for Guillermo's running record.) He was a Spanish-speaking, second-grade student from Mexico who had been in his U.S. school for about three weeks. Although he didn't speak much in English, he spoke in Spanish with other students and enjoyed looking at books in English and Spanish; his intake records indicated that he could read some Spanish. When doing the running record, his teacher, Ms. Carras, used a book about pets written by a student from a previous year as it was short and she had noticed that Guillermo often chose books about animals. She wanted to see what strategies he would use when reading a book in English. (She did not speak Spanish; if she had, she would have also assessed his reading using a text in Spanish.)

Guillermo's running record shows that he made 17 errors while reading 44 words—Ms. Carras did not record *Dis* for *This* as an error as she decided it was due to his pronunciation in English. He self-corrected twice (on *bird* and *my*). When analyzing which cueing systems he used, she saw that he relied most heavily on the visual or graphophonic cueing system, particularly at the beginning of words—in 10 of the 17 errors, he used his knowledge of phonics. However, he also used the meaning cueing system in 7 of the 17 errors and appeared to be reading for meaning. This was reinforced by her observation that he looked at the pictures and paused slightly when he encountered *gerbil* and *rabbit* in the text and on the second occasion that *rabbit* appeared, he read

FIGURE 6.3: Guillermo's Running Record

Text title: My Pets (written by a student) (44 words) Student: Guillermo Grade: 2 Date: Oct. 14	E	SC	Information used	
			E MSV	SC MSV
This is a dog. Dis/This — — ✓ (is a)	✓✓			
This is a cat. Dis/This — — ✓ (is a)	✓✓			
This is a bird. Dis/This ✓ — (a) b-b-bid/bird |sc	✓	✓		Ⓜ S Ⓥ
This is a rabbit. Dis/This ✓ — (a) r-r-r	✓✓		M s Ⓥ	
This is a gerbil. Dis/This ✓ ✓ ger-gerb/gerbil	✓		M s Ⓥ	
These are my pets. Dis/These sc is/are M-m/My |sc p-e-t/pets	✓✓	✓	Ⓜ Ⓢ V Ⓜ Ⓢ Ⓥ	Ⓜ Ⓢ Ⓥ
I like dogs. ✓ ✓ dog/dogs	✓		Ⓜ s Ⓥ	
I like cats. ✓ ✓ cat/cats	✓		Ⓜ s Ⓥ	
I like birds. ✓ ✓ bird/birds	✓		Ⓜ s Ⓥ	
I like rabbits. ✓ ✓ rab, rab, rabbit/rabbits	✓		Ⓜ s Ⓥ	
I like gerbils. ✓ ✓ gerb/gerbils	✓		M s Ⓥ	
I like all my pets. ✓ ✓ a-l/all my pet(?)/pets	✓✓		M s Ⓥ Ⓜ S Ⓥ	
	(17)	(2)	(7) (2) (10)	(2) (2) (2)

Error rate: 1:4
Percent accuracy: 75%
Self correction ratio: One in ten

it correctly, after looking briefly at the picture. She wasn't surprised that he wasn't familiar with *gerbil* but eventually got *rabbit* as there was a rabbit in the classroom, which he loved to help take care of. Ms. Carras also noted that several of his errors were related to omitting the final /s/ in plural nouns (e.g., *dog* for *dogs*), which is not uncommon with newcomers to English. She also noted that he read with expression when parts of sentences were familiar. In addition, after reading the piece, Ms. Carras asked Guillermo to tell her what the story was about. He responded, "It about boy that got dog, cat, bird, rabbit. He like dog, cat, bird, rabbit," which told her that Guillermo had understood the text. All in all, she determined that he was well on the way to becoming a successful reader in English, despite the percentage accuracy rate being only 75%, which is often considered too low a percentage to suggest that the student would be able to make meaning from the text. She didn't think this was the case as she was aware that Guillermo's running record reflected several issues that teachers are likely to encounter when assessing newcomers' reading in English (e.g., apparent errors being related to pronunciation and making the same error repeatedly when omitting the plural /s/, a common occurrence with ELs). She decided that the following instructional/learning experiences would help Guillermo become a more successful reader:

- Join a shared reading/guided reading group made up of newcomers with whom she would meet two to four times a week to read and discuss books and work on reading- and English-related teaching points.
- Teach him about regular plural nouns, probably in the context of the small EL group as other students omitted the final *s* plural in both their reading and writing, which sometimes caused confusion for readers.
- Have him listen to English-medium books on tape and the computer so he could see and hear how English words look and sound while also exposing him to more English vocabulary.
- Encourage him to continue reading in Spanish in order to develop his reading strategies.
- Introduce him to bilingual books so he could use his knowledge of Spanish to help him double-check whether he understood the words and text in English.

Anecdotal Student Records

In addition to gathering data on newcomers' reading processes, strengths, and needs through the previously discussed assessment strategies, it is also important to gather data on their independent reading preferences, experiences, and insights into books and genres. For students who can read in their native language, it is important that they have as much access as possible to books written in the native language as strategies and skills used and developed in the native language often transfer to English reading. Students can keep anecdotal records of their independent reading, including dated logs of the books they have read in which they list the titles, authors, in which language read, length, genre, and brief evaluations of the books. In Chapter 7: Developing Newcomers' Writing, in the section on reflective writing, we discuss a range of journal-writing opportunities, including dialogue journals. These kinds of experiences can also provide teachers with important awareness of students' reading experiences, preferences, and insights.

Familiar Classroom Reading Experiences with a Focus on Newcomers

The following well-known classroom reading experiences can be particularly helpful in developing newcomers' reading in English, so long as teachers make adjustments or modifications to accommodate newcomer students' developing understanding of English:

- Read-alouds;
- Language Experience Approach (LEA);
- Shared reading;
- Guided reading;
- Independent reading;
- Book discussions; and
- Post-reading activities.

Read-alouds

Read-alouds are a very valuable experience for newcomers as read-alouds can model fluid reading, introduce new concepts and vocabulary, and advance critical thinking through the conversations that follow a read-aloud. They can also introduce newcomers to information about the new culture they are immersed in.

In a traditional read-aloud, one of the major goals is to turn students on to books and to enjoy the experience of sharing a book with others. It is also an occasion to introduce students to concepts and vocabulary they may not already be familiar with to develop comprehension. The teacher typically reads the text aloud and periodically shows the illustrations to the students, sometimes followed by an end-of-session debrief. If it is a text that is read over several days, such as a novel, the teacher may begin each session brainstorming with students what occurred in the previous section or chapter to activate students' memories. However, with newcomers, it is often important to modify or enhance the read-aloud experiences through a variety of strategies, such as the following:

- Select texts that contain familiar content for newcomers, such as the following:
  - Family life;
  - Cultures that are similar to those of newcomers;
  - Nonfiction themes that are popular with children around the world, such as animals and sports;
  - Experiences that newcomer students may be familiar with, such as losing a tooth or different kinds of bread; and
  - Familiar stories, such as fairytales—for example, there are more than 30 Cinderella stories from around the world that are available in English and, sometimes, another language (Figure 6.4 lists just a sample of the many available).

FIGURE 6.4: A Sampling of Cinderella Stories from around the World

Louie, Ai-Ling. *Yeh-Shen: A Cinderella Story from China.* (Illus. by Ed Young). (A retelling of a Chinese story)

San Souci, Robert D. *Cendrillon: A Caribbean Cinderella.* (Illus. by Brian Pinkney). (A retelling of an Iraqi story)

Hayes, Joe. *Estrellita de Oro/Little Gold Star.* (Illus. by Gloria Osuna Perez and Lucia Angela Perez.) (A bilingual retelling of a New Mexico story)

Thomas, Joyce Carol. *The Gospel Cinderella.* (Illus. by David Diaz). (An original African American Cinderella story)

- Select texts that have lots of illustrations and make sure that the illustrations actually do relate to the text—in some books, both fiction and nonfiction, illustrations aren't closely aligned with the text. Also, make sure to take time to talk about the illustrations and point to specific features or items in them to clarify meaning as you read.
- Vary the genres read aloud. Fiction is often the most difficult genre for newcomers to understand, particularly if it contains lots of figurative language. In contrast, nonfiction books often have content that is familiar to newcomers and the illustrations help them crosscheck for understanding.
- Do a walk-through of a text before reading it aloud, showing the pictures and pointing out key vocabulary. In this way, students get a heads-up for what will follow.
- Make copies of the text available to newcomers during the readaloud so they have the support of pictures to help them get the gist of the text and so they can follow along as the teacher reads aloud. This helps reinforce the following: what English words and phrases look like; the role of punctuation to support meaning; and connections between the words on the page, the illustrations, and meaning. Also, if newcomers are literate in a language other than English, particularly if it is Latin based, such as Spanish and Portuguese, they are able to use that knowledge to build their vocabularies and enhance understanding. One teacher we know always has three to four extra copies available, which students "borrow" during read-alouds on a rotating basis, if they wish. We have observed how other students will cluster around the students who have the extra copies, so even more children have access. This strategy is particularly helpful for students who are not strong auditory learners.
- If extra copies aren't available, teachers can use a document camera to display the pages as they read aloud, so students can follow along and be supported to make meaning from having easy access to the pictures and the text.
- Read aloud published texts written by students. It can be very interesting and encouraging for newcomers to read texts that other students have written and published. They can be texts that are posted on the wall or in binders. And, they can be texts that have been bound into books or class anthologies and stored in book boxes and the classroom and school libraries.

- While reading aloud, pay attention to whether newcomer students are following along. Although read-alouds benefit from dramatic reading to convey meaning, it is particularly important to do this with newcomers while also using gestures and pointing to images, as needed. See Chapter 5: Developing Newcomers' Listening and Speaking for additional suggestions for enhancing newcomers' understanding of oral language.
- Once newcomers become more fluent in English, it is important to read aloud texts on topics and about cultures they may not be familiar with, in order to expand their knowledge base (schema) and vocabularies.

Language Experience Approach (LEA)

LEA was originally designed as a way to develop reading materials for young, emergent readers (Allen 1976; Stauffer, 1970), but it has been found to also be very effective with ELs (e.g., Rigg, 1989). A key element is that students generate the texts. We have followed these steps when using LEA with ELs:

- A student or group of students orally generates a text. Some suggestions for what the text may be about follow:
    - A personal experience (e.g., a family experience or cultural holiday);
    - A shared experience (e.g., a field trip or when a visitor came to class);
    - A retelling of a story; or
    - What has been learned about a topic in a content-area class (e.g., steps in conducting a science experiment or the rules for playing kickball).

When students are very new to English, the texts are likely to be very short. For example, Lourdes generated this text when looking at a picture of a dog and three pups: "This dog. Dog baby. One, two, ..." (She wasn't sure how to say *three* in English.)

- The teacher acts as a scribe and writes the text exactly as dictated. If a group of students dictates the text, the teacher uses chart paper or a document camera or whiteboard so that all the students can see it.
- The teacher then goes through the text, explaining how to revise

the grammar, words/phrases, and punctuation. The teacher uses a colored pen to show the revisions. The teacher does not change the content. An example of this revision stage is in the dialogue below:

TEACHER: (*Saying the first sentence*) "Plant got water." Is that OK?
JAVIER: Plants?
TEACHER: Yes. It needs an *s*. "Plants." It's plural because there were four plants (*holds up four fingers*). Right?

(*Students nod in agreement.*)

TEACHER: Anything else in this sentence?
AMIRA: The. "The plant got water?"
TEACHER: You're right. It needs an article, *The*. "The plants got water."

The students and teacher continue this process until the entire text has been revised.

- The teacher transcribes the revised text onto a clean sheet of paper (or chart paper, if working with a group of students) so that it is easy to read. A paper copy (vs. a whiteboard or digital projector copy) is best at this stage so that the text is preserved for students to return to regularly to read and to learn about English and writing.
- The student(s) and teacher then read the revised text aloud together. And, over the next several days, the students read it many times.

Although the teacher does the physical writing, newcomers generate the text and are learning how to write in English. The teacher can later type up the text and make it into a book that the students illustrate and read. Because the content is familiar, they are supported as both readers and writers.

Shared Reading

Shared reading is a strategy that is typically used with primary-grade children as they embark on becoming readers. However, it can be very helpful with newcomers of all ages. The following steps are typically followed in a shared reading experience:

- Students sit on the rug (or, with older students, in concentric circles of chairs) in front of the teacher.

- An enlarged text, which all the students can see, is placed on an easel or projected on a document camera. This can be a commercially produced "Big Book," a class book made by students or previous classes, or a chart (either commercially produced or prepared by the teacher). The genre can vary (e.g., fiction, poetry, nonfiction). The text is often predictable as this feature is very helpful to emergent readers. Predictable elements include refrains (e.g., " 'Who's that going over my bridge?' said the troll" in *The Three Billy Goats Gruff*) and a cumulative story structure (e.g., Patricia Polacco's *In Enzo's Splendid Garden* (1997), in which a boy drops his book while watching a bee, which leads to the waiter tripping over the book, then some ladies spilling their tea, then Chef Enzo spilling the spaghetti, and so on.).

- The teacher does a short introduction to the text while turning the pages and showing them to the students to activate students' knowledge and prepare them for the story, poem, or nonfiction content.

- The teacher reads the text aloud, while pointing underneath each word with a pointer (e.g., an expandable pointer or a thin stick or yardstick)—it is important that the pointer not interfere with the ability of students to see and read the text. This helps students associate how words look with how they sound. The pace of this reading is slightly slower than in a typical read-aloud.

- The teacher invites students to collaboratively read the text again while continuing to point underneath each word. This is like a choral reading. Some students may attempt to read the entire text while other students may just read a word or two or the refrain, and some students may simply follow along silently.

- The students and teacher read the text aloud again and may re-read it several times more, depending on how engaged the students are.

- The students and teacher may read one or more enlarged texts that they are already familiar with. Students who may not have joined in on the reading of the new text often join in with this familiar read.

- In advance, the teacher selects one or two reading skills or strategies to focus on (e.g., words that sound alike and have different meanings, such as *bee* and *be*; irregular past tense verbs, such as *to go/went* and *to say/said*; paying attention to the ends of words).

- Students may then work in pairs, triads, or individually to complete a related task (e.g., putting sentence strips of a story in order or completing a cloze text). In a *cloze*, words are deleted from a text and students have to use their knowledge of the content as well as the surrounding text to figure out what belongs in each blank space. A traditional cloze deletes every five or 10 words after the first sentence, but when working with ELs, it is helpful to be very strategic about which words are deleted and to delete words that are grounded in recent learning (e.g., key terminology or the articles *a, an,* and *the*). The following example of a cloze text is from a fourth-grade class that had been studying ecology. First, we show the complete text with the words selected by the teacher for deletion bolded. This is followed by the cloze text.

Ecology is the science that studies living things, the environment, and how they interact. Each environment is called an **ecosystem**. Some of the environments are wetlands, coral reefs, **freshwater** ponds, and forests. While studying about forests, we focused on the four **levels** of that environment. The bottom level is called the forest **floor**. It is a dark and damp place. Gorillas, elephants, and leopards live here. The second level is called the **understory**. It is made up of vines and dense **vegetation**. Birds, snakes, and butterflies live here. The third level is the **canopy**. This is the **thickest** layer, where tall, mature **trees** can be found. This is where birds, monkeys, and many insects live. The final level is called the emergent layer or **overstory**. Only the **tallest** trees live here. Bats, snakes, small monkeys, and lizards live here.

Ecology is the science that studies living things, the environment, and how they interact. Each environment is called an _____. Some of the environments are wetlands, coral reefs, _____ ponds, and forests. While studying about forests, we focused on the four _____ of that environment. The bottom level is called the forest _____. It is a dark and damp place. Gorillas, elephants, and leopards live here. The second level is called the _____. It is made up of vines and dense _____. Birds, snakes, and butterflies live here. The third level is the _____. This is the _____ layer, where tall, mature _____ can be found. This is where birds, monkeys, and many insects live. The final level is called the emergent layer or _____. Only the _____ trees live here. Bats, snakes, small monkeys, and lizards live here.

Guided Reading

Guided reading is small-group reading instruction and is most often found in primary-grade classrooms (Fountas & Pinnell, 2016). Students in a given guided reading group have similar reading needs and the teacher meets with groups several times a week for about 20 minutes each session. All students in the group have their own copy of the text; often, they are *leveled texts* (i.e., texts that have been assessed to be at different reading levels, based on such features as length, sentence complexity, and vocabulary). Guided reading is a very useful learning experience for primary, upper-grade, and middle school students who are newcomers to English reading.

Each guided reading session typically consists of the following components:

- *Selecting the text:* It is critical that teachers select texts that are accessible to newcomers. For example, will students have some prior knowledge of the content? Will the vocabulary, sentence structure, and length of the text be just right and not too long or complex? Is the text appropriate for the age of the students, particularly students in the intermediate grades and middle school? Even though older newcomers may be beginning readers in English, they should not be reading texts that are written for much younger children. The text can be a short story, picture book, poem, or nonfiction book, preferably with pictures to help with understanding.
- *Introducing the text*: The purpose of the text introduction is to help students later read the text on their own and be able to problem solve when they encounter unfamiliar words or terms. It is useful to go through every page, talking about vocabulary and grammatical structures that may be unfamiliar or confusing for the students, including figurative language, complex grammar, and words with multiple meanings. Also, be prepared to use visuals to explain new concepts (e.g., what snow looks like if a class has students who come from hot and arid regions of the world).
- *Reading and supporting effective reading*: Students take turns reading aloud to the teacher while the rest of the students read their own texts silently and independently. Some students may subvocalize, that is, say the words aloud softly, as they are reading independently. The teacher monitors what the student who is reading aloud is doing as a reader and

points to and supports effective reading, such as when a student self-corrects or goes back and re-reads a section that got mixed up.

- *Responding to the text*: This is a time for students to comment on what they have read, such as what they learned and what they particularly liked and why.

- *Teaching and extending meaning*: This is an opportunity to teach to one or two carefully selected points based on what was observed in the students' reading. Examples of this kind of teaching include the following:
  - Focus on a key point in the text by looking for a specific description or piece of information in the text.
  - Help students figure out unfamiliar words by focusing on word parts and/or context clues.
  - Help students interpret information found in graphs, charts, tables, and maps.
  - Work on other reading strategies like questioning, summarizing, inferring, and making connections.

- *Working with words*: This component lasts just a couple of minutes and is grounded in what the teacher observes. Examples of this type of work include the following:
  - Building awareness of sounds that appear in the English text but are not found in the students' native language; and
  - Building word families (e.g., in a nonfiction piece about baseball, *manager* is in the text; *managers, managed, managing, manageable*, and *management* are in the same word family).

Independent Reading

To become a reader, one must read, and this is true for newcomer students, just as it is for other students. Time <u>in</u> school for independent reading is essential—this is true for all students, regardless of age. However, care must be taken to ensure that the texts made available to newcomers for independent reading take into account their emerging status as readers in English; this is particularly the case with upper-grade newcomers as the texts that their non-newcomer peers typically read independently are often much too long and complex for newcomers to have success with alone.

We have observed newcomers having success with independent reading when the following have been available to them:

- *Simpler texts*, particularly for older newcomers: These include photo stories, picture books that are appropriate for older students, graphic novels and nonfiction books, short stories, and magazines. Graphic novels and graphic nonfiction books are often more comprehensible than non-graphic novels and nonfiction books because there are far fewer words and lots of illustrations. Texts with a predictable structure that allow readers to anticipate the next word or sentence are also often good choices (e.g., Shirley Neitzel's *The Bag I'm Taking to Grandma's* [1995] and Walter Dean Myers' *Looking Like Me* [2009]*)*.

- *Texts in the native language*: It is important for newcomers to have success as readers and, if they are able to read in their native language, they should be encouraged to do so. Reading strategies that one uses in one's native language typically transfer to reading in another language, which is just one of the many reasons to encourage reading in the native language. If the text in the native language is available in English, newcomers can later read the English version and are likely to understand this version because of their familiarity with the content that they gained from reading in the native language.

- *Bilingual texts*: For newcomers who can read in their native languages, having access to bilingual texts can be very helpful. The layout of languages in these books varies. For example, sometimes English is on one page and the other language is on a facing page (e.g., Te Ata's *Baby Rattlesnake/Viborita de Cascabel* [1989] and Sandra Cisneros' *Hair/Pelitos* [1994]). In other books, the text in both languages is on the same page (e.g., George Ancona's *The Piñata Maker/El Piñatero* [1994] and Truong Tran's *Going Home, Coming Home/ Về Nhà, Thăm Quê Hưởng* [2003]. Figure 6.5 lists some publishers and distributors of bilingual books and books in languages other than English.

- *Published texts written by other students*: Reading published texts written by other students can be both interesting and encouraging for newcomers, who may find the content and language more familiar than in many commercially published books. These published texts can include papers on the classroom wall placed at a height and in a location that is easily accessible for students to read. They can also be student- or class-authored books that are stored in book boxes and class and school libraries. We have found that, after students have published their writing, it is often hidden from view, which is a great loss as the purpose of

FIGURE 6.5: Publishers and Distributors of Bilingual Books and Books in Languages Other Than English

Publishers
Cinco Puntos Press—https://www.cincopuntos.com An independent book publisher in south Texas that has published many Spanish-English bilingual books and books in Spanish for children.
Del Sol Books—https://www.delsolbooks.com An independent publisher of Spanish-English bilingual books and books in Spanish. Owned by the authors, Alma Flor Ada and Isabel Campoy.
Lee & Low Books—https://www.leeandlow.com An independent multicultural children's and young adult book publisher that is minority owned and committed to increasing diversity in children's book publishing. In addition to many multicultural books, it publishes Chinese-, Hmong-, Japanese-, Korean-, Spanish-, Tagalog-, and Vietnamese-English bilingual books. It acquired the following publishers, which are now imprints of Lee & Low Books: *Shen's Books*, which focuses on books about Asian/Asian American cultures, with an emphasis on the present day. Many books are bilingual. *Children's Book Press*, which focuses on Spanish-English bilingual books.
Distributors
Booklandia—https://booklandiabox.com A small independent distributor located in northern California. It carries books in Spanish and Spanish-English bilingual books for children and young adults.
Lectorum Publications—https://lectorum.com Lectorum is a subsidiary of Scholastic Books. It distributes Spanish-English bilingual books and books in Spanish for children and young adults.

writing should be for more than to show one can do it—students need authentic audiences for their writing.

- *Books on tape*: Listening to fiction and non-fiction books that have lots of illustrations can provide a successful reading experience for newcomers. It is particularly helpful when the hard copy accompanies the CD or tape. There are also websites/online apps where children can read on the screen and the story is read aloud to them, highlighting words as they go. We know teachers who use Raz-Kids: https://www.raz-kids.com/. Teachers can also record books for this purpose, as can students and volunteers. If teachers do this, they will need to make sure to include a signal for page turning (e.g., a bell); it may be necessary to teach students the signal to turn the page. We have found that books that turn the page at the end of a sentence work best with newcomers.

Book Discussions

It is very important that newcomers have many opportunities to talk about books with other students and their teachers. This can occur in a variety of configurations, including the following:

- *Peer conversations*: Newcomers talk with a peer, with two peers in a triad, or with a small group. They can talk about a book they've read in common or about different books. For example, after reading texts that explore different cultural practices and experiences or stories from around the world, such as Cinderella stories, they talk with peers about similarities and differences in the cultural practices and experiences described in the books or how Cinderella stories are similar and different. It is important for ELs, particularly newcomers, to chart these similarities and differences, using sketches whenever possible to help convey meaning.
- *Buddy reading*, in which older students read to and with younger students. It is important to prepare the older students to be buddies or tutors (e.g., how to share a book reading with the younger child, how to talk about pictures, how to ask questions that elicit more than yes/no responses). It is also important to teach the younger students how to interact with their older buddies (e.g., attentive listening, how to respond to a book that has been read aloud, not making fun of their tutors/buddies if they are not fluent in English). For more information about introducing and maintaining a cross-age buddy reading program, see *Buddy Reading: Cross-Age Tutoring in a Multicultural School* (Samway, Whang, & Pippitt, 1995).
- *Teacher/student conversations* about books read with a single student, a small group of students, and the entire class. We have found that when we observe the following suggestions, the conversations are much richer and students are much more engaged:
  - Avoid an initiation-response-evaluation (IRE) sequence in which the teacher initiates a question (often a known-answer question), a student responds, and the teacher evaluates or gives feedback on the response. This is a very common form of discourse in classrooms and it is almost like an interrogation. Instead, we have found that open-ended questions lead to interesting conversations.
  - Wait—after asking a question, even a couple of seconds in wait

time can seem like a long time, but we have learned to wait until a student responds. This is particularly important with newcomers. An encouraging smile and/or looking at a page in the book while waiting can help students figure out what they would like to say. Also, rephrasing the question can help.

- Follow the lead of students. What are their burning questions? What are they particularly excited about? What kinds of connections are they making between the text and their lives and experiences and the world around them?

- Do not correct comments that students make, even if they are not supported by the text. Instead, ask for clarification in order to understand students' thinking and help them figure out what the text is communicating. For example, one day, Katharine was in a book discussion with a group of third- and fourth-grade students who had just read Natalie Babbitt's *Tuck Everlasting* (1975). Toward the end of the discussion, one of the students commented on what it might be like for the main character, a young girl called Winnie, to live forever. In the book, Winnie is given the opportunity to drink magic spring water that would give her eternal life. The author does not clearly state what Winnie does but leaves clues in an epilogue and a headstone for a much older Winnie. Katharine did not tell the students this. Instead, she suggested they go back and read the ending of the book and look for evidence of Winnie drinking the water. Together, and with a little nudging from Katharine (e.g., to look at the picture of the headstone), the students realized that they hadn't paid attention to the headstone and had therefore overlooked the dates on it. Also, they didn't understand what an epilogue is, which provided some clues. The search for meaning was active and the students expressed pleasure to have figured out what actually happened. This conversation also led to a very interesting discussion about the pros and cons of eternal life—the students didn't agree with each other, some preferring eternal life and others seeing problems with it.

- Offer your own insights, particularly in response to what students have said, but do not dominate the conversation. Apart from being a very natural thing to do in a conversation, it can be a way to extend students' thinking and understanding.

- Encourage students to use any language (English, their native language, or another language they speak that is shared by other students). This is very important for newcomers because they almost certainly have more to say in their native or other language spoken than they are able to say in English.

Teacher-student discussions are addressed in some detail in *Literature Study Circles in a Multicultural Classroom* (Samway & Whang, 1996).

Choosing Texts for Newcomers

When selecting books for all kinds of reading, including for the classroom library and reading boxes, it is important to ensure that they are unbiased, that they accurately and respectfully portray people and cultures, and that minority characters have well-developed stories and don't simply serve to save Caucasian characters. Another guiding principle is to look for books that aren't limited to retellings of folktales and legends but also include stories and nonfiction about present-day peoples.

In order to address the potential for bias in books, teachers should be alert to and address the following set of guidelines and considerations when selecting texts and materials to use in classrooms. These guidelines are adapted from "Guide for Selecting Anti-Bias Books for Children" (Derman-Sparks, 2019).

- *Check for negative stereotypes,* and look for books and materials that depict people compassionately as complex human beings. Make sure that images don't convey stereotypical features.
- *Avoid tokenism*, which involves centering on only one representative of a group of people. An example of this is when only one African American child is presented among a group of white children.
- *Avoid invisibility,* whereby entire groups of people who have tended to be marginalized in U.S. society are not present in the materials, books, or images that children have access to. This includes homeless people, transgender people, people with disabilities, and immigrants.
- *Be aware of biases related to the power dimensions* conveyed in the storylines of texts or in the relationships between characters. Are only or mostly white or male characters the protagonists in most books and materials available in the classroom? Are the achievements of particular groups based on stereotypes (e.g., girls are presented as good at domestic activities while boys are seen as lead-

ers)? Make sure that books and materials depict people of different backgrounds in "doer" roles (e.g., as leaders and those that resolve conflicts).

- *Look for negative and generalized messages about different lifestyles.* How are people of color and people living in poverty depicted, particularly in comparison with those who are white and middle class? Are they portrayed as needing to be pitied? Do the books and materials in your classroom present, within a specific racial/ethnic group, a variety of experiences, family structures, types of work, and gender-based roles?

- *Check on how books and materials may affect children's sense of self and identities.* Will children see themselves and their families in your collection of books and materials? Will they see characters with whom they can identify in a positive light?

- *Look for books about people who have been active in social justice issues.* Do the books and materials in your collection include people who have engaged in struggles for justice? Are these people from diverse backgrounds, including those who are impoverished or who have been oppressed?

- *Consider the authors' and illustrators' backgrounds and perspectives.* Make sure that your collection includes books written and illustrated by authors and illustrators from diverse cultural, social, and gender communities and backgrounds. If authors are not members of the ethnic group being written about, it is important to check the author note in the book to establish whether they carefully researched their topic and ethnic group. In Appendix 4, we provide an annotated list of books that we have found work well with newcomers, and many of the authors are members of the cultures written about.

- *Watch for loaded words in books and materials.* A loaded word demeans or renders people invisible because of their identities. For example, using *man* to reference people in general is one such example. The use of adjectives with racist messages to refer to people of color (e.g., *savage*, *primitive*) is another.

- *Consider copyright dates.* Until the 1970s, most books for children were written by Caucasian authors. Although the world of publishing children's literature has changed quite a bit since the 1970s, books by authors from underrepresented groups still lag behind, and there are few books for children about some cultures found among immigrant groups (e.g., Syria, Sudan). It is a good idea to start with the most recently published books.

There may be occasions when available texts and materials contain biases but are otherwise well written. If this occurs, it is important to explore with students the following:

- In what ways are the texts or materials biased?
- What is the possible impact of these kinds of biases on members of the group at the receiving end of the biases?
- Why may these texts and materials be biased (e.g., are there historical or geographic realities that may have affected the author's writing?)? Some questions that can help students explore bias in books include the following:
  - Is the text fair? Why/why not?
  - Which characters are in charge? How do you know?
  - Are there people like you in the book? Should there be? Why?

Post-Reading Activities That Support Newcomers

After reading independently, students often keep a log of what they have read and the number of pages. They may have brief conversations with other students about the book they are reading and/or have just read. Some additional activities that can support newcomers after reading include the following.

Dyadic Belt

The goal of a dyadic belt is to give students opportunities to share what they are reading and to make recommendations. For newcomers and other ELs, it is also an opportunity to use English in an authentic and meaningful way. However, students should feel free to use their native language in order to communicate fully. We have found the following steps to be helpful:

- Students put five to 10 sticky notes in their books, indicating pages they want to talk about and would like other students to see.
- Students sit facing each other in two parallel lines. If the class is large, there can be several parallel lines.
- Students take turns telling the student across from them about their books, using their notes. They have one to two minutes each to do this. A signal from the teacher to switch (e.g., a quiet bell ringing) can be used to ensure that both students have the opportunity to share.

- After both students have had a chance to share (about three to four minutes), the right line in the dyadic belt moves one chair to the right. The person at one end of the right-hand belt comes to the other end of the belt.
- Continue this way until students have had multiple opportunities to talk about their books.

Reading and Writing Book Reviews (<u>Not</u> Book Reports)

Students are often asked to write book reports after reading a book, which is typically read by just the teacher and then graded. A much more meaningful alternative is to write book reviews, which are different from book reports in that they have an authentic audience (other students) and purpose (to share a book that has been liked in hopes that other students may read and enjoy it, too). Because reviews can be short, they can be accessible to newcomers who are coming into English. Also, if newcomers can write in their native language, bilingual or multicultural reviews can be written and shared.

A short, two-week book review unit of study can be a good place to start. For newcomers who are recent arrivals or just beginning to move into English, it is important to support them through using the kinds of strategies described in Chapter 5: Developing Newcomers' Listening and Speaking (e.g., using lots of visuals, sketches, and mime), as well as partnering newcomers with other students. A suggested procedure for teaching students about writing book reviews through an inquiry unit-of-study approach follows:

- *Before the unit of study begins:*
    - The teacher gathers about four to five reviews of books that the students know (e.g., through read-alouds and in independent reading) and have liked. Searching online for "reviews of _____" and naming a book you know your students like is one way to start. Although the wording in a published review may be more complex than is appropriate for many of the students, it can be used as a model for reviews the teacher writes (and can share with other teachers).
    - The teacher makes copies of these reviews for the students.
- *Day 1 of the unit of study:*
    - The teacher explains the following to the class:
        - They will be writing book reviews for a class publication

that will be shared with other students, including possibly online.

- – The publication is intended to be a guide for other students who may be looking for good book suggestions.
- – The books can be any genre (e.g., fiction, nonfiction, poetry, picture books, photo books, books by students, novels, short story collections, and graphic books).
- – Because the published collection of book reviews is intended to offer many suggestions to lots of students, there won't be any duplicates of books reviewed.

- The teacher reads each of the reviews aloud while the students follow along in their own copies—these reviews will become mentor texts for the students when they are writing their own reviews. The teacher can also use a document camera to display the reviews while reading them so that newcomer students are able to follow along. However, the students will also eventually need their own hard copies.

- The students collaboratively generate a list of characteristics of good book reviews, which the teacher charts (e.g., it talks about the story or content of the book; it talks about the illustrations; it includes humor; it mentions the author; it mentions how many pages). Quick sketches are included next to each characteristic to help newcomers; students can help make these sketches. There is no discussion at this point about whether a given characteristic is required in all book reviews. The following scenario illustrates this process of figuring out characteristics of a book review.

SCENE: A fourth-grade class

PARTICIPANTS: The classroom teacher, Ms. Bader, and her class of students from many different language backgrounds. Several students are ELs, some of them newcomers from Spanish-speaking backgrounds. In order to support the newcomer students and help them understand what is being talked about, Ms. Bader uses a lot of mime and gestures (e.g., gesturing to illustrate "lots"), provides alternate words or terms (e.g., "not so good parts" for "weaknesses"), and sometimes offers Spanish for English words (e.g., "*ejemplos*" for "examples").

SCENARIO: Day one in a book review unit of study. The students are collaboratively generating characteristics of a good book review. As Ms. Bader charts the characteristics that students generate, she typically abbreviates their words into a few concise words, using terminology that students have already been introduced to.

MS. BADER:	So, what are some of the characteristics of a good book review? *Las características?*
ANITA:	I think it gotta be kinda short. (*Ms. Bader writes* Short *on the chart while miming* short.)
ANDRÉS:	Well, you gotta' have the name. The book. And the writer.
MS. BADER:	You mean the name of the author and title of the book (*while pointing to the name of the author and then the title of a book*)?
ANDRÉS:	Yeah. (*Ms. Bader writes* Includes the author *and* Title *on the chart.*)

The students and teacher continue this process until they have quite a long list of characteristics. See the left column in Figure 6.6.

- *Day 2 of the unit of study:*
  - The next day, the students go through the list and collaboratively decide if each listed characteristic is required, optional, or not required in a good book review. For example, as the right column in Figure 6.6 shows, some of the characteristics that the students in Ms. Bader's class decided were required included:
    - a) mentioning the author's name and book title, b) giving a summary of the book, and c) mentioning what was good about the book. They couldn't agree on whether a) writing the review as if talking to the reader and b) mentioning any weaknesses in the book were required, so they were classified as optional and recorded as "Maybe." They also decided that a) including lots of descriptive words and
    - b) having more than one paragraph were not required, which was reflective of the reviews they had read.
  - This list may be added to as the unit of study progresses.
  - The teacher then emphasizes to students that this chart of characteristics is there to guide them when they are writing their own book reviews.

FIGURE 6.6: Characteristics of Good Book Reviews: Chart Generated by Students

Characteristics (Características) of a Good Book Review	Required?
Short—not too many words	Yes
Includes the author and title	Yes
Gives a brief summary of the book	Yes
Mentions what was particularly (very) good about this book	Yes
Mentions any weaknesses in the book	Maybe
Gives examples to support points	Maybe
Uses lots of descriptive words	No
Written as if talking to the reader	Maybe
Includes a recommendation	Yes
Has more than one paragraph	No

- *Day 3 of the unit of study:*
  - The teacher displays on the rug or a large table many more books than there are students so that each student will have some choice. These are books that the teacher has observed that students have enjoyed, but they do not include the four to five books the teacher has provided reviews of to the students as mentor texts. Alternatively, each student can select two to three books they particularly like from book boxes, the class library, and the school library and place them on the rug or table; their reading logs can help jog their memories about books they particularly liked. If there are any duplicate books, they can be put to one side.
  - Using a selection process that works for the class, pair the students with the books. Remind students that they need to select books they have read. Some alternate ways to do this selection process follow:
    - Students write their three preferred books on a piece of paper and the teacher later uses these lists to pair students with their books. In the case of newcomer students, they may be paired with another student with whom they work well.
    - The teacher randomly pulls students' name written on popsicle sticks and students come to the rug or table in that order to choose a book. One possible problem with this

randomized selection is that newcomers and struggling readers may not have books available that they can really cope with as more experienced readers may select books that the newcomers and struggling readers have placed on the rug or table.

- The teacher uses a modified random selection process whereby the newcomer students and struggling readers have first choice of the books to help ensure that the books they are able to choose from are books they have read.

- *Days 4–7 of the unit of study:*
  - Over the next four days, the students draft and revise their book reviews. They confer on their drafts with peers and the teacher. The beginning of each writing session begins with a mini-lesson (e.g., how to start a book review or how to list the title and author's name).
- *Days 8–9 of the unit of study:*
  - Students edit their book reviews and confer with their peers on their edits.
  - Students write up or type clean, edited versions of their reviews.
- *Day 10 of the unit of study:*
  - Students display their book reviews along with their books on tables or clusters of desks. Visitors (e.g., caregivers/parents, students from other classes, teachers, librarians, aides, and administrators) visit and talk with the book review writers about their recommendations. It is a time to celebrate their work.
- *After the celebration:*
  - In the days following the celebration, the book reviews are typed (if not already done so by the students) and edited for public consumption. Volunteers can help the teacher with this process.
  - The collection of book reviews is collated and formally presented by the class to other classes, the school library, and other interested people and organizations (e.g., local libraries). If there are resources, each student receives a copy.
  - If the school or class has a website, the collection can be posted online.

Please note how important it is for students to do their own inquiry into the characteristics of a book review rather than the teacher showing them what goes into a book review or providing a list of requirements. In this way, students are able to internalize what they have collaboratively generated and discussed and then use it in their own writing. Professionally published book reviews may share some characteristics (e.g., the author and title are included), but they vary considerably from review to review.

Booktalks (an Alternative to Show and Tell)

Show and tell can be a very helpful way to ensure that all students have an opportunity to speak publicly. However, sometimes these events can be a rather stressful time, particularly for children from low-income and/or immigrant families, when students bring in toys—sometimes quite expensive toys. Teachers we know now use booktalks as an alternative to give students an opportunity to talk briefly about books they have read and enjoyed. It is helpful if students are taught how to do this effectively. One procedure we have found to work well is a demonstration, such as the following:

- The teacher begins by demonstrating a booktalk and asks students to notice what she/he does that works in the booktalk. This is a not-very-good example, but the teacher doesn't tell the students this in advance.
- The students comment on what they saw happening and whether they thought it was helpful. One group of second graders generated this list:
  - <u>What was helpful?</u>—showing pictures from the book.
  - <u>What wasn't helpful?</u>—mumbling; not telling anything about the book.
- The teacher demonstrates a second booktalk—this is a much better example, but the teacher doesn't tell the students this in advance.
- The students comment on what they saw happening and whether they thought it was helpful. The same group of second graders generated this list:
  - <u>What was helpful?</u>—showing pictures from the book, speaking in a lively way, telling a bit about the book, telling why you'd recommend it.
  - <u>What wasn't helpful?</u>—maybe it went on too long.
- In the discussion that follows, the class decides what should be present in a good booktalk, and the teacher charts their insights and posts it in a prominent place in the classroom.
- Students practice giving booktalks with a partner or partners.

- Before students are scheduled to give booktalks, they are reminded to go over the guidelines and also practice, both in school with a partner or the teacher and at home with family members and caregivers.

Vocabulary Development through a Word Consciousness Approach

Vocabulary is at the heart of a language. It is also at the heart of reading comprehension. If a child can decode a word or words but does not understand the meaning of these words, then the child is not really reading. In the U.S., vocabulary is often taught in a routinized way that does little to develop an extensive vocabulary or a love of words. For example, students may be given a list of 10-20 words each week to define and/or memorize. Relying on the dictionary for definitions can often be tricky as a given word may have multiple meanings (e.g., *high*, which has almost a page full of meanings in *The American Heritage Dictionary*). Or, students may be taught a few words or terms in advance of a particular unit of study. In place of this limited approach to vocabulary development, we advocate for a generative approach in which students build an awareness of words and are able to figure out or attempt to figure out word meanings on their own. In the process, they develop an appreciation and love for words and their meanings. This type of approach is often referred to as *word consciousness* (e.g., Graves & Watts-Taffe, 2008; Samway & Taylor, 2009; Scott & Nagy, 2004).

As we mentioned earlier in this chapter, reading, being read to, and talking about texts throughout the day are all very important and powerful ways to develop newcomers' vocabularies and reading. These also support newcomers' development as writers. When we inititate and encourage talk about interesting words and expressions, we can enhance newcomers' vocabularies. When we engage them in specific activities designed to build their observations about words and expressions, we can help to build their curiosity about language.

We have found the following strategies work well when engaging in word consciousness work with newcomers:

- Share your own curiosity about and love for words and expressions throughout the day.
- Use an inquiry approach—that is, instead of telling students what words mean, encourage them to use context and knowledge of other words in a word family to figure out potential meaning(s). In this way, they develop strategies that enable them to learn more vocabulary on their own.

- Use demonstrations to help students understand the differences between similar words.
- Make word-related games available in the class for vocabulary development/ reinforcement work and for free choice time. Games such as *Dictionary, Word Bingo, Word Concentration*, and *It's a . . .* work well and students enjoy playing them.
- In *It's a . . .*, students use their creative thinking to generate as many imagined uses as possible for a simple object—such as a paperclip or a drawing of an imaginary object—such as the following:

FIGURE 6.7: Imaginary Object

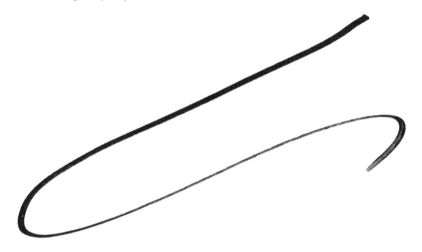

- Keep charts of words and expressions and add to them on an ongoing basis—the examples of activities that follow illustrate what some of the charts may focus on.

Activities for Building Word Consciousness

The following activities are designed to build curiosity and knowledge about words.

Shades of Meaning

Teachers often ask students to look for and use synonyms (i.e., words or expressions that have the same or nearly the same meaning) in place of much-used words. However, there are very few occasions when two or more words have identical meanings. In fact, there are typically significant differences in meanings between words. On a recent trip to Katharine's home town near Manchester, England, she was delighted to observe a poster at light rail stations that encouraged people to walk. The poster was a wonderful example of words with similar (but different) meanings—that is, shades of meaning (see Figure 6.8).

FIGURE 6.8: Walking Shades of Meaning

Greater Manchester
Walking
Festival May 2019 ▶

Strolling
Wandering
Roaming
Ambling
Walking
Striding
Shuffling
Mooching
Exploring
Stepping
Pushing

1st — 31st May 2019
**Over 400 guided walks for everyone.
However you choose.**

Delivered by
Greater Manchester
Moving > ∧ < ∨   Transport for
Greater Manchester

gmwalking.co.uk
#GMWalkingFestival

Source: Greater Manchester Moving Team, Manchester, U.K.

Let's take the word *said*, a word that is used often in students' writing but also in professional writing. If we make a list of words that can be used in place of *said*, it might include *shouted, whispered, announced,* and *claimed*. However, each of these words has a strikingly different meaning and cannot necessarily replace *said* in a text. The task, then, is to collect as many words as possible that <u>could</u> go in place of much-used words and, through visuals and demonstrations, help students internalize the differences and be able to understand them when reading (and writing). The following steps work well when developing awareness of shades of meaning:

- The class collects words with similar meanings from a variety of sources, including books, the environment outside school, and TV, which are posted on a chart (e.g., *laugh, giggle, snicker, guffaw, chuckle*).
- Small groups of students take responsibility for two to three of the words, discuss what each means, and practice demonstrating each word.
- The group posts their words so other members of the class can see them.
- Individual members of the group demonstrate each of the words in turn.
- Class members then have to decide with which word a demonstration corresponds. Interesting discussions often follow.

There are many other groups of words that work well in this activity, including words related to the following:

- Movement (e.g., *walk, stride, crawl, limp*)
- Gestures (e.g., *wave, shrug, beckon, signal*)
- Facial expressions (e.g., *smile, grimace, scowl, grin*)
- Color (e.g., for *red—rose, scarlet, ruby, vermilion*)
- Size (e.g., for *large—big, huge, enormous, gargantuan*)

Charts of words should be added to on an ongoing basis as students encounter new words.

Multiple Meanings

The English language is very rich and one aspect of this richness is how many words have multiple meanings. In fact, there are many, many words in English that have multiple meanings—a quick look in a dictionary will demonstrate this. Words with multiple meanings can be very confusing for newcomers. For example, they may know *run* in the context of playing soccer on the playground and running after a ball but be surprised when they read in a book that a car *ran* downhill or a batter scored a *run*. Some other examples of words with multiple meanings include *box, tie, drive,* and *list.* It is important to keep lists or charts of words with multiple meanings and add to them as students encounter new meanings.

Borrowed Words

Like other languages, English has many words that have been borrowed from other languages. We have found that newcomers are often very excited to discover that their native language has influenced English words. Some examples include the following:

- From *Arabic*: average (*awār*), safari (*safara*), cotton (*quṭn),* hummus (*ḥummuṣ*)
- From *Spanish*: coyote (borrowed by the Spanish from the Nahuatl language), burrito, churro
- From *Vietnamese*—ao dai (traditional Vietnamese dress), pho (Vietnamese soup)
- From Chinese—bok choy (from Cantonese--白菜), chop suey (from Cantonese--雜碎), feng shui (from Mandarin--風水)

Exploring *borrowed words* works particularly well when students elicit the help of their family and community members. Keep in mind that many words in English have multiple origins, so it is entirely possible that a word derived from Arabic, for example, may also derive from other languages, such as French. This can lead to more word consciousness inquiry work, including why that may have happened.

Different Englishes

English is spoken in various countries around the world and the accents differ, both from country to country, and from one region in a country to another. In addition, there are often differences in common words. For example, the U.S. refers to *trucks*, whereas in England, they are called *lorries*. Students are likely to encounter in books English words that are not used in the U.S., and this is a good time to talk about these differences and start a chart of different

Englishes. Also, newcomers will encounter regional differences in vocabulary in the U.S. (e.g., *soda, Coke, pop*).

Cognates, Partial Cognates, and False Cognates

Cognates are words in two or more languages that have the same root and have similar meanings. They may also sound and look alike. There are many cognates in Latin-based languages, such as English, Spanish, Italian, French, and Portuguese. (There are also many English-Germanic languages cognates.) Newcomers who have studied subjects such as science in their home countries may be quite familiar with very complex terms and, if their home language is a Latin-based language, such as Spanish or Portuguese, they may be able to access some meaning through cognates. For example, *geography* in English is written *geografía* in Spanish and *geografia* in Portuguese—there is no accent in Portuguese and the pronunciations in Spanish and Portuguese are quite different from each other and from English. Although the pronunciations of these words in Spanish and Portuguese are very different from the English pronunciation, the written words in the three languages look very similar, have the same root, and have the same meaning—that is, they are cognates.

There are also *partial cognates*, which are words in two languages that have the same meaning but not in all contexts. For example, the Spanish word, *conducir*, means *to conduct* in English. However, it also means *to drive* or *to transport* in Spanish; in addition, in Spanish, the *conductor* on a train is the *driver/engineer*, not the *ticket collector*. To complicate matters further, there are *false cognates*—that is, words that look and sound alike but have quite different meanings. Many people we know who have been living in a Spanish-speaking country and are still relatively new to Spanish have used a false cognate when they have said *"Estoy embarazada,"* intending to say that they are *embarrassed*; in fact, they have said that they are *pregnant*, which left them feeling <u>very</u> embarrassed!

CHAPTER 7

Developing Newcomers' Writing

WRITING IS A BIT LIKE the forgotten friend in literacy instruction as it often gets ignored or is taught in a routinized, unengaging way. This is particularly true with newcomers. Often, they are given tasks such as the following, which all require some kind of writing but aren't writing in the sense of generating original texts and communicating a message through print:

- Copying sentences;
- Completing cloze passages in which they have to fill in missing words;
- Rewriting sentences to reflect different verb tenses (e.g., putting the present tense into the future tense);
- Filling in the missing punctuation and/or capital letters in a short passage; and
- Completing grammar and vocabulary drills in a workbook.

While these activities are not really writing experiences, they sometimes serve a useful purpose. For example, when newcomers are moving into becoming writers in English, they sometimes choose to copy from environmental print (e.g., from posters, maps, and charts on the wall or whiteboard). Also, if newcomers are unfamiliar with a Latin-based script like English, it can help them to copy some of the letters and words in order to practice how the letters are formed. The other activities listed above can be useful when used to reinforce a skill that students appear to be ready to master. However, all too often, these kinds of activities are assigned without any regard to the needs of newcomer students.

In the remainder of this chapter, we will focus on more authentic writing experiences that are appropriate for newcomers, but we will begin with brief discussions of prior writing experiences newcomers may have had, principles of writing instruction that help newcomers, and "stages" in newcomers' writing development in English.

As you read, you may notice that many of the activities we describe rely on more than writing; this illustrates the importance of <u>not</u> teaching language modalities (listening, speaking, reading, writing) in isolation. For example, in a writing workshop, students may read books and other texts that help them figure out how a writer organizes a story or labels an illustrated science essay or how-to book; in writing conferences, students listen, speak, read, and may write; in writing mini-lessons, students listen and may read and write and talk in pair shares.

Prior Writing Experiences Newcomers May Have Had

The degree to which newcomers are able to write, whether in the native language, another language, or English, can affect the kind of writing experiences that are most appropriate for them. The following are just a few examples of the range of experiences with writing that newcomers may have had:

- *Students have experience writing in their native language but have been taught using a very different pedagogy from a learner-centered approach.* Sometimes, they have been taught that writing is copying the writing style and word choice of experts (e.g., in the case of many students from China) or skills practice (e.g., when students have received some instruction in English in their homeland or in a refugee camp).
- *Students can write in their native language, but their written language looks very different from English writing.* This may occur with students from, for example, Arabic-, Urdu-, or Farsi-speaking countries, where the language is alphabetic, but is written right to left.
- *Students are not literate in their native language.* This is sometimes found with students who have had limited or no formal schooling due to living in isolated areas and/or war. However, most will almost certainly have seen environmental print in their wider surroundings, even if they are unable to read it.
- *Students have some experience with writing, but most of their schooling has been in a non-native language.* This is sometimes found with refugees who have spent several years living in a refugee camp. Their instruction may have been in English as a way to prepare them for being resettled in English-speaking countries, such as the U.S. and Canada. This is also the case

with students who speak indigenous languages at home but attend school in their country's official language (e.g., many Guatemalan immigrants who have attended school speak an indigenous language at home and in the community and have been taught in Spanish at school).

"Stages" in Newcomers' Writing Development in English

Although there is no straight path that newcomers take when developing as writers in English, there are some stages through which they may pass, and this progress is typically affected by age and the extent to which they can write in another language. We have put *stages* in quote marks to underscore how the path that ELs take in becoming competent writers isn't linear. The following chart briefly describes stages through which newcomer ELs may pass, along with circumstances or ages where one is likely to encounter a particular stage.

It is important to stress that newcomers' writing development is often recursive—that is, the student may seem to have made progress and then

FIGURE 7.1: Stages of English Learners' Writing Development in English

"Stages" of ELs' Writing Development in English	Circumstances That May Affect the Appearance of This Stage
Drawings	ELs of all ages who are just being exposed to print in English, even ELs who can write in their native language
Scribbles that resemble the native language	Young children who are just becoming writers and have been exposed to print in their native language
Scribbles that resemble English letters	Young ELs who are just becoming writers and have been exposed to print in English
Random letters	Young ELs who are just becoming writers and have been exposed to print in English
Copying environmental print (e.g., charts on the wall)	ELs of all ages who no longer scribble or write random letters or series of letters in English
Drawings labeled in English and/or the native language	ELs of all ages who are moving into writing in English
Short, sustained texts that may not be in fluent English	ELs of all ages who are more experienced writers in English
Longer, more complex texts in English	Often older students who are more experienced writers in English.

seems to have regressed. This is not unusual and is often related to students being introduced to a new genre and/or writing on an unfamiliar topic and/or incorporating new grammatical structures and vocabulary.

Some Features of Writing Instruction That Help Newcomers' Writing Development

It can be enormously helpful to newcomers if the following features of writing instruction are present. More detailed explanations of some of the suggested strategies will be described through scenarios later in the chapter.

Write at Regularly Scheduled, Predictable Times

It is important to have a predictably scheduled time to write, such as a daily writing workshop right after lunch. This helps students come prepared, mentally (e.g., thinking about what they'd like to write about next or what they need to do with an in-process piece) and in terms of being ready with their writing tools (e.g., pens, pencils, writing folders, computers) and resources (e.g., a list of possible topics or guidelines for a unit of study on writing a biography). It is much harder for students to do this when they don't know when they will next be writing. Also, newcomers already have a lot to make sense of in their new school environment, so having predictable routines can be enormously helpful to them. Readers can learn more about a unit of study writing workshop for ELs in *When English Language Learners Write: Connecting Research to Practice, K-8* (Samway, 2006).

Have Opportunities to Write Often

Like any activity, students' writing "muscles" need to be exercised often. The more students write, the better and faster they will develop as writers. Although we advocate for a daily writing workshop, there are also many other times in the school day when students should be writing (e.g., keeping a science journal to record their observations of an experiment they are conducting or writing notes to be deposited in a class mailbox).

Provide Real Purposes for Writing

It is important to offer newcomer students many authentic purposes to write. For example, in the real world, people do not write book reports, except to show a teacher that they (may) have read a book. In contrast, book reviews are read all the time, both in hard copy and online. So, asking students to write a book review (and studying the genre first) is a much more real and purposeful alternative to book reports. The book reviews should be available to be read by other students as a way to make book recommendations. For a description of a book review writing unit of study, see Chapter 6: Developing Newcomers' Reading.

Have Real and Multiple Audiences

Having a real audience makes a huge difference to writers. This act of going public encourages writers to keep their audience in mind and to write as clearly and evocatively as possible. It is very important that students write for many audiences, not just the teacher. The most immediate and authentic audience in schools is other students, who typically enjoy reading and giving feedback on each other's writing. Other audiences may include public officials (e.g., when students write letters about problems that need fixing in the neighborhood), caregivers/parents (e.g., in a class newsletter), and younger students (e.g., when writing books for students in a buddy reading program).

Have Opportunities to Write in Many Genres

In the past, most writing done in elementary schools was story or memoir (personal narrative) writing. With the advent of the Common Core State Standards (CCSS), there has been more emphasis placed on nonfiction writing. It is very important that newcomers have experience writing across a variety of genres (e.g., writing how-to books, science reports, essays, stories, memoirs, letters, and poetry).

Model Steps and the Final Product

When introducing a writing activity, it is important to show students what the final product may look like, explore its component parts, and then model the steps involved in writing it. For example, a group of 14 sixth- and seventh-grade newcomers meet on a daily basis with a pull-out ELD teacher, Ms. Flanders. They are going to host an international music and dance event at the school, to which parents and community members will be invited. They are ready to put together invitations and Ms. Flanders has brought in copies of several invitations to similar past events. The students spend time collaboratively generating a list of the features of and content in these invitations, which Ms. Flanders writes down on chart paper. The list includes the following:

- A greeting (Dear . . .);
- Examples of the kinds of performances (e.g., Mexican Hat Dance, oud playing with singing, drumming from around the world);
- The title of the event; and
- The date of the event.

The students then go through the list and come to a consensus about what needs to appear in their own invitations. Ms. Flanders demonstrates writing an invitation but stresses that the students don't need to copy hers and that they should make their invitations their own.

Have Opportunities to Select Genres and Topics

Published writers of all ages often respond to requests for pieces of writing on a given topic (e.g., a sports story, an urban gardening initiative, the impact of immigration policy on local families) or in a given genre (e.g., letter, response to a blog post, essay, memoir, or poem). However, they have a great deal of choice over what they write about and how they write it. They are also able to generate their own topics and genres. These are features of being a writer that we need to foster in all students, including newcomers. Although there will be genres that students are required to write in, depending on local and state standards and grade level (e.g., an opinion piece in fourth grade) and broad topics that students need to write about (e.g., something related to westward movement), there also need to be opportunities in the school year when students are able to self-select their genres and topics so that they develop these other writing "muscles."

Brainstorm Writing Topics and Genres

If newcomers have had few experiences generating their own writing topics or selecting their own writing genres, it is important to teach them how to do this, such as through demonstrations. For example, Katharine has used the following procedure successfully with students at different ages and with varying levels of English fluency:

- She makes a list of five to six possible topics she thinks would be of interest to the students.
- She projects them one by one, while briefly talking about each one.
- She invites students to collaboratively generate possible topics, which she writes on chart paper.
- Students work with a partner to generate their own lists of topics.
- There is a share-out, after which students select their topics and begin writing.

This procedure can be used for all kinds of topics (e.g., when writing a memoir or poem, when writing a non-fiction picture book, when writing about a famous historical event in a given era, when writing a how-to book). Katharine has also used a similar procedure to demonstrate selecting a genre.

Encourage Writing in the Native Language

A very valuable stepping stone for newcomers who are not yet writing in English is to encourage them to write in their native language, even if you are not able to read it. This underscores for them that the goal is to write. Other students or adults who speak and write the student's native language can translate the text into English, and the bilingual texts can be made available for other students to read.

Have Opportunities to Talk About Writing with Peers and Teachers

We have been in classrooms where students wrote in silence and did not have any opportunities to share their writing with peers and this appeared to affect their enthusiasm for writing. Having an audience and getting feedback on one's writing are both essential for writers, including newcomers. This can be accomplished when students talk with their peers in a writing conference while sharing the piece of writing. In some classrooms, students confer informally during independent writing time while at their tables or desks. In other classrooms, students move to a designated conferring area (e.g., in the classroom library area). In still other classrooms, there is a designated time when all students share their writing with peers.

Focus on Content First

The writing of newcomers may be filled with misspellings, awkward grammar, and a lack of punctuation and capitalization. These surface features easily capture our attention, but it is important to focus first on the student's message—what are they trying to communicate?—and figure that out through talking with them. It is a good idea to keep a record of the surface features/mechanics of a newcomer's writing so you can see if there are patterns and topics that the student would benefit from being taught. It is true that mechanics can get in the way of understanding the message, but correcting surface features is not likely to help the newcomer writer learn how to write better.

Teach Skills and Strategies in Context and as Needed

By keeping a record of what each newcomer accomplishes as a writer, as well as needs, teachers are able to better judge whether a specific skill or strategy is important to teach at that moment. A good rule of thumb is to identify features that recur and/or seriously impact understanding. For example, if newcomers do not use periods and capital letters, it is important to teach them how these conventions help readers make sense of a text. Similarly, if Arabic-speaking newcomers write in English from right to left, it is important to show how, in English, text is written left to write and have the students try writing their texts from left to right.

Use Print (Not Cursive) when Writing

For many newcomers, cursive writing is much more difficult to read and write than print. For this reason, it is best to <u>not</u> require cursive handwriting from newcomers. In fact, they may be more comfortable writing on a computer. Also, it is helpful to print any directions or when giving written feedback to newcomers.

Provide Opportunities to Publish Writing

Writers need audiences, unless they are writing for just themselves, such as in a personal journal, and part of that experience involves publishing writing. Books written by students can be placed in the class library and/or reading boxes on students' tables. The teacher or students themselves can do booktalks about them so that other students are encouraged to read them. (Booktalks are discussed in some depth in Chapter 6.) Pieces of writing can be posted on a bulletin board that is at a height that students can read and in a location that is easy for students to access. Writing can be published in class and school newsletters. Writing can also be published on class and school websites.

Learn about Writers' Processes

It is very helpful for students to learn about the writing processes of their favorite authors. This is enabled through authors' websites, where they often comment on how they go about writing, what their writing routines are, and how they arrive at topics. Videos are also available for many authors. In addition, it is very important for teachers to share their own writing and writing processes.

Read, Read, Read

Possibly the most important resource for writers is reading. By reading a lot, newcomers are exposed to how the English language works, how to express ideas, how texts are organized, and how words and phrases are used. For newcomers with no or very little English or limited literacy skills in any language, books with only a few words per page, books on tape, and reading buddies can be very helpful.

Writing-related Experiences for Newcomers

The writing activities in this section are particularly appropriate for newcomers because they are authentic writing activities and also provide considerable support to the students.

Shared or Interactive Writing

If newcomers are reluctant to write, shared or interactive writing can be a very effective way of supporting them. It is a scaffolded approach to writing in which the student(s) and teacher share the pen. The text may be revised while it is being composed. We find that the following steps are helpful guidelines:

- Student(s) generate the topic (e.g., about a musician who came to class and played Latin American instruments) and collaboratively generate the content.
- The text may be revised in the process of being written.
- At the beginning, the teacher does the physical writing of the text, but students take turns to write what they are able to—it may be a letter, word, or phrase.

An example of a shared writing follows.

SCENE: A fourth-grade class in a suburban neighborhood school that has recently received several newcomers.

PARTICIPANTS: Mr. Acosta and his four newcomer students. The newcomers come from India (Amrita), China (Niki and Bai), and Peru (María Elena) and speak Urdu, Mandarin Chinese, and Spanish, respectively.

SCENARIO: It is independent writing time, and Mr. Acosta is meeting with the four newcomers at a round table. An easel with chart paper is to the left of Mr. Acosta. There had been a fire drill the previous day and the students decide that they want to write about it.

MR. ACOSTA: We're going to write about the fire drill, right? (*Students nod in agreement*) How should we begin? What do you remember about the fire drill?

BAI: Fire drill very noise.

MR. ACOSTA: Right. It was very noisy. What else?

MARÍA ELENA: The bell (*she makes a ringing sound*).

MR. ACOSTA: So, the fire bell was ringing?

MARÍA ELENA: Yes.

BAI: All kid go way.

AMRITA: Kids go out.

NIKI: On playground.

AMRITA: Line up.

MR. ACOSTA: So, the fire bell rang. It was very noisy. All the kids went outside. Just the kids?

(*Students shake their heads.*)

MR. ACOSTA: So, who else went outside?

STUDENTS:	Teacher.
MR. ACOSTA:	Right. All the teachers and students went outside. And then what happened?
NIKI:	Come back here. Bell stop.
MARÍA ELENA:	Teacher count 1, 2, 3 *(pointing to the other students)*.
MR. ACOSTA:	Right. So, the teachers counted the kids. And when the bell stopped, we all came back to our classes. Anything else? *(Silence)* When was this? Today?
STUDENTS:	Noooo! *(In unison)*
MARÍA ELENA:	Yesterday.
MR. ACOSTA:	OK. I think we've got it. "Yesterday, the fire bell rang. It was very noisy. All the kids and teachers went outside. The kids lined up on the playground. The teachers counted the kids. When the bell stopped ringing, we all came back to our classrooms." Is that OK?

(Students nod and say "Yeah" and "Yes.")

MR. ACOSTA:	So let's start writing it. *(He picks up a pen and writes on chart paper:* "Yesterday, the fire bell rang. It was very noisy.")

(While Mr. Acosta writes, he talks through what he's writing and explains points [e.g., "Yesterday" begins with a capital letter because it's the first word in the sentence.].)

MR. ACOSTA:	Second sentence, "It was very noisy." María Elena, can you come and start that sentence? "It was very noisy."

(María Elena writes "It was beri n" and stops.)

MR. ACOSTA:	So "very" begins with another letter. Anyone know which one? *(Silence)* It's a [b], like in baby, *bebé*. And the [i] sound is written with a [y]. v-e-r-y.

(María Elena crosses out beri *and writes* very *and passes the pen back to Mr. Acosta.)*

MR. ACOSTA:	Thank you, María Elena. Anyone want to write *noisy*? "It was very noisy." *(No one responds.)* Niki. It begins with the same letter as your name, Niki. Come on up and give it a try.

(Niki comes to the chart and writes "Noys.")

MR. ACOSTA:	You're very close, Niki. You're right, it starts with [n], but it's a lower-case [n] because it's in the middle of a word. *(Mr. Acosta writes* noisy *above* Noys *and adds a period, while explaining what he's doing.)*

(This process continues until two sentences have been written. Mr. Acosta tells the students that they will finish it the next day as time has run out.)

Reflective Writing

Journaling is a well-established form of writing that people from all kinds of backgrounds engage in. If newcomers are literate in their native language, it is possible that they have already written in personal diaries/journals, which are usually written for the eyes of the writer only. Other forms of reflective writing, however, involve writing to others and they have been used very successfully with ELs, including newcomers (e.g., Peyton & Reed, 1990; Taylor, 1990). We describe some of these options below.

Written Conversations

In a written conversation, students typically write about what happened in class or on a field trip. The teacher gives a topic for students to write about (e.g., gravity or the field trip). Students sit next to or opposite each other and, at first, they do not speak with each other. They are given about two minutes in which to write whatever they wish about the topic on a piece of paper or in their writing notebooks. At the end of the two minutes, they switch papers and respond to each other in writing, again without talking with each other. After this has happened a few times, the students have an opportunity to speak together about their entries and the topic, which allows them to clarify and extend their knowledge. In the following example of a written conversation, the newcomer student, Octavio, who is from Guatemala and is a native speaker of K'iche', is partnered with Antoine, who is a native speaker of English. They are in sixth grade and are studying magnetism. Here is one of their written conversations, the one that Octavio started:

FIGURE 7.2: Students' Written Conversation

Octavio	*magnet stick metal*
Antoine	Yes. *magnets don't attract wood like metal objecs*
Octavio	what attract
Antoine	Attract means the magnet draws metal objects to it
Octavio	I hear pol in class what they
Antoine	there are 2 poles the north and south poles, the opposite poles are attracted to each other. You can't see them but you can see how it work when two magnets get put next to each other.

Dialogue Journals

Journals allow students to reflect upon their learning and their lives. In dialogue journals (DJs), students correspond with the teacher and/or another student, and they have been found to work well with ELs, including newcomers (e.g., Peyton & Reed, 1990). We have found that the following suggestions can help make the experience successful:

- Content may be entirely open ended or focused on a particular subject (e.g., a reading log).
- Newcomers' entries may be pictures only at first, then pictures with labels, then a mixture of unlabeled and labeled pictures, then primarily text.
- When teachers are corresponding with students in DJs, we have found that it is best to keep the following suggestions in mind:
  - Respond authentically, as a reader, to a student's entry. For example, when third-grader María Luisa wrote, "I lik Sandra Cisneros story," her teacher, Ms. Campbell, wrote back, "I also like Cisneros' writing. I like how she captures family life."
  - Be prepared to read your responses aloud to the newcomer student and then leave, so the student can reply on his/her own.
  - Avoid long responses, which can overwhelm newcomers. Writing entries that are about the same length as the newcomer's is a good rule of thumb.
  - Focus on the message and do not correct the newcomer's writing, as this can be very discouraging—and not helpful.
  - If you are corresponding in DJs with a whole class, it is best to stagger when they hand in their journals so you don't get overwhelmed.

Letter Writing

Even in a time of social media and texting, letter writing remains an authentic writing experience, so long as the letters are written for a real audience and read by that audience. We have found that newcomers often respond very enthusiastically to corresponding with others. There are many kinds of letters that can be written, including the following:

- A letter to another student, which is posted in the class mailbox—students love to receive mail. To get this kind of activity off the ground, students can be instructed to write to their writing partner(s) in class;
- A letter of invitation—to caregivers/parents inviting them to an event at school, such as an international food evening or a back-to-school night;
- A letter to a pen pal—to another young person living in the same or a different community, in the U.S., or abroad;
- A thank you—to guides on field trips and visitors to the class;
- A complaint—to school employees, community officials, and businesses;
- A request for information or "freebies"—to magazines, community organizations, and government offices;
- A suggestion—to a local business (e.g., to add flavors to their ice cream selection) or government official (e.g., to convert a nearby town-owned, vacant plot into a community garden or park); and
- A letter to the editor—about a concern that the student or students have (e.g., about library hours being shortened).

Many newcomer students are familiar with texting and email, and several of the suggestions above lend themselves to these forms of correspondence, such as writing to a pen pal, requesting information or "freebies," and writing a letter to the editor (many newspapers prefer online submissions of letters).

Student-authored Books

Students often feel great accomplishment when they author their own books, which are then read by other students—those in their own class as well as students in other classes and grades. These books can be placed in class and school libraries, in reading boxes on tables, and on the ledge under a whiteboard or chalkboard. The important thing is that students know that these books are there to be read, enjoyed, and used as inspiration. For example, in Dorothy Taylor's pullout ELD class, students wrote their own books, which she used as early reading material for newcomers (Taylor, 1990). One of her sixth-grade students, Maya, did not speak a word of English when she came to the U.S. However, after just a few weeks, she wrote *Things That I Love,* which relies on speech bubbles, pictures, labels, and a repetitive refrain (*I love*). It is also a bilingual book as she included Russian words and phrases. This book became a favorite of other newcomers, and it inspired more than a dozen students to independently write their own *Things That I Love* books. Older newcomers can write and illustrate picture books to be read to and by younger students.

There is sometimes a debate over whether the teacher should edit the published writing of newcomers. It is usually a good idea to do this so that the text can be read easily. However, the editing should be very light and not change meaning and, as much as possible, should be done with the student. Also, it is important to keep the original piece of student-edited writing so that the student, the teacher, and caregivers/parents can see progress over time.

Class Books

Class books can provide a very effective entry into writing for newcomers, particularly if the books focus on topics that allow them to fully contribute. Depending on the topic, class books can also broaden all students' knowledge of the world and how people live in different communities. Some examples of these kinds of topics are:

- How marriages are celebrated around the world and across families;
- How birthdays are celebrated around the world and across families;
- How the end of a season is marked around the world; and
- Celebrations that are particular to individual families—for example, we know a family that has a pig roast when a family member leaves for another country, and another family goes to a local restaurant when a child graduates from elementary school.

Class Newspapers

Class newspapers provide a very effective way for students to write in a variety of genres, illustrate, and communicate with caregivers/parents and others. Newcomers can contribute in various ways, including the following:

- Write short pieces in English or the native language.
- Translate information for caregivers and parents into their native language.
- Illustrate the newsletter with labeled drawings and/or photos.

Teach Spelling Strategies as Needed

Rather than utilizing a spelling program, it is advisable to teach spelling strategies as needed. Resources such as *Words Their Way with English Learners: Word Study for Phonics, Vocabulary, and Spelling* (Hellman, Bear, Templeton, Invernizzi, & Johnston, 2012) can be helpful. It is important when teaching spelling strategies to keep in mind that many of the sounds in the English language are not found in other languages (e.g., the *th*) and letters in English that are found in other languages often have different sounds attached to them. For example, whereas in Spanish there are very few vowel sounds, in English there are many (e.g., the *I* can be pronounced in different ways, such as in *high* and *limit)*. In other alphabetic languages, such as Vietnamese, Latin-based letters are used, but not all that are found in English. For example, the letters *f, j, w,* and *z* are not in the Vietnamese alphabet, though Vietnamese speakers may use them when using loan words from another language. Also, Vietnamese is a tonal language—there are six tones, which can dramatically alter the meaning of a word.

Writing Workshop and Newcomer Students

Many teachers have commented to us that they love to read but don't like or are not confident writers, and they usually credit that disposition to the actions of a teacher they once had. For example, one teacher told Katharine that her first-grade teacher had told her that she wasn't a good writer and this had stayed with her until then. This may help explain why writing gets so little attention in schools. Fortunately, there have been efforts since the 1970s to introduce teachers and students to a learner-centered approach to teaching writing that supports writers and encourages students to enjoy writing (e.g., Atwell, 1987; Calkins, 1986; Graves, 1983; Ray, 1999, 2001). This writing workshop approach is consistent with our book's goal of teachers acting as instructional advocates for their newcomer students because the writing workshop is grounded in a learner-centered approach.

We were introduced to writing workshop through the work of Donald Graves, who conducted the first longitudinal research project investigating the writing processes of children (1975). Although Graves' work did not focus on ELs, we have considerable experience with this approach to teaching writing with ELs, and research confirms that this approach can be successful with ELs, including newcomers (e.g., Edelsky, 1986; Hudelson, 1984; Samway, 1987, 1993; Urzúa, 1987).

Features of a Traditional Writing Workshop

A traditional writing workshop approach includes the following features:

- The workshop has a regularly scheduled time, often each day.
- The workshop begins with a short (e.g., five to 10 minutes) whole-class mini-lesson when the teacher teaches to a specific skill or strategy, such as the following:
  - Alternate leads in a piece of writing
  - Alternatives to the word "said"
  - How to revise one's writing and
  - When to use the present and past tense.
- The mini-lesson is followed by independent writing time. While students are writing and conferring, the teacher goes around and confers with individual students and small groups of students.
- The content of mini-lessons and conferences are grounded in the observed needs of students.
- Students select their own topics and genres.
- Students publish their writing (e.g., in individual and class books, on the walls, in class newspapers).

An Inquiry, Unit of Study Approach to Writing Workshop

Lucy Calkins worked on Graves' research project. Later, she initiated and is presently the director of the Teachers College Reading and Writing Project (TCRWP), which has played a major role in introducing thousands of teachers to an inquiry approach to writing workshop. This approach to teaching writing is very similar to a traditional writing workshop, but there are several ways in which it is different, reflecting the growing knowledge about how to teach writing to K–8 students. Some of the differences include the following:

- In advance of the school year, the teacher plans a year-long series of units of study lasting from two to six weeks that includes a variety of genres (e.g., information books, poetry, persuasive essay, and a student-selected genre); author studies (e.g., Pat Mora, Donald Crews, or Jacqueline Woodson); and technical issues (e.g., when to use colons, how to edit one's writing).
- At the beginning of a unit of study, students are immersed in the topic or genre through reading, such as reading (and having read to them) a lot of nonfiction texts before embarking on a nonfiction writing unit. This reading often occurs about two weeks earlier in a reading workshop.
- Through inquiry, students establish characteristics of well-written texts representative of the unit of study's focus. They do this collaboratively, through looking at the texts representative of the unit and brainstorming characteristics, which the teacher writes on chart paper. Through discussion and with the guidance of the teacher, the students decide whether an individual characteristic (e.g., humor, an interesting lead, dialogue) is required or optional in a well-written piece. This chart is then posted and is available as a resource to students while they are writing.
- The students use books and other texts that align with the unit as mentor texts. In this way, they are able to learn from experts. They learn about many things, including how to structure pieces, how to use evocative language, how to use dialogue, when to use colons and semicolons, and possible topics.

The goals of an inquiry, unit of study approach to writing workshop are varied and include the following:

- *To support writers* in becoming more effective, independent, confident writers, who are able to find their writing voices and interests and write across multiple genres.
- *To teach students about writing* through using inquiry to explore what writers do that makes their writing so effective.

- *To celebrate writing and writers* through publishing students' writing and having regular celebrations of their writing.

The following scenario illustrates the start of a poetry unit of study—in particular, the role of inquiry in a writing workshop.

SCENE: A third-grade classroom in an inner city, low-income neighborhood that has many ELs

PARTICIPANTS: Mr. Jacobi and his 26 students. A majority of the students are African American, but 12 are ELs, including four newcomers, who come from Somalia (Mustafa and Yasmin) and El Salvador (Marta and Diego).

SCENARIO: The class is beginning a four-week study on writing poetry.

BACKGROUND: In reading workshop over the past two weeks, students have read a lot of poetry and Mr. Jacobi has focused on poetry in read-alouds. Because Mr. Jacobi knows that children often associate poetry with rhyming poetry and because he knows how hard it is to write good rhyming poetry, he has brought in lots of books of poetry that are non-rhyming, including many books of poetry written by African American authors (e.g., Jacqueline Woodson, Nikki Giovanni) and authors from other underrepresented groups (e.g., Gary Soto, Sandra Cisneros, Naomi Shihab Nye). He is also thinking of following up with a rap-writing unit later in the semester as he knows how much his students, particularly the African American students, are familiar with and love rap, with its rhyming lyrics.

Writing workshop: The students are sitting on the rug in front of the whiteboard. Mr. Jacobi begins the day's writing workshop.

MR. JACOBI: Good morning, writers. As you know, we're beginning a new writing unit today. A poetry unit. (*He holds up some of the poetry books the students are already familiar with.*)

STUDENTS: Yeah! Oh, good. (*Many students express excitement about the new unit.*)

MR. JACOBI: I can see you're excited. So am I. That's great. The first thing we need to do is figure out what some of the characteristics of good poetry are. What features do they share in common? You've already done this kind of thing with your memoirs and non-fiction books. What I want you to do is work with your partner and start listing in your writing notebooks anything you notice in these books of poetry. (*He*

holds up his writing notebook and mimes reading, thinking, and writ-
ing in the notebook.) Maybe it's something about the way the poems
are laid out *(pointing to two poems that have different kinds of layout).*
Maybe it's about the themes. What the poems are about. Maybe it's
the language that's used. Anything that you notice. You have 20 minutes and then we'll come back on the rug and share out. There are
poetry books on your tables that you can go through. (*He goes over*
to a nearby table and holds up the six or seven books on that table.)
Questions?

ANDRÉ: How many we gotta list?

MR. JACOBI: As many as you can. (*He writes "20 minutes" on the board and*
includes the time when the class will come back together.)

The students are dismissed back to their table clusters, where they meet with
their writing partners and begin reading the poetry books and jotting down
ideas in their writing notebooks. In some cases, the students read randomly
selected poems from their books, but in other cases, the students go through
their two to three books more systematically. In still other cases, students
choose poems that they remember and liked in each book. Before moving
around the classroom to check in with the class, Mr. Jacobi meets with Mustafa, Yasmin, Marta, Diego, and their writing partners to make sure that
they all know what they are going to do. He has paired the newcomers with
other students who speak their native languages, which has been working
out well.

While the students are involved in this inquiry work, Mr. Jacobi moves
around the classroom, checking in briefly with students. After about 17 minutes, he tells the class that they have three more minutes. When the students
return to the rug with their notebooks and poetry books, there is a sheet of
chart paper on an easel in front of them. It has three columns. The left column
is labeled "Characteristics of Poetry"; the middle column is left blank and will
be used to help make the meaning of the characteristic clear to students, especially the newcomers; and the right column is labeled "Required?" The students
offer their insights, which Mr. Jacobi lists on the chart, sometimes clarifying
and rewording to make meaning clear. He also uses sketches, symbols, gestures, and mime to make meaning clear; for example, he uses his hands and

face to indicate *short* as opposed to *long*. At this point, there is no discussion about whether a characteristic is shared by all the poems and may be required when writing a good poem. The chart begins to look like the chart below in Figure 7.3.

On the following day, the class returns to the rug and they go through each characteristic, discussing whether the characteristic is required or optional. They agree that strong, evocative language is required in good poetry, but they decide that the remainder of the characteristics listed on the chart below are optional. This chart is posted on a wall that is easily seen by all the students— it is intended as a resource for the students when they write their own poems. As the unit progresses and students read poetry, they suggest additional characteristics, which are briefly discussed as they come up and are then added to the chart.

FIGURE 7.3: Inquiry Chart of Characteristics of Good Poetry Generated by Students

Characteristics of Poetry	Examples and (Possible Visuals)	Required?
About people	*(Sketch of people)*	
About sports	*(Sketch of sports equipment)*	
About animals	*(Sketch of animals)*	
Short		
Includes a question	?	
Strong language	e.g., fantastic, amazing	
No punctuation	harriet tubman coming down the river	
No capital letters	harriet tubman	
Line breaks in middle of sentences	The sun rose in the sky	
No paragraphs	(¶)	
Funny	Ha ha ha	

(*Source:* for excerpt from poem about Harriet Tubman: *Cross over the River* by Sam Cornish, in Arnold Adoff (ed.) *My Black Me: A Beginning Book of Black Poetry*)

Writing Workshop with Newcomer ELs

You may be wondering how newcomer students fit into this complex, learner-centered approach to teaching writing. You may be asking, "If they can't read or write English, how are they going to participate in or benefit from being in a writing workshop?" We have learned that it is very important for newcomers to be included in these kinds of major classroom events in order to learn from their peers and to feel part of the class. Although they may feel lost at times, the predictable routines inherent in a writing workshop, along with opportunities to work with peers and confer with the teacher, help them make sense of what is often a very different way of learning from anything they have experienced before. We have found that the following strategies help newcomers succeed in a writing workshop.

Meet Regularly with Newcomers

It is important to check in briefly with newcomer students each workshop, particularly once the independent writing time in the workshop gets under-way. If you've established a buddy system, that can help newcomers, but it is still important to check in, to make sure that they understand the task at hand.

Keep Conferences Short

There is a temptation when conferring with newcomers to let a writing conference drag on too long because it takes time for newcomers to formulate their comments, questions, and answers. However, a good rule of thumb is to keep the conference five minutes at most. It is sometimes helpful to hold group conferences with students who have similar needs, and these will last a bit longer. Also, when conferring, limit the number of teaching points to one or two at most, and make sure that they are the most important for that student. More than that is likely to overwhelm newcomers.

Encourage Students to Write in Their Native Language

If newcomers are able to write in their native language, encourage them to do so. In this way, they can participate more fully in the workshop as they transition into being able to write in English. There are several ways in which this can be facilitated, including the following:

- If there are other students in the class who speak the same language(s) as the newcomer student(s), they can work together on writing and illustrating bilingual texts.
- As students become more fluent in English, they can write bilingually. They may write first in their home language and then translate into English. They can use Google Translate to translate from their native language version to English and then work with a more fluent speaker of English to make sure that the words carry the intended meaning.
- If newcomers aren't able to write in their native language(s) or English, they can verbally co-compose with English-speaking students who speak their language(s) and do the writing and then take responsibility for some or all of the illustrations.

Have Bilingual Texts and Native Language Texts Available in the Classroom

It is very encouraging for newcomers to see books and magazines in the classroom that are written in their native languages. See Figure 6.5 in Chapter 6 for a list of publishers and distributors of bilingual books and books in languages other than English. This includes texts that are bilingual or multilingual. Also, whenever possible, refer to these books when teaching during mini-lessons and writing conferences. You may also want to consider teaching a unit of study on bilingual books in which students work in pairs and groups to compose texts in English and another language or languages. Depending on how many students are biliterate or multiliterate, the book may be initially written in English or another language.

Encourage Newcomers to Draw

When newcomers are very new to English, encourage them to draw and then label their drawings as much as they can. For example, seventh-grader, Ivan, drew a wordless story (or almost wordless as he included *HOME* and *The end*) (see Figure 7.4). The frames describe how he watched TV late at night (1), woke up late (2), and was late to school (3). His teacher yelled at him (4). As punishment, his teacher gave him a lot of homework (5). He went home (6), it took him a long time to do his homework (7a and 7b), and he wasn't able to watch TV that evening (8), which made him sad and gave him a headache (9).

FIGURE 7.4: Ivan's Wordless Story

Source: Katharine Davies Samway and Dorothy Taylor. (2008). *Teaching English Language Learners, grades 6 and up: Strategies that work.* Reprinted by permission of Scholastic Teaching Resources.

Beware of Imposing a Silent Workshop Time

Newcomers (and other ELs) need to hear English around them and have opportunities to interact verbally with peers as it is through talk that learning is often mediated. We have observed that students tend to talk more about the content of their writing when their pieces focus on topics that clearly matter to them, such as these two examples:

- The unit was of great interest to the class (e.g., when fourth graders were engaged in a unit on informational writing, which resulted in letters to their city council member about local issues, such as drug selling in their neighborhood, a lack of playgrounds, and not many after-school activities)

- Individual or small groups of students were particularly interested in a topic (e.g., when a group of second graders was writing about sharks; when a fourth-grader, Wilfredo, who visited a local boxing gym with his father, was writing a biography about the world-famous boxer, Muhammad Ali).

Devote Units of Study to Nonfiction

Reading and writing illustrated nonfiction can often be much easier for new-comers than fiction as they may already be familiar with the concepts in non-fiction (e.g., wild animals, geographic features, the solar system). Also, the illustrations in books can help clarify meaning. In addition, newcomers may have great interest in nonfiction topics and be especially motivated to do the reading research involved as well as the writing.

Offer Units of Study Focused on Children's Literature

Teachers of older newcomer students have told us how successful teaching a children's literature unit of study has been with their newcomer students. This includes both fiction and nonfiction picture books and wordless picture books, which they publish and then read to younger students. These units appear to be particularly successful with newcomers because the length of texts that they read in the inquiry aspect of the study and the research they do for their own books is more manageable than longer and more complex texts.

Challenge Students, But Have Realistic Expectations

A word of caution is needed in an age of the Common Core State Standards (CCSS). We have observed teachers who are concerned that their ELs, including newcomers, have the same kind of challenging learning experiences as other, non-EL students and, in the process, neglect to pay attention to what is appropriate and attainable for their ELs, particularly newcomer students. The following scenario illustrates this dilemma:

SCENE: A fourth grade classroom in a large school in an inner city, low-income neighborhood that has many ELs

PARTICIPANTS: Ms. Alexander and her 26 students. Fifteen students are fluent English speakers, nine are ELs who have been in the U.S. for two to three years, and two are newcomers. Students' native languages include English, Spanish, Thai, Laotian, Mam (an indigenous Guatemalan language), Arabic, and Tagalog. Carlos and Mikaela are the newcomer students and both speak Spanish.

SCENARIO: The students are in the middle of an essay-writing unit of study and Mrs. Alexander is conducting a mini-lesson on how to elaborate. The students are sitting on the rug at the front of the classroom, under the whiteboard. Ms. Alexander has projected a short essay that she has written and is talking through how she would elaborate on points she makes, using carets and inserting text as she talks. Many of the students are restless, and Ms. Alexander repeatedly reminds the students of the importance of paying attention. Carlos is sitting in the middle row on the rug and turns to his rug partner, Javier, and whispers "*¿Qué está diciendo la maestra?*/What's the teacher saying?*" Javier shrugs his shoulders and says, "*No sé*/Don't know." Later in the day, Ms. Alexander talks with her fourth-grade partner teacher, Mr. Dixon, who had observed the class, about how hard this unit of study is and how many of the students didn't seem to get how to write an essay. He wonders if some of it is related to the ELs, especially the newcomers, not understanding what she's asking them to do—w hether maybe it's too hard for them at this point in their English language development. "But," Ms. Alexander replies, "I feel, I think I have to give them the same content as the other fourth graders. That they need to be exposed to the same standards. They need to be challenged. Otherwise I'm not doing my job." This leads into a discussion about how to challenge students but in ways that are commensurate with their understanding of English.

Assessing Writing

In Chapter 4: Assessing Newcomer Students, we shared a range of assessment strategies, some of which are particularly appropriate when assessing writing (e.g., checklists). When assessing the writing of students, particularly newcomer ELs, the temptation is to focus on what we see on the page, which, with newcomers, is likely to be very limited and non-standardized. As the writing expert Carl Anderson suggests in his book, *Assessing Writers* (2005), it is much more useful to focus on the following three elements: a) assessing students as initiators of writing, b) assessing how well students write, and c) assessing students' writing processes. Each element requires careful observation on the part of the teacher and conversations with students, as well as reflection on the part of students.

Assessing Students as Initiators of Writing

This category looks at how engaged the student is with writing. Issues to consider include the following:

- *Purpose*—How well does the student use writing workshop time? Do they get to work right away? Are they prepared? Do they have a hard time getting going? Do they write outside of school?
- *Genres*—Does the student write in clearly observable genres?
- *Audience*—Does the student have an audience other than the teacher in mind? Do they share their writing with others?

Assessing How Well Students Write

Multiple issues need to be assessed in this category, including the following:

- *Meaning*—Does the student communicate meaning in their writing?
- *Genre*—Does the student's writing include features associated with the genre?
- *Structure*—Do the parts of the student's writing help develop meaning? Does the student use transitions effectively (e.g., *However*)?
- *Details*—Does the student include details that develop meaning? Does the student use specific words in the details?
- *Voice*—Does the student use a variety of sentence structures that give voice to their writing? Does the student use a variety of punctuation marks that give voice to their writing?
- *Conventions*—Does the student use punctuation marks correctly in the kinds of sentences they are writing? Does the student use capitalization correctly in the kinds of texts/genres they are writing?
- *Grammar*—Does the student use verb tenses that are appropriate for the texts they are writing? Does the student use a variety of verb tenses appropriately in their writing?
- *Word choice*—Does the student use appropriate words and terms in the kind of writing they are doing? Does the student use evocative language in their writing that enhances meaning?

Assessing Students' Writing Processes

This category focuses on the individual student's writing processes and how effective they are.

- *Rehearsal*—Does the writer use strategies successfully that help them find topics?
- *Drafting and Revision*—Does the student use writing tools to help them draft and revise (e.g., different colored pens)? Does the student use drafting and revision strategies successfully (e.g., carets and sticky notes for adding to a draft; strikeouts for deletions)?
- *Editing*—Does the student use writing tools to help them edit effectively (e.g., dictionary, thesaurus, spell checker)?

Although Anderson's book was not written for teachers of newcomers, we know from experience how valuable this advice can be as it allows us to look more closely at very important aspects of our students as writers, while also giving us guidance on what to teach them and how to individualize instruction.

CHAPTER 8

Engaging Newcomers in Content Learning

WHEN NEWCOMERS ARRIVE in our classrooms, they face a daunting task: learning to understand and express themselves in spoken English, learning to read and write in English, learning the academic content that their grade-level peers are studying, and negotiating a new country and culture. When trying to support their newcomer students, teachers often have many questions: *What should I focus on first? How can I teach my newcomers math or science or history if they don't speak English? How do I support my newcomers with what they need while also teaching the rest of my class?* Consider the following scenarios from two different sixth-grade science classes, both of which have several newcomer students. Which one do you think is supporting these newcomers in learning science and English?

SCENARIO 1

The majority of students are seated facing one another at rectangular tables. Three newcomers, Ramón, Juana, and Samuel, who have recently arrived from Mexico, occupy one table. They are coloring in pictures of objects labeled in English, while their classmates are building circuits.

RAMÓN: ¿Qué tenemos que hacer? (*What do we need to do?*)

JUANA: Colorear estes dibujos usando los colores en la caja. (*Color these pictures using the crayons in the box.*)

SAMUEL: ¿Por qué tenemos que hacer eso? (*Why do we need to do that?*)

JUANA: No sé. Así dijo la maestra. (*I don't know. That's what the teacher said.*)

A few minutes pass during which the three students diligently color in the drawings on the worksheet.

RAMÓN: Pssst, psst *(trying to get the attention of Jaime who is working at a nearby table).* ¿Qué estás haciendo? ¿Me puedes contar? ¿Qué es eso? *(What are you doing? Can you tell me? What's that?)* *(Ramón points to a wire that Jaime has in his hands.)*

TEACHER: Ramón! Ramón! Finish your worksheet. You can talk with Jaime at recess. Right now is work time. Now *trabajar* (work). *(She points to the worksheet in front of Ramón.)*

SCENARIO 2

The students are similarly seated in groups at rectangular tables. The class includes six students who are newcomers from Mexico, El Salvador, Guatemala, and Cuba. At one table, two newcomers, Jorge and Abel, work with Vivian, who is African American and a native speaker of English who has some understanding of Spanish. Each group is drawing a model of the energy-efficient house they are designing and will begin prototyping and testing the next week. Vivian has just finished making a simple line drawing of a house on a piece of poster paper that is positioned in the center of the table.

VIVIAN: So what should we use for the walls? *(Vivian points to the sketch of the house in front of her.)*

JORGE: De ladrillo *(of brick).* Of '*drillo.*

VIVAN: You mean out of brick. *(She draws a row of small rectangular boxes on the wall of the house.)*

JORGE: *Sí.* Breek.

ABEL: *Pero aquí va a entrar el aire.* (But the air will come in here.) *(Abel makes a shushing sound as he points to a space between the bricks that Vivian has drawn.)*

VIVIAN: We can put cement between the bricks to keep out the air. *(Vivian uses her pencil to fill in the spaces between the bricks.)*

JORGE: No. *Plástico* walls. *Paredes de plástico. Así no entra el aire.* (Plastic walls. That way that air won't get in). *(Jorge taps Vivian's plastic lunch box.)*

VIVAN: Plastic. What do you mean? Like sheets of plastic that hang from a roof? Like a tent? *(Vivan makes a sketch of what appears to be a four-sided triangle.)*

ABEL: A *carpa* (a tent). It's good. No air.

Let's go back to our question—in which scenario are newcomer students being supported to learn content and English? It is clear that Scenario 2 provides newcomers with many more opportunities to engage with science content and to interact with English-speaking classmates. In Scenario 1, the newcomers are isolated from their peers and excluded from science activities. We have seen well-intentioned teachers using activities like those described in Scenario 1 (e.g., worksheets or online language learning applications) with their newcomers because they want to make sure newcomers acquire basic English skills. However, this approach limits newcomers' learning opportunities in several ways:

- It isolates newcomers from their English-speaking peers, who can play a valuable role in helping them learn English. Learning a new language requires lots of opportunities to engage with "input" in the new language (opportunities to hear the language and engage with text), as well as opportunities to interact in the new language with their developing proficiencies. While there are definitely times that newcomers need to be pulled for specialized instruction, they also need lots of opportunities to interact with their English-speaking peers. English-speaking students also benefit from engaging with and establishing relationships with newcomers who have experiences and insights that are different from their own.
- Students don't need a high level of English to start learning content through English. With support and thoughtfully planned instruction, newcomers can start learning content in English. Below, we outline many instructional strategies for integrating content, literacy, and language learning.
- Finally, newcomers simply don't have time to wait to start English literacy instruction or to learn grade-level content. If we hold off on teaching reading, writing, and content, newcomers will fall even further behind academically.

Scenario 2 provides a more productive content- and language-learning experience for newcomers, in which we see the following:

- Newcomers are engaged in making meaning of and applying grade-level science content using their emergent English.
- The teacher has thoughtfully grouped newcomers so that they are

integrated with English-speaking peers and have many opportunities to interact with and learn from their classmates. She has
strategically placed Jorge and Abel with Vivian, who has the language skills to support her newcomer peers and is helpful and
collaborative.

- The engineering task is hands-on, so that newcomers can learn and
  use English in context. As we see in the interactions above, language is clarified as students work together to design their houses.

This chapter describes how to integrate language, literacy, and content instruction for newcomer students so that students are engaged in learning grade-
level content and developing disciplinary language and literacy skills. In the
following pages, we will address these topics:

- Planning for content instruction with newcomers;
- Taking an inquiry approach;
- Using multi-modal resources and experiences;
- Reading and listening to learn;
- Teaching language in context; and
- Providing multiple ways for students to show learning.

We then dedicate a section to specific issues and strategies to consider when
teaching math to newcomers. Although the strategies described throughout the
chapter also apply to math, we discuss math separately because of the unique
challenges and opportunities that math instruction raises with newcomers.

Planning for Content Instruction with Newcomers

Articulating Clear and Strategic Learning Objectives

Foundational to all good teaching is being clear about your learning goals for
students. When planning for a class with newcomer students, it is important
to be clear about which grade-level standards or learning objectives are most
essential to address. Because you are teaching both content and language, you
may not be able to cover as much material with newcomers. This will often
require taking a "less is more" approach and making some judgment calls
about which standards or content objectives are most important to focus on
with your newcomer students. In making these decisions, consider the following questions:

- What content is most foundational for future learning? For example, understanding the phases of matter (i.e., solid, liquid, gas) is foundational to a great deal of science learning later on. We would want to dedicate time for students to develop a strong understanding of this content standard, as opposed to trying to expose them to a lot of science standards. This may mean that the sixth-grade teacher described above may pass over a standard on genetic variation because she knows students will loop back to this when they study heredity and adaptation in eighth grade. When we focus on covering as many standards as possible, we might expose students to a lot of material that they don't fully grasp and can't then use or apply as a foundation for future learning.

- What content or phenomenon will be most relevant or engaging to students? For example, in the case of history, can we study content through looking at a local case study or example in the community? This is important as history learning is often most meaningful when we can help students make connections between historical issues and contemporary issues. For example, a class might study the concept of national borders by looking both at how borders were expanded and established in a few historical case studies and then investigating how and why the U.S. has established and tried to secure its border with Mexico and the impact of these efforts.

Going back to Scenario 2, the sixth-grade students were focused on understanding the concept of energy and how energy moves or is transferred through different materials or types of matter. Energy and matter and how they flow through different systems is identified as a Crosscutting Concept in the Next Generation Science Standards (NGSS), meaning that it is a foundational concept that students will continue to build on as they study different areas of science and different scientific phenomena. For more information about the NGSS, go to https://www.nextgenscience.org.

The students were learning about thermal energy and energy transfer through creating energy-efficient houses that would trap heat. This engineering task addresses a relevant problem in our world today—how to create energy-efficient buildings so that we can reduce our use of energy and our impact on the planet. In sum, the teacher had selected foundational science concepts to focus on and had engaged students in applying those concepts to address a real-world problem. The hands-on and interactive nature of the task also helped engage and motivate students.

Integrating Newcomers

When we are teaching newcomers in the context of a larger class, there are strategic moments when we will plan to work with newcomers in a small group so we can provide targeted instruction. However, we want to make sure that they also spend time integrated with their peers to support their English learning and to help them integrate into the school community. For example, in the sixth-grade science class from Scenario 2, newcomers worked with their peers in groups to design their homes and then build and test prototypes with infrared thermometers to see if they would, in fact, trap heat. After testing their prototypes, they revised them, adding new insulating materials and sealing cracks, and then retested them to see if their improvements were successful.

As described in the scenario, the newcomers fully participated in their groups' work to design, build, test, and re-design their energy-efficient house prototypes. As will be described, the readings they engaged with and their final products were modified and the teacher worked with them in small, differentiated groups, but they were still engaged in collaborative and interactive work with their English-speaking peers. Through this interaction, they were able to learn some English terms and phrases that are useful in science and in regular settings. They used their emergent English as they made sense of their teacher's instructions and their peers' discussions. Finally, the newcomers in this scenario were engaged in the buzz and activity of the class and developed relationships with their peers rather than being segregated to work on ESL worksheets or online apps without any opportunities to learn content or interact in English, as we saw in the first scenario.

It is important to point out that this intentional integration takes planning and is different from a sink-or-swim approach to language instruction. The teacher planned specific moments when she would work with the newcomers in a small group to provide targeted support and planned for how to modify the reading and writing tasks for the newcomers. She was also strategic about how she grouped students and planned opportunities for students to reflect on and debrief their group work to make sure collaboration was productive and that all students were involved.

Taking an Inquiry Approach

When we are teaching history, geography, science, math, physical education, or visual and performing arts, we are not only teaching specific content, we are also bringing students into the discipline and the ways knowledge is generated and expressed in that discipline. We advocate for taking an inquiry approach so that students are actively engaged in constructing knowledge and doing the work of the discipline. The importance of engaging students in disciplinary practices can be seen in recent standards reforms that focus not solely on content, but also on disciplinary practices. For example, the NGSS articulate eight Science and Engineering Practices, such as "Developing and Using Models" and "Arguing from Evidence," which describe how scientists investigate the natural world and how engineers design and build solutions. Like scientists, students should be engaged in the Science and Engineering Practices as they investigate and deepen their understandings of the natural world. Similarly, the Common Core State Standards (CCSS) for math articulate eight Standards for Mathematical Practice, such as "Make sense of problems and persevere in solving them" and "Construct viable arguments and critique the reasoning of others," which are key competencies students should develop and practice throughout their K–12 math education.

Drawing on Family and Community-based Funds of Knowledge

The funds of knowledge approach developed by Moll and colleagues (e.g., Gonzalez, Moll, & Amanti, 2005; Moll, 1992; Moll & Greenberg, 1990) enables teachers to integrate resources that are part of newcomer students' home and community networks into inquiry-based units in their classrooms. Building on this approach, teachers working with students from immigrant backgrounds, including newcomer students, engage parents and community members in research activities to learn about the knowledge and practices that are available in students' social networks outside of school. Moll and his colleagues use the term *funds of knowledge* when referencing the "cultural practices and bodies of knowledge and information that households use to survive, to get ahead or to thrive" (Moll & Greenberg, 1990, p. 321). Figure 8.1 offers example topics for study that teachers have identified during home visits.

In Chapter 9, we describe how teachers can learn about the funds of knowledge in their students' families and communities. Teachers can develop units that draw on these funds of knowledge and connect family members with students' academic studies, as seen in the following scenario from a kindergarten science class.

FIGURE 8.1: Drawing on Community Funds of Knowledge

Field of Study	Specific Topic or Fund of Knowledge
Economics	Patterns of employment that affect children's families Making purchases that accommodate family budgets
Farming	Information about growing vegetables and fruits in family gardens The care of animals Specific agricultural practices used in the community Distribution of water in a particular community
Sciences	Chemical reactions that are used in cooking and preparing food (e.g., in the case of baking and pickling)
Mathematics	Mathematical skills and practices used in construction (e.g., measuring, using ratios and proportions to create scale drawings) Using ratios and proportions to make purchasing decisions
Medicine	Herbal cures for the treatment of specific conditions Use of massage for the treatment of specific conditions
Government	Ways of engaging in collective decision making utilized in countries of origin Information about elections

SCENE: Ms. Wu's kindergarten class

PARTICIPANTS: A class of 23 kindergarteners, most of whom come from Middle Eastern, Southeast Asian, and Latino immigrant families and were born in the U.S. Because, for most students, this is their first year in school, they are beginning to learn English. Ms. Wu also has three students who have arrived from Yemen and Vietnam this school year.

SCENARIO: Ms. Wu noticed that her students frequently came in from their afternoon recess thirsty and sweaty, complaining that the asphalt playground was too hot. She asked them why they thought it was so hot during the afternoon recess and what they could do about it. Ahmed, a newcomer from Yemen, pointed outside the window at the blazing sun.

"The sun," said Ms. Wu. "You think it's so hot because of the sun." She wrote *the sun* on the board and drew a picture of the sun. Other students agreed, explaining through words and gestures how they had to shield their eyes from the sun and how the sun made the asphalt, slide, and monkey bars hot to the touch.

To understand what was causing the heat, the class spent two weeks observing the weather and taking temperature measurements three times a day—at 9 a.m., 12 p.m., and 2 p.m. They found that, on sunny afternoons, the asphalt reached the highest temperatures. In the morning and on cloudy afternoons, the asphalt was not as hot. They realized that Ahmed was right—the sunlight was causing the asphalt to warm up.

Ms. Wu asked the class what they could do to address the problem. She gave each pair of students a piece of paper and asked them to draw a solution. Some pairs like Mireya and Thien drew a picture of a tree and students underneath enjoying the shade. Others, like Carlos and Asha drew a shade canopy over the playground, and a few pairs drew water features like sprinkler systems that students could run through to cool down. Ms. Wu then brought the class to the carpet to discuss their solutions and decide which they could most feasibly pursue. The students decided that a shade canopy was the most feasible solution since a tree would take a long time to grow big enough to provide shade and sprinkler systems would waste water and could lead to very wet students. From home visits and parent conferences earlier in the year, Ms. Wu knew that several of her students' parents worked in construction and invited a few to come in and consult with individual groups about their canopy designs. Small groups shared their draft designs with the parents, and parents asked questions and gave advice about how to create stable structures (see Figure 8.2). The students then revised their designs and built prototypes with the help of parent volunteers. Finally, the class decided on the design they thought was the most stable and feasible, and the families built the structure with students' help on a Saturday.

FIGURE 8.2: Kindergarten Shade Structure Design

Connecting Content to Relevant Social Issues

One way to make content more meaningful for all students is to connect it to issues that are relevant to students' lives and their community. In this way, learning becomes a tool to understand, address, and take action aimed at solving urgent problems that students are experiencing. Further, when the curriculum focuses on issues of social justice, students come to realize the role they can assume in fostering a society that is committed to the wellbeing and equality of all its members. This can be particularly relevant for newcomers who have lived through the many social and political issues that are facing the world today, either in their home countries or in their neighborhoods in the United States, such as climate change, migration, and civil war. Many newcomers and students from marginalized communities have experienced the kind of oppression that has constrained their voices, rights, and ability to have an impact on their environment. As Shawn Ginwright (2016) argues, this has contributed to their trauma and sense of hopelessness, particularly in regards to their future opportunities. Ginwright advocates that teachers employ a range of practices and strategies focused on addressing the structural causes of oppression that lead to the trauma and damage so many youngsters face in U.S. society. Through their involvement in social justice analysis and actions, teachers and students can restore a sense of hope that counters the damage caused by poverty, violence, and oppression.

There are many opportunities to tie history, science, art, theater, and math to relevant issues of social justice. Figure 8.3 provides some examples as a starting place.

As noted in Figure 8.3, the arts can engage newcomer students in analyzing and acting on social issues. For example, Augusto Boal's Theater of the Oppressed (TO), which is grounded in Paulo Freire's perspectives on democratic education (Freire, 1970), provides participants with opportunities to reflect and act on the oppression they experience in their lives. Boal has used two particular approaches that we have found useful with newcomers: a) Image Theater and b) Forum Theater. In the case of Image Theater, participants are given a task, such as:

- Create an image of a fun time on the playground.
- Create an image of a time when you were unhappy on the playground.

FIGURE 8.3: Connecting Content to Relevant Social Issues

Discipline	Example Connections to Contemporary Issues That May Be Relevant to Newcomers

History	• Pairing a study of trade, colonization, migration, and/or civil war with contemporary examples, such as:
	  ▪ Border conflicts and border security
	  ▪ Causes of migration in particular regions
	  ▪ Current wars and conflicts that lead to immigration
	  ▪ Global trade and whether products are "fair trade"

Science	• Climate change and its consequences in different parts of the world • Access to healthy food in low-income communities • Water crises due to drought and contamination • Engineering solutions to issues (e.g., saving energy by creating energy-efficient homes, filtering, or desalinating water) • Environmental issues in students' communities (e.g., cleaning up local creeks and the watershed, lobbying against companies that pollute the neighborhood)
Math	• Learning to read data in different forms (charts, graphs, tables) to learn about various issues • Collecting and analyzing survey or demographic data related to various topics
Art	• Analyzing how artists communicate social and political messages through their artwork • Creating artwork to communicate their own messages
Theater	• Role-playing different conflicts and possible just solutions • Stakeholder meetings, where groups of students take on the perspectives of different stakeholders connected to an issue and debate • Creating a play or skit to teach about or draw attention to an issue

• Create an image of how you felt when you first came to this school.
• Create an image of how you now feel when you come to school.

Students create a frozen image, assuming the characters' poses as if they were clay. They then discuss their image, including what the characters are doing, why they are doing what they're doing, and how they feel.

In the case of Forum Theater, which may be easier to facilitate with newcomers who are not new to English and have lived in the U.S. for a year or more, students role-play dilemmas that they have faced in which they or someone they know has been treated unfairly. Examples of these kinds of experiences include the following:

- An encounter in a store when a clerk stops a group of children before they leave the store and demands that they empty their pockets to prove that they haven't taken any candy; or
- A classmate used an ethnic slur when referring to a newcomer.

After they have enacted the dilemma, spect-actors (other students in the audience) are invited to enter into the role-play to change the course of the role-play. A facilitator asks the spect-actors to participate in another enactment of the dilemma by taking over a role or adding a new character and changing what transpires. For example, in the case of the store dilemma, a child may decide to assume the role of a customer who asks the clerk to offer a reason for requesting that the children empty their pockets. After each enactment, the teacher facilitates a discussion, posing questions such as the following:

- What happened in the enactment/drama/play?
- Why did the characters do what they did?
- Was what they did fair? Why/why not?

Structuring Inquiry-based Units

We have found the following instructional sequence helpful when structuring inquiry-based content units in different disciplines :

- Engage students' curiosity and wonder.
- Facilitate hands-on learning.
- Make meaning of hands-on experiences.
- Support students in engaging with resources (e.g., texts, videos, lectures) to learn.
- Involve students in organizing, applying, and communicating what they've learned.

In this section, we will describe different ways to launch an inquiry and engage students' curiosity and wonder about a phenomenon. In the rest of the chapter, we will address the other components of the instructional sequence mentioned above.

When launching an inquiry-based unit, it is important to pique students' curiosity and wonder about the topic. All of the strategies below begin by having students activate and share relevant background knowledge and then generate questions to guide their inquiry. In the first two strategies, visuals or objects are used to engage and surface students' background knowledge, which is particularly helpful for newcomers.

- *Looking closely at an image, a video, or an artifact and engaging students in a See-Think-Wonder protocol:* As described in Chapter 3, this protocol first engages students in observing and describing all the things they notice. Students then make and discuss inferences based on their observations. Finally, they generate questions, brainstorming all the things they're wondering about after looking at the image. These questions can then serve as a springboard for and frame their inquiry throughout the unit.
- *A gallery walk of images related to what students will be studying:* A teacher posts photos or other intriguing images around the room related to the topic the class will be studying. Students circulate in pairs or triads to discuss the images and record their thinking, either on a note-taking sheet or on charts posted next to the images. For example, in the sixth-grade science class described above, students launched their study of energy with a gallery walk. The teacher posted several images related to energy around the room, such as images of the sun, electrical wires, solar panels, windmills, sunflowers stretching toward the sun, and a thermal image of a house. Students walked around in triads with a note-taking sheet on which they recorded what they saw and wondered about (see Figure 8.4).

FIGURE 8.4: Gallery Walk Note-Taking Sheet

Image number	I see . . .	I wonder . . .
1		
2		

As they walked, the students discussed and recorded their thinking in triads, as seen in the example (Figure 8.5).

FIGURE 8.5: Example of Completed Gallery Walk Note-Taking Sheet

Image number	I see . . .	I wonder . . .
1	I see the sun is big and glowing. The middle is really bright yellow and there are lines coming out of it.	Will you go blind right away if you look at it? How hot is the sun?
2	I see some kind of cable plugged into the outlet.	What is it? How come sometimes when you plug things in you see a little spark?
3	I see solar panels on a house. They look shiny and they're pointed toward the sun.	What happens when it's raining or cloudy? Does their power go out?

Through this activity, students were introduced to an abstract concept—energy—through concrete images, many of which were already familiar to them. Newcomers were supported because discussion was grounded in visuals and the teacher and other students referred to these images as they spoke, helping newcomers comprehend the class discussion and learn new language. When the class came together to share what they discussed, the teacher labeled key objects in the images and charted students' ideas next to the images to create a repository of environmental print that they would be drawing on in the following weeks.

- *KWL charts:* A simple but effective routine for delving into a new topic is to have students surface and share what they already *know* and what they *want to know*. For newcomers, it is really helpful to bring in some visuals or realia to help them understand and participate in the discussion. For example, in a second-grade class, the teacher launched a study of bees. In order to help newcomers and other ELs generate ideas and questions, the teacher projected images of bees. As students explored the topic throughout the unit, they returned to the chart to address the third column, what they *learned*. Teachers can also add a fourth column, addressing *how* the class learned. See Figure 8.6 for a sample KWLH chart.
- *Clustering questions:* The strategies above describe different ways for students to generate questions. We've found that children are extremely curious and often push our thinking by posing fascinating and authentic questions. Sometimes, a helpful next step is to have students organize

FIGURE 8.6: KWLH Chart

We know . . .	We want to know . . .	We learned . . .	How did we learn it?

their questions, grouping or clustering them together. This is easier to do if students have written their questions on sticky notes, index cards, or sentence strips that can be moved around on a piece of chart paper, a board, or a pocket chart. We've found that a bottom-up approach to categorizing works well with students. For example, a teacher can display all the questions students generated and choose one to begin, re-reading the question and asking if there is another question that is similar. Students can then identify questions that go together and then, with teacher support, attach a label to the category. For example, with the help of the teacher who used arrows and circles to connect similar questions, the second graders studying bees categorized their questions as shown in Figure 8.7:

FIGURE 8.7: Second Graders' Questions about Bees

Bees' life cycle	How bees get food	Where bees live	Bees and humans
• How do bees die? • How do bees have babies? • How do bees feed and take care of their babies? • Do bees have nests? • Do bees lay eggs? • What is a queen bee? • Is there a king?	• What do bees eat? • How do bees get pollen out of flowers? • Do bees share food? • Do bees fight over food? • Do bees eat meat?	• Where do bees live? • Do they live alone or in groups? • Where do killer bees live?	• Are there killer bees? • Can bees kill humans? • Can you die from a bee sting? • Do we need bees? • What should you do if you get stung by a bee? • How can you avoid getting stung by a bee? • Are bees dangerous? • What should you do if a bee is bothering you?

- Students, particularly older students who can read English, can be given a sheet of paper with all of the questions, cut them apart, and then work with a partner to group them into categories.

In all of the above strategies for launching an inquiry, students are actively engaged in their learning. Starting in this way sets a tone for the unit—that we are investigating and learning together—as well as a purpose for future investigations and readings. In the sections that follow, we will describe ways of engaging students in hands-on learning and in learning from texts and other resources, as well as how to modify tasks so newcomers can show what they've learned.

Using Multi-Modal Resources and Experiences

In all content areas, it's important to engage newcomers in different types of learning activities, instead of relying solely on text and verbal explanations. Figure 8.8 below describes many different types of multi-modal resources and experiences that can support newcomers in different disciplines. For example, in both science and social studies, all students can be engaged in "reading" by examining visual texts that are important to the disciplines, such as scientific models or diagrams, mathematical graphs, wordless books, graphic novels, and historical maps, images, and artifacts. The work of reading and analyzing texts shouldn't be limited to written text, and students can learn disciplinary analysis by examining visuals. These visuals often include minimal text and have strong visual cues to communicate meaning and support students' comprehension. Visual texts also support ELs by keeping talk and writing grounded in images.

In all content areas, we want to provide students with a range of multi-modal experiences. To illustrate this, let's go back to Scenario 2 at the beginning of this chapter, in which the sixth graders were studying thermal energy, and see how multi-modal experiences were used to support newcomers' learning during that unit:

- *Hands-on investigations:* The engineering task described in the scenario engaged students in hands-on learning since they were actively building, troubleshooting, testing, and revising their house prototypes. Before embarking on the engineering project, they had conducted several scientific experiments to learn about how energy moves through

FIGURE 8.8: Multi-Modal Resources and Experiences for Content Instruction

Modality	Science	History	Math
Hands-on investigations	• Science experiments • Engineering tasks • Closely observing natural objects like shells, fossils, feathers, and leaves • Field trips • Fieldwork	• Examining historical artifacts • Field trips • Fieldwork	• Using math manipulatives
Visuals	• Scientific models or diagrams • Graphs • Computer simulations • Pictures, photos, charts • Video inputs	• Examining historical images • Maps and mapping activities • Pictures, photos, charts • Videos	• Drawing models and diagrams to understand math word problems • Graphs
Kinesthetic	• Modeling scientific concepts by acting them out, such as magnets attracting and repelling or planets orbiting the sun	• Writing and acting out historical scenarios • Historical simulations	• Acting out math word problems

different materials and to determine if materials are conductors or insulators.

- *Visuals:* When students started reading about thermal energy, the newcomer students "read" scientific models, or diagrams, to learn content using a *See-Think-Wonder* protocol with the model/diagram (Figure 8.9).
  - First, the teacher gave the newcomer students, all of whom were Spanish speakers, copies of the model and pointed out that, as is often the case in science, many words are cognates from Spanish (e.g., gas/*gas*, liquid/*líquido*, solid/*sólido*, energy/*energía*, molecules/*moléculas*). (See Chapter 6 for more information about using cognates with newcomers.)
  - Then she asked students to look closely at the model and

FIGURE 8.9: Molecules in Solids, Liquids, and Gases

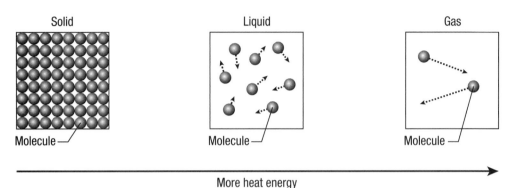

Source: the authors

brainstorm what they saw. The teacher recorded all their ideas in the *I see* column on a piece of chart paper (see column one in Figure 8.10). When students used Spanish, the teacher translated their ideas and charted them in English. If the teacher had not spoken the students' native language, she would have relied on bilingual students to translate, if they were present, or inferred from students' gesturing and use of visuals. To support comprehension, she frequently pointed to the model when she spoke English or charted ideas and when other students spoke.

- After noting everything they saw in the model, they moved on to identify what the model made them think and charted that in the second column below, *I think* (see Figure 8.10, middle column). This step required them to pull together information from the images, text, and their prior knowledge and make inferences about what the model was communicating.

- Finally, they brainstormed questions they had about the model, and the teacher charted them in the third column, *I wonder* (see Figure 8.10, right column).

- Through this activity, students learned some big ideas about energy and phase changes (e.g., how matter turns from solid to liquid or vice versa), as well as some important language in English that they would need as they continued learning and reading about the topic (e.g., *molecules, solids, liquids, gas, vibrate*). They also looked closely at an example of a scientific model/diagram, which would help them build their understanding of how to create their own scientific models later on in the unit when they created models of their house prototypes.

FIGURE 8.10: Example See-Think-Wonder Chart

I see . . .	I think . . .	I wonder . . .
• Three squares—gas, liquid, solid • Little circles • Red arrow • Two little circles in gas • More little circles in gas • A lot of circles in solid • Little arrows in liquid and gas	• The little circles are molecules • The molecules are moving in liquid and gas • Solid gets hotter and becomes liquid • Liquid gets hotter and becomes gas	• What are molecules? • Why are there only two molecules in gas? • Why are there more molecules in liquids and solids? • Why are the molecules moving?

- *Computer simulations:* The teacher showed students a simple computer simulation of molecule movement at different temperatures. The simulation started at a low temperature, and the molecules vibrated minimally in place. When she increased the temperature on the simulation, the molecules began to vibrate more. When she increased it further, the molecules began moving, spreading around, and bouncing into each other.
- *Kinesthetic activities:* The teacher used kinesthetic activities to further solidify students' understandings of how heat affects molecule movement. She brought the students together in the front of the room and drew a simple thermometer on the board. At first, she drew a low temperature in blue marker and explained, "Now it's cold." She put her arms over her torso and pretended to shiver. She asked, "How will the molecules move?" Students had previously seen the computer simulation, and they drew on this experience as they moved closer together; they were mostly still, only wiggling (or vibrating) in their places. Then she gradually increased the tempera-

ture on her thermometer. Students acted out the molecules moving and spread around the room.

While teachers often integrate hands-on and multi-modal experiences in science, it is equally important to provide these experiences in other subject areas, such as math and history. The scenario below describes a multi-modal learning sequence in a first-grade math class.

SCENE: Ms. Allen's first-grade class

PARTICIPANTS: A class of 24 first-graders, the majority of whom are English learners. Three students are newcomers who arrived earlier that school year.

SCENARIO: Ms. Allen's first-graders are learning to solve simple word problems with addition and subtraction. Each day, she uses the same protocol to solve a word problem, using kinesthetic activities, manipulatives, and models to make sure students understand the situation before writing and solving equations. First, they chorally read the problem. Today's problem is:

Together Megan and Jason decorated 12 cookies on Sunday. Megan decorated 5 cookies. How many cookies did Jason decorate?

Then Ms. Allen takes out a box of yellow hexagonal pattern blocks and asks for two volunteers to be Megan and Jason. She explains that the pattern blocks will be cookies and asks how many "cookies" they should take out to act out today's problem. Some students say 5, and others say 12.

"Hmm, let's re-read the problem," Ms. Allen says. "How many cookies did they make altogether?"

The class chorally reads the problem again and decides they need 12. Ms. Allen underlines 12. "So the two kids, Megan and Jason, decorated 12 cookies. How many cookies should we give each one? Let's read it again to see."

Again, the class re-reads the problem and the students realize Megan needs five of the cookies because she decorated five. They chorally count out five cookies and Ms. Allen hands them to the student pretending to be Megan.

"What's our question? What are we trying to find out? Let's read it again and see." After determining that they need to figure out how many cookies Jason decorated, they decide to give the student pretending to be Jason the remaining cookies and count them out together to see how many he decorated.

After acting out the scenario, Ms. Allen's students move to their tables, where they have smaller boxes of pattern blocks. They work with partners to create a model with the pattern blocks to represent the situation and then to draw their model on a paper.

Ms. Allen brings the class together and has some of the partners share their diagrams with the class, such as in Figure 8.11. They talk through any differences or discrepancies. Then the pairs go to their tables again and write equations to represent the problem.

FIGURE 8.11: Word Problem Model and Equation

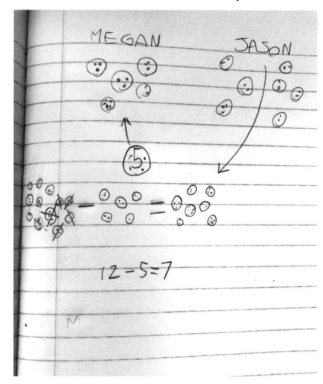

Reading and Listening to Learn

Preparing Students to Read and Listen to Learn

Students are expected to learn a great deal of content through reading and listening activities, and both reading and listening activities can be important venues for language acquisition. Newcomers who come with some literacy in another language besides English can and should start engaging with English reading early on. Scaffolded reading activities provide access to English that is sometimes easier to manage than fast-flowing conversational English. A peer or teacher may say something quickly and then that speech is gone, whereas a newcomer can engage with text at his or her own pace and return to it multiple times to make sense of it.

Although newcomers can and should be engaged in reading and listening activities to develop their English and learn content, there are important steps that need to happen beforehand to prepare them to grapple productively with reading and listening activities. When planning pre-reading or pre-listening activities, it's important to keep in mind a few important goals:

- Activate key background knowledge that will create a schema to support students' comprehension.
- Plant a few key terms that students will encounter. You do not want to pre-teach a list of words, but rather introduce the terms in context.
- Help students acquire pre-reading or pre-listening strategies, such as using images and section titles in a text to make predictions before reading, which will help them comprehend other texts in the future.
- Set a clear purpose for reading or listening. Articulate for yourself what the key information is that you want students to learn from the experience and make sure to set that purpose for students (e.g., *We've been wondering how bees get their food. We're going to read this article to learn about where bees find food and how they get it*).

There are many different types of pre-reading activities teachers can use to prepare newcomers to engage with different types of text, including the following:

- *See-Think-Wonder protocols:* You can use any images that accompany the text—photos, maps, graphs, models—or still images from a video. See Chapter 3 and the preceding section in this chapter for detailed descriptions of the *See-Think-Wonder* protocol. If a text doesn't have images, you can search for a relevant image online and print or project it.
- *Sequencing protocols to predict what will happen in the text or video*: This works well with narrative texts or videos, as well as texts that describe historical or scientific processes. Teachers can give students a set of images to discuss and sequence based on their prior knowledge or predictions; the images can come from the text or elsewhere. For example, before read-

ing a picture book version of a Native American legend, fourth graders were given four key illustrations from the story. They worked in a group to sequence them and then each group explained what they thought the story's sequence would be.

- *Sorting protocols*: If a text focuses on describing a key concept or contrasting two different concepts, teachers can give students a set of images to sort before reading. For example, before reading a text about the characteristics of life, sixth graders sorted a set of images of different living and nonliving objects. They worked in pairs to sort them based on their own emergent definitions of living and nonliving, which included a lot of lively debate about whether fire or clouds were living. They returned to and re-sorted the images after reading.
- *Using images and titles to predict:* Students need to learn strategies to preview texts and make predictions to help them comprehend texts or videos. Teachers can draw students' attention to the text or video title and section headers and ask them to generate predictions about what they will learn or questions they think they will be able to answer. Afterward, they can return to these predictions and questions to confirm/disconfirm or answer them.

All of these protocols can be used either with the whole class or with a group of newcomer students. The scenario below describes a fifth-grade class preparing to read a history text.

SCENE: Sarah's fifth-grade class

PARTICIPANTS: Thirty fifth-graders, including five newcomer students

SCENARIO: Sarah's class is studying early U.S. history and the role of tobacco in expanding the early colonies. The class will be reading a text about how tobacco plantations and the tobacco trade helped expand and strengthen the Virginia colony. Sarah brings her students to the carpet and shows them three images printed and taped onto three pieces of chart paper (see Figure 8.12).

They use the *See-Think-Wonder* protocol to explore the three images, and Sarah annotates each image with their ideas. Through this, her newcomer students learn several key terms they will encounter in their modified version of the text, including *tobacco*, *ship*, *barrels, smoking*, and *plantation*.

FIGURE 8.12: Jamestown Images for Sequencing Task

Source: Tabaco, Anthony Chute, 1595

She explains that the images represent three main events in the text they'll read and gives each triad a copy of each image. Then she asks the students to talk in triads about what they think the order of events will be. When possible, she places her newcomers in groups with one student who is bilingual in their native language and one student who is not. She has told the groups to use English as much as possible and to translate only if the newcomer student is not able to understand. One of her newcomers, Aisha, speaks Arabic, and there are no other Arabic speakers in her class. Aisha physically moves the images around to show her group the order she predicts. She gestures and points to show how she thinks the plants shown in the second image are the same plants in the man's pipe. The students talk through their predictions and share them with the class. Most think that the plants show tobacco growing on a farm or plantation, then tobacco is placed in barrels and put on ships to England, and finally, a man in England smokes the tobacco. Students now have a schema that will support their sense making as they read the article.

Sometimes, the temptation is to pre-teach a list of words, to prepare ELs or newcomers to read, or to provide a summary or synopsis of the text before students read. However, learning lists of words without context is not helpful, and telling students what they will read ahead of time takes away the purpose of reading to learn. The goal is to make strategic moves before reading that will prepare students to grapple productively with the text.

Choosing and Modifying Texts and Videos Strategically

In an upper elementary or middle school classroom, in particular, teachers will need to choose and modify texts strategically to make sure they are accessible to newcomer students. History and science textbooks often pack a great deal of information and concepts into a single paragraph, making it very hard for students, particularly newcomers, to make sense of the content. Newcomers should be introduced to English reading early on, but the task needs to be within reach to make it a productive and successful learning opportunity. Here are some steps to take when modifying texts for beginning newcomers:

- Decide what you want students to learn from the text. In the case of a narrative text, what are the most important ideas or events?
- Reduce the amount of text newcomers must read, eliminating paragraphs and sentences with unnecessary details.
- Take out sections of the text that make confusing connections or analogies, such as "For example, the water molecules in solid ice are tightly packed together, *like marbles in a jar.*" While the analogy to marbles would be helpful for a student who understands the phrase *marbles in a jar*, it is likely to be confusing to a newcomer and detracts from their sense making.
- Adjust vocabulary so that the language reflects the language students have been learning in class. For example, in the original text that middle school students read, *particles, molecules,* and *atoms* were all used. However, in the modified text, only *molecules* was used as this was a term that the class had been using.
- Shorten and simplify complex sentences. As can be seen in Figure 8.13, right column, the sentences in the modified text are less complex, making them more accessible to newcomers.
- Make use of cognates if students' primary language shares cognates with English, so students see how they can use their primary

language to support their English reading. (See Chapter 6 for more information about cognates.)

Figure 8.13 is an example of a modified text for beginning newcomer students in a middle school earth science class and it illustrates several of the steps listed above. In the left column is the original text and in the right column is the modified text. The teacher kept words that are important in a study of earth formation (e.g., *erosion, glaciers, V-shaped,* and *U-shaped*); she used visuals and gestures to clarify these concepts. The teacher also shortened sentences and used language that she thought students would be familiar with (e.g., *made* in place of *formed*; *different shapes* in place of *variety of forms*; *dig out* in place of *carve*). Teachers can modify text by retyping it, or by simply using scissors and glue and literally cutting and pasting together a new version.

A caution about modifying text: This kind of rewriting and simplifying should only be done for very beginning ELs, not for students who have been here for more than one or two years. ELs who are not at the very beginning stages of language acquisition need access to this more complex language to develop their language and literacy abilities. Teachers can limit the amount of text they grapple with, but they should still be engaging with grade-level text, concepts, and terminology.

Similarly, teachers will want to modify videos to support students in listening. We recommend shortening videos to focus on the most essential ideas or events we want newcomers to learn and having students view them multiple times. This will cut down on the amount of extraneous content they have to listen to. For older newcomers who are literate, it can be helpful to use

FIGURE 8.13: Original and Modified Text

Original text	Modified text for newcomers
A **valley** is a natural depression in the earth's surface that has hills or mountains on either side. Valleys can be found in all kinds of landscapes, including mountains, hills, and plains, and they are formed by erosion from water and/or ice. They have a variety of forms. Some are V-shaped and have steep sides; and are formed by water erosion from rivers. Other valleys are U-shaped and are formed by glaciers as they carve their way through the existing V-shaped valley.	A **valley** is a low area in the earth's surface. Valleys are made when water and/or ice wear away rock; this is called erosion. Valleys have different shapes. Some are V-shaped; these have steep sides and are made by rivers. Other valleys are U-shaped; these are made by glaciers as they move down valleys.

closed captioning so there are English subtitles reinforcing what the speakers are saying.

Focusing Students on Understanding Key Ideas

Newcomers—as well as all students—need to learn to make meaning when they do not understand every word. This requires developing stamina and the ability to make good guesses and inferences in context. As with modifying text, teachers need to take a little time before teaching to identify the key ideas and events they want students to learn from the text. Once teachers have this clarity, they can use different strategies to help focus newcomers' attention on these key ideas and events, including the following:

- *Setting a specific purpose*: For example, before watching a video about the solar system, the teacher can tell students, "There's going to be a lot of information here, but what I really want you to listen for is the names of the planets that orbit the sun. When you hear one, write it down. Don't worry about spelling." As the teacher explains the task, s/he jots down *names of the planets* and sketches planets orbiting the sun. Similarly, before reading, teachers or students can identify a focus question and highlight any information that seems relevant to answering that question.
- *Margin questions*: Teachers can write questions in the margin to help newcomers focus on the main ideas or events in the text. Students both underline the information in the text and write their responses to the questions in the margins. It is important to create these questions strategically, only asking about events that are important, placing them next to the relevant line or paragraph, and using language that reflects the language used in the text rather than introducing new, unfamiliar terms. You can also use yes/no (e.g., *Did Fred go to Japan?*), closed answer (e.g., *How many sons did they have?*), or choice questions to support newcomers (e.g., *Did Fred speak English or Japanese?*). Figure 8.14 provides an example of margin questions.
- *Annotating for a specific purpose:* Setting a clear purpose for reading can support newcomers to make sense of challenging text and identify the key information they need to learn. Students can be directed to annotate the text with this purpose in mind. For example, in the context of a science unit on animal adaptations, a class might do readings on different animals and how they adapt to their habitat. For a first read of an article about crayfish, a teacher might direct students to use a

FIGURE 8.14: Example of Margin Questions (text modified from Atkins & Yogi, 2017)

Pruning Roses	
Why did Fred's father and mother move to the United States? *opportunities*	Fred's father and mother moved to the United States from Japan looking for new opportunities.
How many sons did they have? *four sons* When was Fred born? *1919* What was his name in Japanese? *Toyosaburo* Who gave him the name "Fred"? *Teacher*	They have four sons. Born in 1919. Fred is third. His parents name him Toyosaburo. His first-grade teacher can't pronounce his name in Japanese. Your new name is Fred, she says.
Where did Fred's family work? *the Flower nursery* What were the names of Fred's brothers? *Hi, Harry, Joe*	Everyone in Fred's family works hard at the flower nursery. Fred and his brothers work all the time Fred's oldest brother, Hi, is the favorite. Harry, the second, is smart. Baby brother Joe is cute.
Did Fred want to work at the flower nursery? *Not*	Fred does not want to work at the flower nursery. He dreams of another future.
Who loved Japan? *Freds Parents Love Japan*	Fred's parents love Japan, the country of their childhood. Fred's parents speak Japanese at home They want to teach their sons Japanese.
Did Fred speak English or Japanese? *Fred speaks English* Did Fred go to Japan? *Not*	But Fred speaks English. Japan is so far away He has not gone to Japan He is an American.

colored pencil to underline all the information in the article about the crayfish's habitat. Then they can bring the class together to share out and chart everything they learned about where crayfish live. On a second read, students can now use a new color and underline information about crayfish's body parts that help them survive in that habitat. This purposeful reading and annotating helps newcomers hone in on the key information they need to glean from the article without being overwhelmed by extra details.

- *Re-sorting or re-sequencing images*: After reading, students can re-sequence or re-sort images they interacted with before reading. For example, after Sarah's fifth grade students read about Jamestown, they returned to the three images to see if the order they predicted made sense. Similarly, after reading a narrative, students can go back to the images they sequenced and see if that order did match the key events in the book.

- *Reconstructing summaries or retellings:* Another strategy to help newcomers who are not yet producing a lot of English engage with the language of a text is to write a shared summary and then have students re-order the events. For example, Laura read the picture book *I'm New Here* by Anne Sibley O'Brien (2015) with a group of third- through fifth-grade newcomers, chunking the book into three parts, which they engaged with over multiple days. After reading each part of the book, Laura scribed and supported the group as they did a shared retelling of that day's part of the story (see Figure 8.15). They then chorally read their retelling.

FIGURE 8.15: Shared Retelling of *I'm New Here*

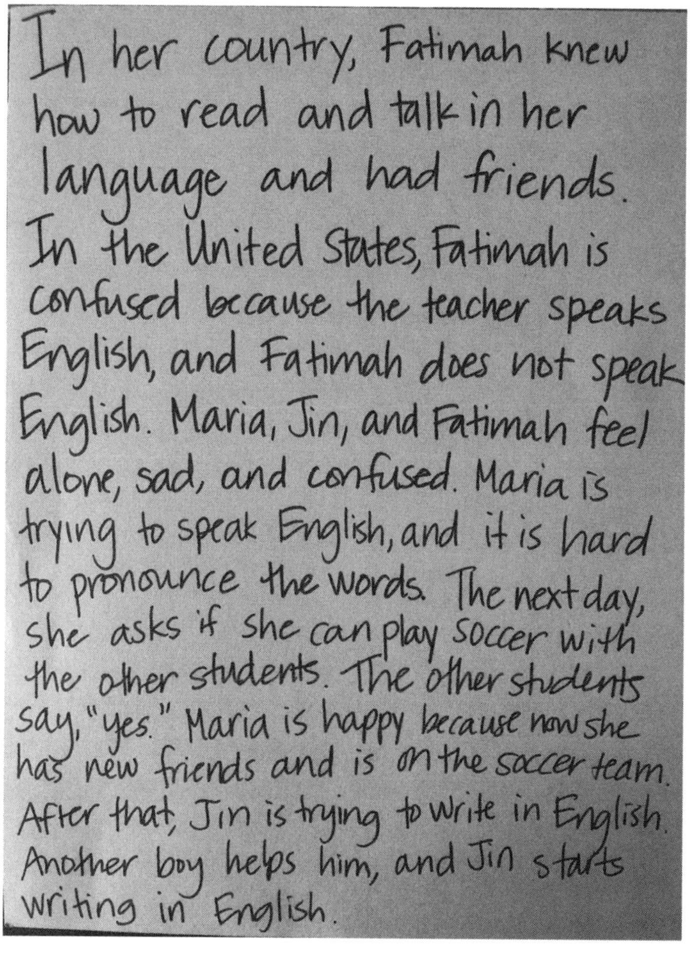

In her country, Fatimah knew how to read and talk in her language and had friends. In the United States, Fatimah is confused because the teacher speaks English, and Fatimah does not speak English. Maria, Jin, and Fatimah feel alone, sad, and confused. Maria is trying to speak English, and it is hard to pronounce the words. The next day, she asks if she can play soccer with the other students. The other students say, "yes." Maria is happy because now she has new friends and is on the soccer team. After that, Jin is trying to write in English. Another boy helps him, and Jin starts writing in English.

The next day, Laura gave each student a typed-up version of the group's retelling with some minor edits and the sentences written out of order. The students cut the sentences apart, re-read them, and re-sequenced them (see Figure 8.16). As they did this, they looked through the copies of the books and matched the events in the sentences to the pictures and text.

- *Graphic organizers:* Students can use graphic organizers that match their purpose in listening or reading to record key information. For example, if students will be watching a short video explaining the causes of wild-fires, they can use the cause-effect graphic organizer shown in Figure 8.17 to note different things that contribute to wildfires.

In contrast, if students are watching a video comparing aquatic and

FIGURE 8.16: Reconstructing a Shared Retelling

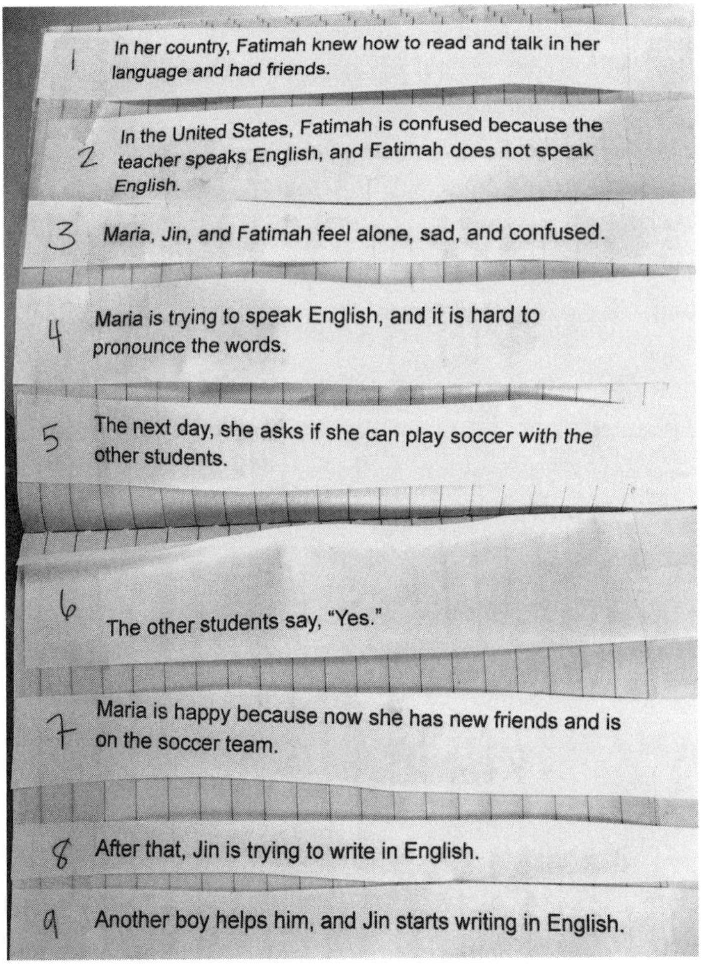

1   In her country, Fatimah knew how to read and talk in her language and had friends.

2   In the United States, Fatimah is confused because the teacher speaks English, and Fatimah does not speak English.

3   Maria, Jin, and Fatimah feel alone, sad, and confused.

4   Maria is trying to speak English, and it is hard to pronounce the words.

5   The next day, she asks if she can play soccer with the other students.

6   The other students say, "Yes."

7   Maria is happy because now she has new friends and is on the soccer team.

8   After that, Jin is trying to write in English.

9   Another boy helps him, and Jin starts writing in English.

FIGURE 8.17: Cause-Effect Graphic Organizer

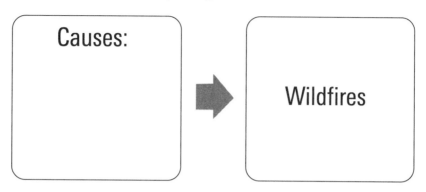

terrestrial plants, a Venn diagram would be more useful to capture insights (see Figure 8.18).

Whatever the format, it is important to preview the graphic organizer and make sure students understand how to fill it out, so that they can use it as a tool.

The following scenario describes how a teacher brings together several of the strategies described above to support her seventh-grade newcomers as they read and analyze a challenging novel, focusing their attention on understanding the main events and ideas in the chapter, rather than getting bogged down by all of the details or words they did not yet understand.

FIGURE 8.18: Venn Diagram Graphic Organizer

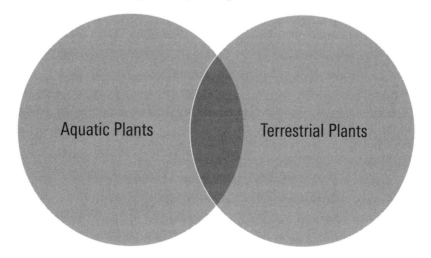

SCENE: Laura's seventh-grade newcomer intervention group.

PARTICIPANTS: Seven newcomers from Mexico and Central America, who had arrived in the U.S. within the last year.

SCENARIO: The class was reading *A Long Walk to Water* by Linda Sue Park (2010), a novel that interweaves the story of two Sudanese young people, a girl named Nya and a teenaged boy named Salva. Each chapter is divided into a short section about Nya and a longer section about Salva's story. Laura adapted the text by having the newcomers only read the sections about Nya, which themselves create a complete narrative. She also cut some paragraphs and sentences from the chapters when they dealt with details that weren't essential to understanding the main events of the narrative. Then she created margin questions to focus their attention on key events in the plot. Students underlined the evidence in the text that helped them answer each question and wrote their responses below each question, borrowing key phrases from the text.

After students had read and responded to the questions, they were given a short summary of the key events out of order, as seen below.

Chapter 17
Nya will learn to read and write.
No one will have to walk to the pond to get water.
All the children will be able to go to school.
The men are building a school.

Students then cut apart the sentences and used the text to re-order the main events, finding key words and phrases in the chapter that matched those in the summary.

To support the development of students' inferring and use of evidence, students then matched quotes with inferences. First, they cut out the following four quotes:

Chapters 12 and 14: Learning Target: I can find evidence to support inferences.
Evidence
"Everyone cheered at the sight of the water."
"Nya clapped her hands along with all the other children."
"They collected piles of rocks and stones and tied them up into bundles using sturdy cloth . . . Other villagers, using tools borrowed from the visitors, pounded the rocks to break them up into gravel."
"But as Nya watched the water spraying out of the borehole, she frowned. The water wasn't clear. It was brown and heavy-looking."

Then, they identified which quote would serve as evidence to support each inference below:

Inference
Everyone in the village is collaborating to build the well.
The people are happy to see the water.
At first, Nya is happy to see the water.
Nya is disappointed that the water is brown and full of mud.

Through all of these activities, students were supported to grapple with English text by focusing their efforts on the key events in the chapter rather than all of the details, which could have made the reading task overwhelming and unattainable for newcomer students.

Teaching Language in Context

Integrating language and content instruction also means strategically drawing attention to particular language structures that will help students read, talk, and write about what they're learning. Direct language instruction should always be in the context of meaningful use and for the purpose of enabling students to engage in a task rather than disconnected grammar lessons. When thinking about what to focus on, consider the following: What language structures do students need for this assignment or genre? For example, if students are writing lab reports, focusing on sequence words or past-tense verbs is likely to be important for them so they can clearly communicate the steps they took in conducting an investigation. Figure 8.19 outlines organization structures and language features that may be helpful to focus on with newcomers who are writing in different genres.

When teaching language, do not be surprised if students can use language features correctly during a lesson, only to misuse the language feature in their writing or speech. This is to be expected as developing grammatical accuracy takes time. Rather than interrupting students' writing process to focus on conventions, save this for a final editing step after the rough draft has been completed. In an editing mini-lesson or conference, draw attention to select language features and engage students in reviewing and editing their own writing. The result may not be perfect, but students will learn more from

FIGURE 8.19: Organizational Structures and Language Features for Different Genres

Genre and purpose	Typical organizational structure	Language features to focus on with newcomers
Recounts: to tell what happened	• Introduction • Series of events • Personal comment	• Action verbs • Past tense • Naming specific participants • First-person pronouns • Linking words and phrases (e.g., *next*, *then*, *later on*)
Narratives: to entertain, imagine, reflect on an experience, or teach or inform, based on experience	• Orientation that sets the scene and introduces characters • Often has a complication or problem • Resolution or may be left unresolved • Events are usually told in chronological order	• Specific named participants • Usually past tense • Action verbs • First-person or third-person and consistent use of pronouns • Descriptive language
Information reports: to communicate factual information on a topic	• Opening general statement introducing the topic • Facts about the topic, organized into categories or subtopics • Diagrams, photos, or illustrations with captions	• Present or past tense • Technical vocabulary
Instructions: to explain how to do something	• Goal • Materials • Directions/procedure	• Present tense • Action verbs • Linking words or phrases that communicate time and sequence (e.g., *first*, *next*, *finally*) • Specific information about materials, what to do, and how to do it
Arguments: to take a position on an issue and justify it	• Statement of position—claim or thesis statement • Reasons and evidence, tying back to the author's position • Summing up of the position • Call to action	• Technical vocabulary related to the issue • Modal verbs (e.g., *should*, *must*) • Connecting words (e.g., *because*, *so*, *therefore*)

Explanations: to explain how something works or reasons for a phenomenon	• Orienting statement about the topic • Sequenced explanation of the process	• Technical vocabulary • Action verbs • Present tense • Cause-effect connecting words (e.g., *if/then*, *so*, *because*, *since*)

Source: Adapted from Derewianka, 1990

applying what they're learning about language to edit their own writing than having it corrected by the teacher.

As students are beginning to write in English, using shared writing activities can support their production and language learning. For example, a teacher can use shared writing to engage newcomers in explaining a science experiment, retelling or summarizing a text, or describing an historical image. As students offer ideas for the shared text, the teacher can fill in and rephrase needed language. After creating the shared text, students can re-engage with it to learn language from it in a variety of ways. The teacher can type up the shared text and mix up the sentences, then have students sequence it without looking at the original text. Through this activity, students have to work on comprehending the ideas and structure of the text to sequence it. Students can also search for language features they're learning how to use (e.g., past tense verbs, sequence words, words with the *th* sound, or possessive pronouns).

Providing Multiple Ways for Students to Show Learning

Although newcomers can and should work toward age-appropriate content standards, they will often need to show their learning through modified tasks. Here are some approaches to modifying tasks so that newcomers can demonstrate content learning with emergent English:

- *Creating visuals:* Students can create visual representations to show their understanding of key ideas or concepts. For example, in science, newcomers can create a visual model or diagram with labels and short explanations in English. In language arts or history, students can draw the main events of a text or historical situation, labeling key actors and writing a short explanation.

- *Sequencing:* Often, students are learning about different types of processes—scientific processes, historical events, or events in a story. Newcomers can take illustrations of key events in a process and sequence them. For example, a teacher can give a newcomer illustrations of each step in the water cycle (e.g., evaporation, condensation, precipitation) and ask them to put the pictures in order and use arrows to show how the elements transform.
- *Sorting*: At other times, content learning may be focused on understanding important categories, such as types of living things or causes vs. effects of an historical event or scientific concept. Newcomers can be given images, realia, or cards with names of phrases to sort, demonstrating their understanding of disciplinary categories and relationships. For example, in a first-grade class studying insects and spiders, newcomers can sort photos of different creatures and use what they've learned to classify them as either insects or spiders. In a middle school class, after learning about the difference between chemical and physical changes, students can sort labeled images of different types of changes (e.g., cutting an apple, cooking an egg, dissolving salt in water) and use what they learned to decide if they are chemical or physical changes.
- *Writing*: Writing in English with supports can be easier and feel safer than trying to speak in English. Some newcomers, particularly those who are literate in their native language, can often show much more understanding by writing than through oral expression. (See Chapter 7 for strategies to support newcomers in writing.)
- *Using the native language*: Most second language learners comprehend much more English when listening or reading than they can produce. If you understand students' native language, you can have students use their primary languages to convey what they have learned. If you don't understand your newcomer students' language, you can still have the children write in their native language and use colleagues and/or translation software such as Google Translate to interpret whether they comprehended the content they were studying.

For an example of how newcomers can demonstrate learning, let's go back to the sixth-grade science class described at the beginning of the chapter, in which students were designing and prototyping houses that conserve thermal

FIGURE 8.20: **Model of Energy-Efficient House Design**

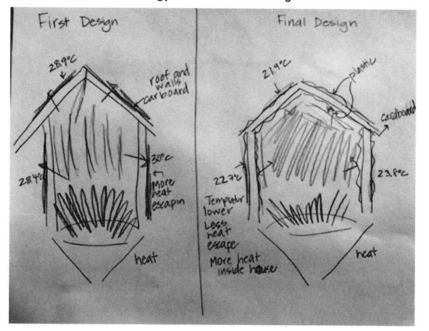

energy. At the end of the unit, most of the students wrote a report explaining their designs and using data to make claims about whether their prototype did, in fact, minimize energy transfer. The newcomers, instead, turned in annotated models of their initial and revised prototypes using arrows, labels, and color to show how the heat did or did not travel through the walls and roof of their initial prototype and revised prototype. See Figure 8.20 for an example.

While the final assignment was modified to make it appropriate for recently arrived newcomer students, the students were still working on grade-level science content and scientific practices. Their models demonstrated that they were able to "design, construct, and test a device that either minimizes or maximizes thermal energy transfer." In the process, they developed key scientific understandings about thermal energy and how it moves in the world, as well as real-life engineering applications of thermal energy. They were also engaged in several of the NGSS Science and Engineering Practices: "Developing and Using Models," "Planning and Carrying Out Investigations," "Analyzing and Interpreting Data," and "Designing Solutions."

Supporting Newcomers in Math

The strategies described previously apply to math as well. Newcomers will benefit from using visuals and manipulatives to learn math and make sense of word problems, and written tasks will need to be modified strategically. Just as in other content areas, students need to be engaged in multiple types of activities through an instructional sequence.

It is also important to be aware that although math is often described as a

FIGURE 8.21: English and Nepali Numerals

Numerals		Written Numerals	
In English	In Nepali	In English	In Nepali
0	०	Zero	शुन्य
1	१	One	एक
2	२	Two	दुई
3	३	Three	तीन
4	४	Four	चार
5	५	Five	पाँच
6	६	Six	छ
7	७	Seven	सात
8	८	Eight	आठ

Source: Katharine Davies Samway and Phulam Lam

"universal language," there are regional and national differences in mathematical notations and algorithms. For example, many countries use different separators instead of commas. Whereas in English one million is written as 1,000,000, in Arabic it is written as 1,000,000, and in Sudanese, it is written as 1.000.000. Some countries, such as Nepal, have different written numerals than those we are familiar with in the United States. For example, in Figure 8.21, English numerals are in the first column, Nepali numerals are in the second column, written numerals in English are in the third column, and written numerals in Nepali are in the fourth column. Also, in many countries, students are taught different algorithms for the four operations and for manipulating fractions.

Newcomers may come with strong mathematical skills and conceptual understanding, but their teachers may not recognize that at first because of these differences in notation and algorithms. Students may also be confused because their teachers and peers use different processes or notations to work through problems. In these cases, it can be helpful to ask newcomers to walk you or the class through how they solve a problem. Learning different algorithms and understanding how they work can strengthen students' (and our own) mathematical understandings.

In other cases, newcomers with interrupted formal education may have gaps in their math learning or may not have studied mathematical concepts and skills that their new classmates learned in previous grades. In these cases, it is helpful to use a diagnostic math assessment, such as Excel Math Placement Tests (2015), which assess math concepts considered appropriate for grades one through six. In this way, it is possible to identify learning objectives that would be appropriate for a student. Some newcomers in upper elementary or middle school with interrupted schooling may need to work on foundational math skills through individualized instruction. It can be helpful to consult with primary teachers and borrow manipulatives to use with newcomers who have had little and/or interrupted schooling. There are also online math applications that can be useful for newcomers to practice early math skills, such as ST Math, Front Row, and Khan Academy. These apps allow teachers to assign specific skills and concepts for students to practice and to monitor students' progress so they can adjust assignments accordingly.

At some points, newcomers who are behind in math can join math instruction to study the same concepts as the rest of the class but use "friendlier numbers." For example, let's consider a fifth-grade class that is learning how to multiply and divide decimals. Newcomer students who have not yet studied decimals can also work on the same operations but use whole numbers instead of decimals. Also, they can work on the same word problems and applied tasks as the rest of the class, substituting whole numbers for decimals. For example, in a sixth-grade class learning about ratios and proportions, newcomers may not have yet learned about decimals and fractions. However, they can still work on ratios and proportions using scenarios with whole numbers, while the rest of the class uses decimals, fractions, and whole numbers. At another time, the teacher could provide small group instruction focused on fractions and decimals.

CHAPTER 9

Teachers Advocating for Newcomers Beyond the Classroom

IN LIGHT OF THE current anti-immigrant and nationalistic political climate, we believe that teachers must be advocates for their newcomer students now more than ever. In this book so far, we have suggested strategies for teachers that view newcomers as active and engaged agents in their learning. This teaching focus is inherently one of advocacy as this type of instruction is not directed by teachers but part of a collaborative approach to learning and teaching that is guided by the needs, resources, and interests of students and their families. In line with the collaborative view of advocacy that we endorse, we see our role as teachers as centered on working *with* students and their families so that we all can ultimately benefit from, contribute to, and transform the larger society. In this chapter, we will focus on what teachers can and have done beyond classroom settings as advocates for newcomer students and their families by addressing the following topics:

- Taking a collaborative approach when working with caregivers, family members, and the larger community;
- Communicating with family members;
- Supporting and establishing partnerships with newcomer families;
- Fostering teacher activism; and
- Legislative work.

Taking a Collaborative Approach when Working with Caregivers, Family Members, and the Larger Community

Children live and learn in a range of different contexts with a variety of people who are invested in their learning and wellbeing. The family is an important context in which they are socialized that usually extends over much of their lifetimes. Through their involvement in schools and classrooms, communities, the larger society, and the social networks that operate in these contexts, newcomer students gain access to needed resources and knowledge. This relationship is not one way (i.e., from parent to child, community to child, teacher to child, or school to child). Newcomer students support and influence their families, communities, teachers, schools, and the larger society. Indeed, many family and community members rely on newcomer children to help them negotiate their lives in a new and unfamiliar country. For example, newcomer students often help translate for elders who speak little or no English. Research that Cindy and others have conducted underscores the prevalence of this practice in many settings, including in clinics and hospitals, work places, and schools (Orellana, 2009; Pease-Alvarez, 2003; Valdés, 2003). Further, as they grow and prosper in the United States, newcomer students become resources for others as they obtain jobs and assume important roles and relationships (e.g., friends, confidants, colleagues, spouses, in-laws, stepsiblings, aunts, uncles).

We endorse a vision that builds on and strengthens the relationships among the various stakeholders involved in the education of newcomer students. According to this vision, teachers, families, community members, and representatives of institutions like schools *collaborate* on the goal of fostering the growth and wellbeing of newcomers and their families. In the next section of this chapter, we will focus on one aspect of this collaboration: establishing supportive relationships between teachers and newcomer families, as both are invested in the education of newcomer children.

Unfortunately, many people, including some teachers, think that newcomer caregivers/parents are not interested in their children's schooling because they may not volunteer in class or come to school-related events, such as back-to-school nights. However, this is usually not the case (Delgado-Gaitan, 2004; Lareau, 2011). As newcomers struggle to make ends meet in an unfamiliar country, there are many reasons why they do not participate in these events, including the following:

- They do not speak much English and think that the adults who work there speak only English at school.
- They have not understood written notices or invitations sent to them in English.
- They do not have childcare for younger children.

- They may not be able to take time off work without losing pay, which they cannot afford to do.
- They may be working more than one job and are unable to attend school events that conflict with their work schedules.
- They do not have a way to get to the school—this is often the case with families who can't access transportation or live far away from the school.
- They do not feel comfortable going to meetings in the evening, especially if they do not drive and must pass through neighborhoods where they feel unsafe.
- If undocumented, they may be afraid that they will be arrested.

Caregivers/parents may see themselves as contributing to their children's education in ways that do not include participating in school-related events. For example, a number of researchers have found that many caregivers/parents of Latinx backgrounds see their role as one of fostering the social and moral development of their children in the home setting rather than engaging in school-related activities (e.g., Reese, Balzano, Gallimore & Goldenberg, 1995; Valdés, 1996; Zentella, 2005). For example, in her work with Mexican-descent families, Guadalupe Valdés (1996) found that parents focused on raising children who, to use her term, are *bien educados*, meaning children who have strong moral values and social behaviors, including acting in ways that were appropriate within the context of their families and communities. While they also valued academic learning, many conceived of teachers as the ones who were best equipped to support their children's academic development.

Based on our experiences working with newcomer caregivers/parents, we have been impressed with their commitment to their children's schooling. Indeed, many, including the two people quoted below, who we have spoken to, came to the United States in hopes of obtaining a better education for their children.

> Estamos aquí porque no habia escuelas donde vivíamos.
>
> *We are here because there were no schools were we lived before.*
>
> (Ana Gutiérrez)

> Venimos a los Estados Unidos para encontrar una vida mejor para nuestros hijos. Aquí pueden estudiar más que la primaria.
>
> *We came to the United States in order to find a better life for our children. Here they can study more than just grade school.*
>
> (Ernesto García)

While parents like Ana and Ernesto above may not participate in their children's schooling in ways that are familiar to U.S.-born caregivers/parents (e.g., by volunteering in class or attending school-related events), they care about their children's education. As Alexander (2019) argues, one of the main reasons that many newcomer caregivers decided to come to the U.S.—to obtain a better education for their children—represents an important type of involvement in their children's education that is often overlooked in schools. Moreover, this decision reflects their deep commitment to the role schooling plays in the lives of their children.

Communicating with Caregivers/Family Members

If we are to have collaborative and trusting relations with newcomer families, we must be able to communicate with them. This can be challenging given that most teachers do not share the languages of many, if any, of their newcomer students, which is clearly the case when teachers are working in a classroom with students who speak a variety of languages. The U.S. Department of Justice, Civil Rights Division, and the U.S Department of Education, Office for Civil Rights, (2015) have been proactive when it comes to urging schools and districts to communicate with parents in languages parents understand. Further, the courts have consistently ruled in favor of family members having access to translation and interpretation services. Under the Obama administration, the Department of Education was quite assertive in requiring that schools have a process for identifying caregivers/parents who need language assistance and for assigning resources to provide this assistance via trained interpreters and translators (Mathewson, 2016). Consequently, many school districts have a central office that arranges for translators for written and phone communications, as well as for parent-teacher conferences.

In some cases, districts and schools have been quite resourceful when it comes to obtaining translation and interpretation services. For example, Olive

Grove Union School District in California, which serves immigrant students from Russia, Croatia, Korea, Mexico, and El Salvador, established a partnership with a local university's foreign language department that enabled them to identify faculty, staff, students, and community members who could serve as translators (Samway & McKeon, 2007). The district paid for the school-related translation services that these people provided.

There are other ways to facilitate communication between teachers and family members. If official interpreters are not available or if caregivers/parents are uncomfortable with these people, let them know that they can invite a trusted family member or friend to school to interpret for them. For many, that trusted family member may be an older child or even the student in your class. If that is the case, make sure that the student is comfortable in assuming this role. While we have worked in communities where children are proud of taking on the role of family interpreter (Pease-Alvarez, 2003), there are children in these communities who resent having to interpret or who find it embarrassing.

When no one is available to interpret, teachers may have to rely on other strategies. Samway and Taylor (2008) suggest that teachers keep the following points in mind when this is the case:

- Smile.
- Express regret that you don't speak their language.
- Speak slowly and clearly but not loudly or in an exaggerated way.
- Strive to use common language (e.g., say *talk* instead of *communicate*).
- Use gestures.
- Pause frequently so that caregivers/parents can process what you are saying and ask questions.
- Show samples of their child's work.
- Keep a bilingual dictionary handy. Illustrated dictionaries may be useful for caregivers/parents who are not literate. Google Translate may be a helpful tool as well, although it is important to remember that Internet and computer programs do not provide perfect translations. However, when using these programs on our phones with caregivers/parents, we have found that incorrect translations can be a source of humor, which can lighten the mood or make those involved feel more comfortable with one another.
- Draw sketches of words or concepts.
- Make a list of talking points that caregivers/parents can take with them so that someone can explain them later on.

It is important for teachers to know that differences in cultural norms and expectations can hinder communication between teachers and caregivers/parents. For example, during a visit, Cindy learned that the father of one of the newcomer kindergartners she was working with thought that his child's teacher, Ms. Ward, was rude and dismissive whenever he dropped his child off at school. He told Cindy that Ms. Ward didn't like him as she didn't greet him. When Cindy mentioned this to Ms. Ward, she told Cindy that she felt like she was bombarded with parents at the door when they were dropping off their children and she had to hurry them out of the room in order to start class on time. Ms. Ward and Cindy thought about how they could address this issue. Ms. Ward began to think of ways that she could make caregivers/parents an official part of the start of school by greeting them at the door and inviting them to spend 15 minutes listening to their child read or showing them a favorite picture book from the classroom library. She also developed a file full of intriguing pictures and photographs that caregivers/parents and children could choose from and talk about.

Supporting and Establishing Partnerships with Newcomer Families

As teachers strive to establish collaborative and trusting relationships with newcomer families, they need to do the following:

- Get to know families.
- Develop meaningful ways for families to participate in learning/teaching activities.
- Establish partnerships with community organizations and other entities.

Get to Know Families

Caregivers and teachers can be important allies, but we need to get to know each other so that we can have positive relationships with one another that enhance children's learning. This can be accomplished in many ways, some of which an individual teacher can embark on, whereas others involve colleagues and school administrators in planning school-wide activities or events. We would like to stress that we believe that schools and districts should compensate teachers for taking steps to get to know families.

Making Home Visits

When Katharine was a new teacher in inner city London, England, she got to know some of the caregivers/parents who came to the classroom to pick up their children at the end of the school day. She was invited by one of the mothers to go to their home for a cup of tea. Katharine was very pleased to have been invited and wanted to go, but she was unsure about whether it would be considered okay, and she asked around and was advised not to go. She was told that teachers didn't do that—that it wasn't appropriate—and so she didn't go. Some years later, Katharine was working in a migrant program in Upstate New York, and it was a program policy that all teachers had to regularly visit families. Some families had resettled and lived in houses, whereas other families were "true" migrants, meaning they were following the crops and tended to live in camps located in very rural, isolated areas. These family visits were very powerful as they allowed the migrant program teachers, including Katharine, an opportunity to get to know the children better, to learn about their strengths and interests outside of school, and to learn about family members' skills and interests, which the teachers could tap into in their teaching.

Teachers are sometimes reluctant to make home visits, sometimes because they are worried that it will be an imposition on families and sometimes because they are unfamiliar with and possibly afraid to enter the community, particularly in the evening, when caregivers/parents may be more likely to be at home. We have made many home visits and have not found them to be an imposition on families; in fact, the families we have visited at home are typically very grateful that we have shown interest in their children and their families. Drawing on our own experience and other resources (e.g., Allen, 2007; Ernst-Slavit & Mason, n.d.), we have found it helpful to keep the following in mind:

- Find out about community and family expectations regarding visits and conversations. In some communities, it may not be appropriate for male teachers to visit homes at times of the day when only women are at home. There may be topics that are taboo in some homes and communities (e.g., religion). It may be deemed appropriate to engage in certain formalities before asking questions (e.g., extended greetings and inquiries about the health and wellbeing of individuals). Community members, including school-based personnel, who have lived in the U.S. for a number of years, can provide some of this information. Also, be alert to cultural practices during your visit. For example, you may notice that some people remove their shoes at the door when in a home.

- Conduct home and community-based visits with someone who is a member of the community and able to interpret, if needed. This person should be compensated by the district and may be an official interpreter or another teacher, school administrator, paraprofessional, or community liaison who speaks the family's native language. We have found that when the family knows that we are coming and they do not speak much English, they will often arrange with a friend or relative who speaks English to join them.
- If caregivers/parents are hesitant about having you in their home, offer or ask them about another place where you could meet. Perhaps they would prefer to meet at a library or other public venue in their community.
- Plan home visits by determining a purpose for the visit (e.g., learning more about students, gaining caregivers'/parents' views on a particular topic), which you communicate to families prior to the visit. Initial visits may be occasions to orient families to school practices, including school routines, curricula, and expectations. If that is the case, be sure not to dominate the conversation. Listen to what family members have to say and don't focus on or raise negative issues. In fact, we recommend that negative issues never be a focus of conversations when conducting home visits.
- Home visits are an opportunity to establish rapport with the family and to get to know them. It is also a time when we tell parents about their children's successes and express our appreciation for their children's contributions to the class. Hence, we make sure that we have a few very positive, genuine comments to make about the child (e.g., how hard the child works; how much progress the child has made in English; how the child knows a lot about a specific topic, such as planets, plants, or animals). It is very helpful to take samples of the child's work to accompany and/or illustrate our comments (e.g., a drawing, chart, piece of writing, or list of books the child has read).
- Schedule visits seven to 10 days in advance of the visit and follow up with a reminder about the time of the meeting and its length that is written in the family's native language.
- Prior to the visit, make sure you know the names of family members and learn a few words or expressions in their language so that you can greet them and thank them for letting you into their home.
- Be sure to introduce yourself and anyone accompanying you. Try to establish some rapport via small talk rather than beginning a conversa-

tion with a series of questions about the family and their children. Once you feel rapport has been established, you may want to use the following ways to initiate a conversation, particularly if it is your first visit:

- Tell me about your child.
- What does your child like best about school?
- What are schools like in _____ (*country of origin*)?

- If an interpreter isn't available, use sketching, mime, and gestures to communicate. We have found that this often leads to laughter, which has typically helped relax everyone.

- In many cultures, a good host offers refreshments and a teacher is often a respected person and honored guest, so it is a good idea to anticipate being offered refreshments. We have also often taken a small gift of food, such as a packet of cookies or some fruit, to share with the family.

- When we have been unsure about how safe we might feel, which has occurred only rarely, we have taken a companion.

- At these visits, we also let family members know about and invite them to upcoming events. Wherever possible, we leave bilingual invitations and go over them before we leave.

Funds of Knowledge Approach

As we mentioned in Chapter 8, teachers have drawn on what they have learned about families to organize their curriculum around their funds of knowledge. In doing so, they have sought out and used the expertise of community members to teach teachers and students skills and practices that are part of their everyday lives. For example, Moll (1992) writes about a teacher who involved students' parents and relatives in developing and teaching a curricular unit on construction. These experts in construction shared their experiences and helped students design and implement their own construction projects.

While some teachers have worked collaboratively with researchers to engage in fieldwork to learn about funds of knowledge in their students' communities, others have visited students' homes, community centers, and community-based organization to engage parents and community members in interviews and conversations. Also, many teachers have enlisted the help of their newcomer students in learning about funds of knowledge by asking them to interview their parents and/or take and share photographs of family and community events. Like ethnographers, teachers develop ways of gaining understandings that may help them identify knowledge and practices they can draw on in their teaching. This may take the form of observations focused on children, families, and community members in and out of school contexts (Gonzalez, Moll, & Amanti, 2005). During home visits, teachers can focus on noticing aspects of family life, including the following:

- The presence of family members (e.g., grandparents, extended family);
- Material possessions (e.g., family photos, clothing, household items); and
- Activities (e.g., children's play, childcare activities like older children caring for younger children).

We advise teachers to check in with community and/or, if possible, family members, to ask if the assumptions they are making about the families' cultural practices based on these observations are valid. Visits to community centers may provide teachers with insights into the various practices and knowledge sources that community members value.

Interviews with community members and parents also provide teachers with another important venue for learning about community-based funds of knowledge. As Gonzalez et al. (2005) describe in their work, these interviews are similar to open-ended conversations focused on specific topics. Possible topics that are the focus of these conversations may include the following:

- Family history;
- Labor history, including ways of earning money outside of the more formal context of a job (e.g., selling food or products made at home, working at home);
- Routine household practices, including those involving children and family members with people outside of the immediate family (e.g., car repair, childcare, hobbies, music);
- Views about childrearing and schooling, including those practices that are valued within the family and the aspirations parents have regarding their children's futures and schooling;
- Language use practices (e.g., when specific languages are spoken; jokes in the native language); and
- Immigration journeys, unless families do not wish to talk about them.

While the actual questions should take into account community and cultural norms, those who have engaged in this kind of work tend to use open-ended questions to begin conversations about parents and community members' funds of knowledge. Questions or prompts that we have used include the following:

- What are you particularly good at doing?
- What do you like to do in your spare time?
- Tell me about your family background.
- Where do you come from?
- What was life like in _____ (*country of origin or most recent home, such as in a refugee camp*)?
- How did life in your home country differ from your life in the U.S.?
- Tell me about the jobs you had in your home country.
- How did you get to the United States? Why did you come?

Keeping a Record of What You Know about Families

Donald Graves (1987), a very influential and inspiring educator who initiated the move toward teaching writing through a workshop approach in the late 1970s, urged teachers to make a list of their students and write next to each name what they know about each child. Many of us have found this to be both enlightening and empowering . . . and sobering. What often happens is that we learn that we know quite a bit about some students and relatively little about others. Graves urged teachers to then focus on getting to know more about the less-known students, which often provides very beneficial results (e.g., learning about children's interests can help in making book suggestions for students or read-aloud selections and can help students to discover their writing topics).

A similar strategy can be helpful when considering newcomer students and their families. The following example of just 10 families shows what Ms. Davies knew about her students' families after three weeks of school (see Figure 9.1). A star (*) next to a name indicates a newcomer family. As can be seen, although Ms. Davies knew something about the non-newcomer students' families, particularly the Andrews, Davis, and Johnston families, she didn't know very much about the newcomer students' families. For example, she wasn't always sure which languages the families spoke at home and she didn't know anything about newcomer family members' skills and interests.

FIGURE 9.1: What Ms. Davies Knew about Families after Three Weeks in School

Family name (and student)	Languages spoken at home	Special family skills/interests
Andrews (Jennifer)	English	Mom is library aide
Dabiri (Adunni)	English	
Davis (Aiesha)	English	Family raises animals
Johnston (DeShawn)	English	Family has plumbing business
Kazemi (Homa)*	Arabic (?)	
Lopez-Gomez (Toni)*	Spanish	
Morales (Eduardo)*	Spanish (?)	
Morales (Lila)*	Spanish (?)	
Nasrallah (Abdullah)*	Arabic (?)	
Tamimi (Fatima)*	Arabic (?)	

Newcomer family

About 10 weeks later, after making home visits and talking with family members when they came to school to pick up their children, she knew much more about the families, both languages spoken at home and special skills and interests (see Figure 9.2).

What this second figure reveals is that, whereas Ms. Davies had thought that Eduardo Morales' family spoke Spanish, she learned that they spoke an indigenous language at home, Mam, and they actually knew just a little Spanish. In the case of the Kazemi family, she knew they came from Afghanistan and thought they spoke Arabic, but learned that they spoke Farsi at home and could speak some English (as the father had worked for the U.S. government in Afghanistan).

Just as important, Ms. Davies learned something about the special interests and skills of family members, which she drew on later in class and school projects. (See Chapter 8 regarding the use of a funds of knowledge approach when teaching content.) For example, when the school started a gardening project, Eduardo Morales' family was a major contributor to how the school (and Ms. Davies' class) went about establishing and maintaining gardens. When the school decided to hold a holiday international music concert in December, the Dabiri, Lopez-Gomez, Nasrallah, and Tamimi families all participated in entertaining the school community. Also, later in the school year, family members

FIGURE 9.2: What Ms. Davies Knew about Families after about 13 Weeks in School

Family name (& student)	Languages spoken at home	Special family skills/interests
Andrews (Jennifer)	English	Mom is library aide
Dabiri (Adunni)	Yoruba, English	Grandma is great singer (and storyteller?)
Davis (Aiesha)	English	Family raise rabbits; father is carpenter
Johnston (DeShawn)	English	Family has plumbing business
Kazemi (Homa)*	Farsi, some English	Have homing pigeons; father worked for U.S. government
Lopez-Gomez (Toni)*	Spanish, a little English	Mom was lawyer in Mexico; dad is musician
Morales (Eduardo)*	Mam, some Spanish	Family has beautiful vegetable garden
Morales (Lila)*	Spanish, English	Mom is dressmaker
Nasrallah (Abdullah)*	Arabic	All sing; father writes poetry
Tamimi (Fatima)*	Arabic, a little English	All play musical instruments

* Newcomer family

of the Nasrallah, Lopez-Garcia, and Tamimi families came to the class to teach the students about their musical instruments and how to play them.

Attending Family Celebrations and Events

Over the course of our careers, newcomer families have invited us to numerous celebrations and events. We have attended weddings, birthdays, christenings, quinceañeras, sports games, and music and dance performances, to name a few. When we haven't been able to fit these events into our busy schedules, we have let family members know how much we have appreciated their invitations. Attending these events has been enjoyable and insightful. For example, after attending ten-year-old Jessica's birthday party, which involved her extended family from Michoacán, Mexico, Cindy became aware of just how prevalent verbal word play was in Jessica's family circle. Throughout the party, Jessica's uncles, aunts, and cousins engaged in repartee characterized by *dichos*/sayings and rhymes, including the following:

- Barriga llena, corazón contento. (*Full stomach, happy heart.*)
- No hay mal que por bien no venga. (*There is nothing bad that doesn't come with good./With the bad comes the good./Every cloud has a silver lining.*)
- En boca cerrada, no entran moscas. (*Flies don't enter a closed mouth./ Silence is golden.*)

Not only did this help Cindy understand Jessica's tendency to use similar *dichos* when talking with her friends at school on the playground, it inspired Cindy to work with Jessica's classmates, all of whom were recent arrivals of Mexican descent, and teacher to develop a list of limericks and rhymes in Spanish that they translated into English. Eventually, the class decided to develop an anthology of Spanish and English jokes and riddles.

Designing More Inclusive School Events Involving Caregivers/Parents

As we mentioned in Chapter 2, newcomers and their families must be made to feel welcome at school. This is fundamental if they are to develop a sense of belonging and a trusting relationship between themselves, their teachers, and other school-based personnel. While caregivers are often required or expected to attend back-to-school nights and parent-teacher conferences, they are not always welcoming events. Instead of being occasions when they are greeted and asked to share their views and experiences, back-to-school nights are often more akin to mini-lectures, in which teachers and administrators inform caregivers/parents about rules or concerns they may have. Similarly, instead of asking caregivers/parents to share what they know about their children, as well as the hopes and expectations they have for them, conferences are often times when teachers dispense their judgments about students. That is, caregivers/parents are treated as an audience rather than part of a dialogue or conversation involving teachers, administrators, and sometimes the children themselves.

There have been efforts to make teacher/parent events more responsive to the needs of caregivers/parents. For example, King and Goodwin (2002) emphasize the importance of obtaining family members' feedback on children's experiences at school, and they have suggested that a series of questions like the following could be the focus of a school-related event, workshop, or parent-teacher conference.

- What is working well for you and your child in this class and/or in this school?
- What do you think we should do differently?
- What kinds of experiences or instructional materials would you like us to use with your child?

In addition to developing interactive formats for school-related events like those above, we have found that it helps when the following procedures are in place when planning school events involving caregivers/parents:

- Make the event festive and inviting. Have students decorate the site and display their written work and art. Make sure that food and beverages are available.
- Provide childcare if the event is geared to adults.
- Make sure that important written information and invitations are available in the native languages of newcomer families. Designing and producing personalized written invitations with students can be an enjoyable classroom project that can generate interest in the event.
- Go over notices and invitations with students before they leave school so they know what they are about and can better inform their caregivers/parents.
- Attendance can be improved, often dramatically, if a written invitation is followed up with a phone call made by someone who speaks the caregivers'/parents' native languages.
- Hold meetings at times when caregivers/parents are more likely to be able to attend (e.g., on Saturdays or Sundays, when parents may have the day off).
- Have a group of students welcome caregivers/parents at the door and show them where to go. In preparing for this activity, students can role-play what they can do to make caregivers/parents feel welcome and comfortable.

The following approaches and events provide caregivers/parents and, in some cases, their children, with opportunities to actively engage with teachers and school personnel on topics of interest to all.

Mini-Workshops

Some schools have abandoned the traditional back-to-school lecture format in favor of events that involve family members and children in mini-workshops focused on different types of learning activities. Children often plan and lead these activities. For example, students may lead their parents through an agenda, show them important things in the room, and involve them in class-room routines and assignments. They usually also share the work that they have done in class, providing explanations of the work and assessments about what they learned. Because students take responsibility for orienting their caregivers/parents to their class, teachers have more time to interact with caregivers/parents on a one-to-one basis, when they can express their appreciation for students and what they have learned and accomplished in class.

Family Literacy Evenings

JoBeth Allen (2007) describes how teachers in various communities she has worked in engage in family literacy evenings. These are occasions when teachers, students, and family members produce and/or share their written or oral texts. During these events, everyone spends time writing, dictating, or telling stories on topics of interest to them. When children and adults share their writing or tell a story, they often inspire others to write or tell about similar topics. Sometimes participants invite everyone to write or tell about a particular theme or in response to a prompt, which is translated into the care-givers'/parents' native languages. The following are some examples of these kinds of prompts:

- What would you like your child to know about your family's country of origin?
- Map and write or tell about the places where your family has traveled.
- Pick something that is of great value to you and write or talk about it (participants may be asked to bring a special object or photograph with them to a workshop).
- Share the best advice your parents ever gave you.
- Share a favorite *dicho* or proverb, and tell what it means to you.

These mini-workshops can be organized so that adults and children share written and/or oral texts in their native languages in small language-alike groupings. Participants may draw or use technology to produce and illustrate texts and then share those texts in mixed-language groupings, ideally with the support of interpreters. The texts themselves can be shared with a wider audience in a written or oral anthology that is part of the school library. Also, written stories, photographs, and artistic representations may be displayed throughout the school.

Family Math Evenings

Family math evenings are occasions when families engage in math tasks together. These tasks are not traditional algorithmic problems. Rather, they are open ended and often involve manipulatives or visuals. It is also helpful to provide written translations of the tasks or visuals. Students who are already familiar with the tasks support caregivers/parents as they engage with them together. Examples of math tasks that focus on math concepts may be found at https://www.youcubed.org/tasks/.

Student-led Parent-teacher Conferences

Many teachers use student-led formats for conferences involving teachers, students, and parents/caregivers. In Laura's school, students prepare for and lead their own conferences, choosing work to share with their parents or caregivers, explaining their work, and self-assessing their learning. When selecting work to share, Laura asks students to include samples of work that they are the most proud of, as well as samples that they would like to improve upon. She supports students in evaluating their work by developing rubrics with them that they use to assess their work. During the conference, students share future learning goals and next steps they need to take to reach their goals and articulate the support they need from teachers and parents to achieve these goals. This then becomes a collaborative action plan.

Meaningful Ways for Families to Participate in Learning/Teaching Activities

As we have mentioned, in many countries caregivers/parents do not volunteer in their children's classrooms or help with children's homework. Further, because they may have long work schedules or multiple jobs, newcomer caregivers/parents may not be available during those times when children are working on homework. In addition, they may feel unable to help children with homework that is in English, a language they may not know, or regarding concepts and skills they did not study or studied many years ago. For this reason, we suggest that teachers consider alternative ways to involve caregivers/parents in learning/teaching events. The following are some suggestions for accomplishing this:

- Assign homework children can do without the support of an adult, such as reading or perusing a book on their own or with a younger sibling, writing or drawing in a journal, or doing math review problems teachers are sure students can do independently.
- Have children and their caregivers/parents conduct family projects. Possibilities include the following:
  - *Interviewing* or asking a family member to share something related to what the class is studying (e.g., ecological environments found in different regions in the world). Some teachers we know routinely ask their students to ask family members how they got their name or about a cultural tradition.
  - *Observation logs,* in which children count and record objects in their home or neighborhood (e.g., trees, fire hydrants, windows in a building, steps on a staircase). These logs can be the basis for future projects. For example, after having fifth-grade newcomers in her ELD class come up with counts of the number of grocery stores in their neighborhoods, Ms. Leland and her students wanted to know more about the kinds of groceries sold in these stores. Each student accompanied a family member to the grocery store to note down the fruits and vegetables sold there. They reported their findings on a chart. They noted interesting discrepancies in the types of fruits and vegetables sold in the different stores. For example, they noted that a greater diversity of produce was sold in local Mexican and Asian markets when compared to national chains. In addition, they found that there were entire neighborhoods where little or no produce was for sale in markets. This led to a community activism project in which students contacted not-for-profits and local news outlets, shared their concerns, and explored possible solutions. The project involved all language modalities (listening, speaking, reading, and writing).
  - *Collaborative writing projects* involving family members and newcomer students. For example, Ada and Campoy (2004) describe a process in which caregivers and children wrote about a favorite object that had special meaning for their family. To help them compose their pieces, which they did in their native languages, teachers used the following prompts:
    - What is the object?

— What size, color, and shape is it?

— Where did you get it?

— Where does it come from?

— Why is it important to you and your family?

Teachers can also ask caregivers and children to draw or take a picture of the object. Their pictures and accompanying text can be organized into a class anthology.

- *Book bag projects.* Each week, students fill and take home a book bag containing books, DVDs, math games, and objects or activities centered around a book for families to read and enjoy. A journal for caregivers/parents, siblings, and the student may be included, in which they can write observations in English and/or students' native languages about a book. It is important to include paper and colored pencils or crayons so that the children and adults can draw pictures related to the particular book. The books in the bag should be in English and the native language, whenever possible. It is very helpful if a note in the families' native languages is included in the bags describing the purpose of the book bag and what is to be done with objects in the bag.

- *Family inquiry projects.* These projects involve students in an activity in which they learn about a topic or phenomenon with the support of a family member. For example, students may interview family members on topics related to their interests and traditions (e.g., a family treasure, celebrations, favorite activities, how they got their name). Once interviews are shared with the class, they can provide teachers and class members with insights into the students' backgrounds and family life and inspire meaningful discussions. Students may also interview family members about topics that are related to what they are studying in class (e.g., immigration, energy consumption, nutrition).

Partnering with Community Organizations

Many newcomers and their families have experienced great traumas before embarking on and during their journey to the U.S. and they may have emotional, physical, and financial needs. Most teachers aren't trained social workers or counselors, but by reaching out and working collaboratively with local community and service organizations, teachers can be powerful advocates for students and families. Some suggestions include the following:

- *Partner with local food banks* to provide food for immigrant families. For example, Oakland International High School does this. For information about their program, visit https://www.eastbayexpress .com/SevenDays/archives/2018/05/21/innovative-oakland-high -school-for-new-immigrant-students-a-model-in-california.
- *Arrange for volunteer tutors* from community organizations, churches, high schools, and colleges. Tutors will probably need some training in how to interact with newcomers, including on topics such as the following:
  - What to focus on when working with newcomers;
  - Strategies for making one's meaning clear;
  - Focusing on what newcomers are trying to communicate, not how they say it;
  - Not correcting newcomers' English;
  - Different ways of asking questions; and
  - The importance of giving plenty of wait time so newcomers have time to process and compose their responses.
    Teaching strategies discussed in the rest of the book, such as in Chapter 5: Developing Newcomers' Listening and Speaking, apply equally well to tutors.
- *Seek out connections with agencies* so that they can provide workshops or services for newcomer families and students. Workshops can focus on caregivers'/parents' rights, including their rights as immigrants, and strategies to help adults and children adjust to a new environment. We know of schools that have obtained support for newcomer students and families from agencies that provide mental health counselors and other medical services. Some states provide funding for these activities, such as the California Newcomer Education and Well-Being (CalNEW) project (http://www.cdss.ca .gov/inforesources/Refugees/Programs-and-Info/Youth-Initiatives/ CalNEW).
- *Advocate for establishing a full-service community school* with a community library, English language and literacy classes for adults, guidance counselors, mental health counselors, and other medical services.

Fostering Teacher Activism

As teacher advocates, we are not mere conduits of educational policies or decisions made by school-based administrators and educational policymakers. As professionals and advocates committed to enhancing the wellbeing and academic development of our newcomer students, we seek opportunities to influence, shape, and initiate educational policies and decisions that affect the lives of our students, including newcomer students. We can do this at our schools by participating in and/or providing input to school site councils, instructional leadership teams, hiring committees, and other decision-making bodies. Through these bodies, teachers can advocate for spending money in ways that will support newcomers, such as the following:

- Teachers who can provide push-in or pull-out ELD services;
- Professional development (PD) to build teachers' capacity to work with newcomers;
- Counseling services that provide individual or group therapy to newcomers who are dealing with trauma; and
- Outreach services to help connect newcomer families to the school community and other needed resources in the community (e.g., health services, legal aid, social networks, ESL classes for parents)

Unfortunately, schools are often underfunded and must make difficult decisions about how to allocate limited funds. Advocating for spending funds in ways that support newcomer students is key. If funds are not available, schools and teachers can look into grant opportunities or partnerships with local agencies.

Teachers can also assert their views on scheduling and programmatic decisions. Often, newcomers are like an afterthought when these decisions are made. Particularly if a school has many newcomers, it is important to consider their needs and how programming can be built to support them. For example, some teachers we have worked with who know newcomers need lots of opportunities to interact with English speakers have advocated for master schedules that provide them with opportunities to take classes with native English speakers instead of spending much of their school day in segregated ELD classes. Scheduling should also be organized in such a way as to facilitate interactions between newcomers and English speakers on the playground and during lunch.

In schools that are receiving many newcomers, there may be tensions. For example, teachers may hear colleagues, parents, and/or students complaining about the resources that are being allocated to newcomers and "taken away" from other programs or complaining that the teachers' attention is going to newcomers instead of their own children. It is important that teachers actively interrupt such talk, pointing out how much students are gaining from attending a diverse school and how much they can learn from their newcomer peers, including opportunities to become more knowledgeable about the world and the importance of diverse viewpoints and cultures.

Collective Activism

Teachers in the United States have often faced obstacles when asserting the kind of professional and political agency that enables them to advocate for the wellbeing and learning of their students. Schools, districts, and governmental entities often expect teachers to comply with policies about how they should teach and assess their students that may not be in newcomer students' best interests. For example, under NCLB, low-income students, including ELs, were often taught using instructional programs that focused almost exclusively on the acquisition of discrete literacy skills in English (Pease-Alvarez & Samway, 2012). These students had few opportunities to read demanding and varied texts or write more than a few lines other than filling in the blanks on worksheets. Despite these mandated programs, the performance of these students did not reveal an improvement in their academic performance.

We and other researchers have found that many teachers are not passive implementers of educational policies that they do not agree with (e.g., Pease-Alvarez & Samway, 2012; Santoro & Cain, 2018). In many cases, they make adaptations to policies that are more aligned with their commitments about learning and teaching. For example, we have known many teachers who have not fully implemented required programs in their classrooms because they did not address the needs of their newcomer students. This was the case for many California teachers who were required to use the commercial reading program known as Open Court with students who were deemed to be English learners.

As we (Pease-Alvarez & Samway, 2012) and others have argued (e.g., Gunderson, 2018; Picower, 2012), teachers who are part of collectives and/or networks have more of an impact on policy than those who resist or attempt to influence policy individually within the confines of their classrooms. By collectively asserting their views in the policy arena, they also combated the isolation and marginalization that so many teachers have experienced.

We have known of and/or participated in teacher collectives that have publicly resisted policies that jeopardize students' opportunities to learn in schools. For example, Cindy has been involved with a grassroots teacher group known as Educators Advocating for Students (EAS) that has successfully advocated for teachers' voices in developing school district policies. Members of the group have included teachers of immigrant students who met monthly to share issues they were having with standardized approaches to instruction and assessment that were mandated in their district, including the following:

- Tests provide little information that informs instruction.
- Preparing for and administering tests takes valuable time away from instruction.
- Tests are given in English, a language that many students struggle with.

Initially, meetings were informal and held in different members' homes. The group engaged in a variety of activities, including the following:

- Writing letters to local newspapers describing teachers' concerns about state- and district-mandated testing and assessment policies;
- Appearing on local community television programs describing these concerns; and
- Participating in collective bargaining efforts that led to including a clause in their contract requiring the district to obtain teacher input on testing and assessment policies.

After a couple of years, teachers in EAS became members of a subcommittee of the union focused on curriculum and assessment issues (EAS, 2011).

Teachers' unions have become increasingly more involved in making sure that low-income students, including newcomers, have access to necessary resources and student supports. For example, beginning in 2016, as part of their contract, members of the Oakland Educators Association (OEA), the union serving teachers in the Oakland Unified School District, called for a variety of demands to enhance the educational experiences of Oakland students, as well as an increase in wages (Oakland teachers are among the lowest paid teachers in the state of California). It is important to note that a large number of students in Oakland are of immigrant backgrounds, with at least one-third being officially designated as ELs. Union demands included an increase in the number of teachers working specifically with newcomers, smaller class sizes, and an increase in the number of school psychologists and nurses. After contract negotiations reached an impasse, teachers went on strike in March of 2019. Community support for the week-long strike was evident in the involvement of caregivers/parents on picket lines, the fact that very few sent their children to school (97% of Oakland students stayed at home during the week-long strike), and backing from various organizations (e.g., other unions, local businesses, and churches). While the contract that was negotiated with district administrators did not include all of the terms that the union supported, a number of conditions were met, including an increase in the number of teachers responsible for working with newcomer students, decreases in class size, and an increase in teachers' salaries. In recent years, similar actions have occurred in other districts around the country, including those serving large numbers of English learners in the Los Angeles, Chicago, and New Jersey areas, suggesting that many teachers are using involvement in their unions and collective bargaining to improve and preserve public schooling, including ways to support newcomer students.

In addition to organized teacher unions, many teachers have formed activist groups and collectives focused on developing and implementing school and classroom practices and engaging in political movements that value diversity and promote equity and social justice (Niesz, 2018). These groups, which have increased over the last two decades, are composed of teachers, counselors, social workers, community members, and caregivers/parents who meet to engage in a range of activities, including joint inquiry about pedagogy and policy, conferences, and collective action (Niesz, 2018). In addition to focusing on practices and policies in schools and classrooms, many of the groups are engaged in consciousness raising and collective action, including organizing rallies and protests, lawsuits, letter-writing campaigns, and radio and television interviews, all intended to influence state and local policy. Many teacher collectives rely on social media as a means to share information, organize, and resist policies that threaten marginalized students, including newcomers.

Increasingly, these groups and collectives are working in collaboration and solidarity on a variety of social issues affecting the lives of newcomer students. Some examples follow:

- An inquiry group organized by NYCORE (the New York Collective of Radical Educators) developed a guide that specifies ways to support undocumented students in K-12 classrooms (https:// teachdreamnyc.com/about/).
- San Francisco-based Immigrants Rising (https://immigrantsrising .org/#) is an organization that involves educators and others in efforts to enhance the educational and life opportunities of immigrant students. Their work includes providing undocumented youth with scholarships that enable them to attend college and opportunities to share their stories.
- Teachers Against Child Detention (TACD) (https://www .teachersagainstchilddetention.org) works with educator groups as well as other organizations, such as not-for-profits and faith-based organizations, to actively work for the end of the detention and criminalization of immigrant children and their families and provide them with certain protections that they are entitled to under the 1997 Flores Decree, which was a settlement agreement pursuant to the Supreme Court decision in Reno v. Flores. The Flores Decree set standards for the federal government's detention of undocumented unaccompanied minors that are supposed to remain in effect until the government finalizes regulations that comply with the settlement's requirements. (For additional information, go to https://www.aclu.org/sites/default/files/assets/flores_settlement_ final_plus_extension_of_settlement011797.pdf). Under the Flores Decree, if and while minors are held in detention:
  - They shall be held in the least restrictive setting appropriate to each minor's age and special needs.
  - The INS shall keep careful records relating to their detention.
  - The INS shall make prompt and continuous efforts to reunify the minors with their families.
  - The INS shall hold them in facilities that are safe and sanitary.

There are a number of ways to become involved in teacher collectives and organizations aimed at enhancing the educational and life opportunities of newcomer students and families. Figure 9.3 lists some organizations that provide these kinds of opportunities:

FIGURE 9.3: Teacher Collectives and Organizations

Association of RAZA Educators (A.R.E.) (Los Angeles)	http://www.razaeducators.org/about.html
Bad Ass Teachers Association	http://www.badassteacher.org
Education for Liberation Network	https://www.edliberation.org
Immigrants Rising (San Francisco)	https://immigrantsrising.org
New York Collective of Radical Educators (NYCoRE)	http://www.nycore.org
Rethinking Schools	https://www.rethinkingschools.org
Teachers 4 Social Justice (San Francisco)	https://t4sj.org
Teachers Against Child Detention	https://www.teachersagainstchilddetention.org
Teachers for Social Justice (Chicago)	http://www.teachersforjustice.org
The National Network of Teacher Activists Groups	https://teacheractivists.org

Legislative Work

Like others living in the U.S., where money has such an influence on political decisions at the local, state, and national levels, educators often feel helpless when it comes to legislative decisions and laws that affect the lives of our students—including newcomers—and our own lives as educators. However, if we do not speak up and put pressure on our legislators, our knowledge and the needs of our students can be easily ignored. For this reason, we strongly urge educators to get involved with legislative work and to do this as collaboratively as possible. The greater the number of voices speaking with one voice, the greater the chance that legislators will listen to us. We offer a few suggestions below, all of which require some action(s):

- Pay attention to upcoming legislation around issues that affect newcomer students, such as standards, testing, and the use of money allocated for textbook adoptions. Then, organize around them. This often means holding informational meetings for colleagues and parents/community members, as well as using social media, telephone trees, and flyers in English and other languages spoken by caregivers/parents/community members to inform them of the issue and encourage them to attend. It is very helpful if childcare and snacks are provided when an information meeting is held. At these information meetings, have an ASK—something that we want attendees to so, such as the following:

- Sign cards to legislators with the demand clearly specified (e.g., that the legislator either sponsor or co-sponsor a bill and/or vote to allow districts to use textbook money to purchase trade books for use in language, literacy, and content learning and teaching). Unions will often provide these kinds of cards.
- Go to the next school board meeting (or county supervisors' meeting, state legislators' offices, or congressperson's local office) <u>and</u> bring three to five other people.
- Go to legislators' offices at all levels, local, state, and federal—state and federal legislators will usually have local offices as well as ones located in state capitols and Congress. Going in large groups can be more effective than going as an individual.

• Get to know reporters and editors at local newspapers and TV stations, including those who work in the languages spoken in the communities of newcomer students. Meet with them, invite them into schools, and keep them informed on key issues and actions. Whenever there is an action, prepare a one-page, one-sided press release that covers key points and demands and includes contact person information (name, email, and phone number). This contact person needs to be articulate and very well-versed in the issue; speaking English and one or more of the other languages in the community can be helpful.

• Figure out who the "natural" local leaders are in the community. That is, the people who can bring a lot of people to an action. In many cases, the natural community leaders are not the elected officials or those who have official titles, such as a chairperson of a parish council. We have found that these natural leaders are often women. Then work closely with these natural leaders to strategize and lead actions.

• Run for public office or support other educators whom you respect and who are knowledgeable about key educational issues, such as the teaching of English learners. Participating on commissions and committees at the local level and running for school board are good places to start. A couple of years ago, Katharine was doing research for an article about her local school district's decision to close schools in primarily low-income, often heavily immigrant, neighborhoods. She attended board meetings and looked into the backgrounds of school board members—only one board member had any background in education. That background was minimal and didn't involve K–12 teaching/schooling. This reality is not at all unusual and it underscored for her how important it is for knowledgeable, informed educators to become school board members.

- Be active in your union. Many have legislative committees and professional lobbyists who can support actions such as those listed above, and this is a place where teachers can become advocates for their students and profession. We recognize that teaching itself is extremely demanding work, and encourage educators to partner with unions and other established organizations in their political advocacy work.

APPENDIX 1

Sanctuary Cities and School Districts

In recent years, with the rise of zero tolerance immigration policies and anti-immigrant rhetoric, a number of cities, school districts, and schools throughout the United States have asserted their commitment to newcomers and immigrants by declaring themselves sanctuary sites that welcome all children regardless of their immigration status. This commitment is available to caregivers/parents and the public at large via their websites and formal and informal modes of communication. For example, Oakland Unified School District (OUSD) has the following statement on their website regarding their sanctuary status, along with other resources for caregivers/parents; it is in six languages (English, Spanish, Arabic, Chinese, Khmer, and Vietnamese).

When we say *Every Student Thrives!* at OUSD it means we stand behind our students no matter where they were born or the barriers they have overcome to be here. We cherish the cultural richness in our district and make no exceptions when it comes to including learners with a wide variety of backgrounds and needs.

It's important to know that Oakland is a Sanctuary City and OUSD is a Sanctuary District. We do not ask for or require proof of legal immigration status upon enrollment, nor is any such information gathered by a school. Hundreds of undocumented, newcomer and refugee students are thriving in our schools with help of the Office of English Language Learners and Multilingual Achievement (ELLMA) and we want to keep it that way.

Together, we will continue to exemplify the OUSD Core Values of *Students First, Equity, Excellence, Integrity, Cultural Responsiveness* and *Joy* in support of all of our students.

Source: www.ousd.org/page/16314

APPENDIX 2

Oakland USD Protocol for Responding to ICE

OAKLAND UNIFIED SCHOOL DISTRICT
Community Schools, Thriving Students

Sanctuary District ICE Protocol Overview and Recommendations for Families

OUSD stands behind a commitment to do everything possible to ensure schools are safe and inclusive environments for all students and families, regardless of immigration status as outlined in the OUSD Sanctuary Resolution. In keeping with the resolution, schools in OUSD are trained to follow protocols if Immigration Customs Enforcement (ICE) actions occur.

Many schools have a customized plan that is more detailed, however the following expectations apply to all schools. This overview also shares community and legal resources to support families with immigration questions, concerns or needs (page 2).

OUSD school protocol for responding to ICE

If contacted directly by ICE, staff, teachers, parents and students should refer ICE agents to the school Principal (or Designated Secondary Responder) to activate protocol.

ALL staff are directed to not provide any information about individual students, families or employee regardless of the reason given and unless directed to by the Legal Office.

In the unlikely event ICE comes to a school,

- ICE officers may present a warrant, subpoena or legal document to the school site. Whether or not they do so, a school site should always call the Chief of the Oakland School Police first.

- If a legal document is provided, the school should contact OUSD Legal for review. If information is requested without a legal document, schools should contact the OUSD Superintendent as well as Legal.

- In all scenarios, schools are directed to provide ICE personnel with a copy of the OUSD Sanctuary Resolution and Board Policy.

- As mandated by the OUSD Sanctuary Resolution, District staff should NOT provide any access or information to ICE unless legally obligated by a warrant or subpoena.

If a school receives reports of a detained family member

- Staff should collect as many details as possible, then call the Rapid Response Hotline.

- The school Principal is directed to inform the Sanctuary Task Force leads in key District offices as well as activate social-emotional supports for the student and family.

If a school receives reports of ICE in the area

- Staff should collect as many details as possible, then call the Rapid Response Hotline and Oakland School Police.

- If ICE activity is confirmed, schools may send a recorded call to alert the community and remind about supports.

- School Principal should inform Sanctuary Task Force leads in key District offices.

(*Source:* https://www.ousd.org/cms/lib/CA01001176/Centricity/Domain/1766/ICE%20Protocols%20for%20 Family.pdf)

APPENDIX 3

Cooperative Activities Involving Newcomers

The activities listed here provide students with opportunities to interact with one another, which is important for integrating newcomers into the class and making sure they have opportunities to interact with other students, including English speakers. Indeed, all students should have access to peers who vary in terms of language abilities; cultural, racial, and social backgrounds; and academic experience, so that they can get to know one another, establish friendships, and benefit from a diverse set of experiences and abilities. In addition to providing students with important opportunities to develop language and content, these groupings may enhance their understanding about students from backgrounds that are different from their own. Keep in mind that it may be necessary to demonstrate these activities first, unless students are already familiar with them.

Think-Pair-Share

A think-pair-share takes the following general format :

- Ask a question or provide a prompt of interest to students where there is an open-ended answer and they can answer visually or through actions (e.g., *What do you think is going to happen on the next page in a book? What do you think will happen when we mix these two chemicals?*).
- Give students time to think about and quickly jot down ideas, draw a sketch, or think about an action that provides a response. Students may ask a partner for help.
- Students turn to a partner and share their thoughts/answers related to the prompt.
- Bring the class together and ask students to share out their ideas or their partners' ideas.
- A think-pair-share provides newcomers with time to reflect on, pro-

cess, and possibly revise their thoughts before sharing out with the class. When working with a peer, they can clarify and revise their responses, while interacting in ways that are useful for their language development.

Gallery Walk

Gallery walks provide students with opportunities to interact with one another as they jointly reflect on and respond to topics that they are studying. We have found that the following procedure works well:

- Post five or six questions, quotes, images, or other prompts about a topic the class is studying on pieces of chart paper or on white boards. Each piece of chart paper or white board is numbered and has a different prompt on it and is placed on the walls of the classroom or on tables spaced several feet away from each other so that they are spread around the room.
- Group students so that they form teams of two to three. Direct each group to start at a different numbered station and give members of each group a colored marker.
- At their first station, each group reads or looks at the prompt and then uses their marker to write an answer or comment in response. As different groups pass through each station, their group responses will be shown through the color of the marker.
- After three to five minutes, groups rotate to the next station. At that station, students read and discuss the comments or answers of the other group and add their own comments and answers. This process is repeated until each group has visited every station.
- After students have visited all of the stations, they quickly revisit all of the stations to see the contributions of their peers.

This activity can also be used for students to give feedback on their peers' work. For example, students can post their science models or diagrams around the classroom and small groups of their peers can provide feedback.

Information Gap Activities

These tasks involve two or more students. One student has access to information or an image, and the other uses language to discover what that information or image is. Two examples follow.

Follow the Directions

- One student looks at a drawing or pattern block design that their companion cannot see—a folder can hide the pattern from this second student.

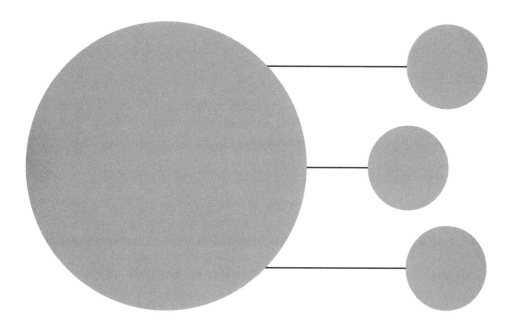

- The person who can see the drawing or pattern block design directs the other student on how to create it, using oral language. For example, in the case of the following image, a student may say, "Draw a big circle. Now draw three small circles next to it."
- It is possible that the directions aren't specific enough, which will become evident when the students compare the prompt with what the other student drew. This can lead to very interesting and important discussions about the need for specificity when giving directions. Another example of this type of activity can be found in Chapter 5.

Who Is It?

- One student has access to a picture of someone who all of the other students know (e.g., the principal, another student in the class).
- The person who doesn't have access to the picture asks questions to

help figure out the identity of the person in the picture (e.g., "Is it a boy or a girl? How old is she? Does she work here?")

Group Solutions

Group solutions are occasions when groups of three to five students work together to come up with a solution to a problem or dilemma to complete a simple project (e.g., construct a tower with blocks of different colors). The following outlines a general format for conducting a group solution of a construction activity.

- Give each group of students a set of six blocks of multiple colors.
- Each group constructs an object with the set of blocks according to a specific set of guidelines or hints, which are written on a card. A sample set of guidelines follows:
  - Card 1: There are six blocks in all. One of the blocks is yellow.
  - Card 2 : The two blue blocks do not touch each other.
  - Card 3: Each red block shares one edge with the yellow block.
- Students work together to construct the object, drawing on the guidelines.
- It is helpful if students address each card separately and in order.

APPENDIX 4

A Selection of Children's Books That Work Well with Newcomers

This appendix provides a selection of children's books that we have used successfully with newcomer students in elementary and middle schools. The list is not intended to be exhaustive, but rather to serve as a starting place for teachers who are looking for quality children's literature to use with their newcomer students.

We have included statements regarding the grade-level appropriateness of these books, which are based on our own experiences with students. However, we do so with some hesitation as so much depends on the students themselves. For example, if a picture book intended for primary grades is on a topic that is of particular interest to older newcomers and/or is about an experience that older students have had, that book may be appropriate for those students. Also, if older students are working with younger students in a cross-age buddy program and/or are writing picture books for younger students, such books can be very appropriate for them.

The bottom line is that students we have worked with like these books, we like these books, and we hope that you and your students do, too.

Nonfiction

- Ancona, George. (1994). *The Piñata Maker/El Piñatero*. San Diego, CA: Harcourt Brace.

  A Spanish/English photo essay about a piñata maker in southern Mexico, which is told like a story. The language can be challenging for newcomers, but the Spanish text and the stunning photos help newcomers understand the content. (Can be used in grades 2–8.)
- Cameron, Eileen. (2002). *Canyon*. New York: Mikaya Press.

  This poetic nonfiction picture book is about the making of a canyon over millions of years. The language can be difficult for newcomers, but vivid photographs lend themselves to discussion and help make meaning for newcomers. It is also a book that lends itself to vocabulary development through a word consciousness approach—see Chapter 6 for a discussion of word consciousness. (Can be used in grades 3–8.)

- George, Jean Craighead. (1997). *Look to the North: A Wolf Pup Diary.* New York: Harper Collins.

  Using brief diary entries, this book describes the lives of three wolf pups from birth to seven months. Expansive, beautiful illustrations complement the text and make it more comprehensible to newcomers. (Can be used in grades K–8.)

- Fanelli, Sara. (1995). *My Map Book.* HarperCollins.

  Written from the perspective of a young child, this is a collection of labeled, hand-drawn maps of real and imagined places (e.g., the narrator's family, day, tummy, playground, bedroom, colors, and school). (Can be used in grades K–8.)

- Kamkwamba, William, & Mealer, Bryan. (2012). *The Boy Who Harnessed the Wind.* New York: Dial Books for Young Readers.

  A picture book adaptation of the books with the same title for older readers. It recounts William Kamkwamba's experience surviving drought and famine in Malawi and, as a teenager, engineering a windmill to bring electricity and water to his community. The language is challenging for newcomers, but the clear and vibrant illustrations can support newcomers in understanding the storyline. (Can be used in grades 4–8.)

- Kerley, Barbara. (2002). *A Cool Drink of Water.* Washington, D.C.: National Geographic Society.

  With just a few words, beautiful photographs, and no preaching, this book shows how people all around the world are unified in their need for water. Endnotes provide information on: a) where the photos were taken, and b) water conservation. (Can be used in grades K–8.)

- Lomas Garza, C. (1990). *Family Pictures/Cuadros de Familia.* San Francisco: Children's Book Press.

  _____. (2000). *In My Family/En Mi Familia.* San Francisco: Children's Book Press.

  Both of these books are collections of paintings by the author, each one depicting a family event or tradition from her childhood. Every painting is accompanied by a brief, one- or two-paragraph description of the event in English and Spanish. The images are engaging and can serve as a springboard for careful observation and discussion before reading the text. The books can also serve as a model for similar art and writing by students about their own family traditions. (Can be used in grades K–8.)

- Morales, Y. (2018). *Dreamers*. New York: Neal Porter Books.

  This picture book recounts the author's experience immigrating to the United States from Mexico with her infant son and adapting to their new life in San Francisco. The illustrations are detailed and vibrant and encourage close observation and discussion. (Can be used in grades 2–8.)

- Pinkney, S. L. (2000). *Shades of Black: A Celebration of Our Children*. New York: Scholastic.

  This picture book of photographs and descriptions of different skin tones, hair textures, and eye colors celebrates the diversity of African Americans. The text is clearly represented in the striking photographs used to portray this diversity. (Can be used in grades K–8.)

- Reyes, M. (2015). *I am Sausal Creek/Soy el Arroyo Sausal*. Oakland, CA: Nomadic Press.

  This bilingual picture book describes the history of an urban creek running through Oakland, California, including its use by Native Americans, the impact of urbanization and pollution, and current efforts to restore the natural habitat. While the language is quite complex, the clear illustrations can be used to support newcomers' comprehension. (Can be used in grades 3–8.)

- Sill, Cathryn. (2007). *About Habitats: Deserts*. Atlanta, GA: Peachtree.

  The short texts on each page with stunning paintings on facing pages describe the geography, flora, and fauna in desert environments around the world. The combination of text and illustrations lend themselves to a lot of discussion. An afterword provides additional information about the content of each picture. (Can be used in grades K–8.)

Fiction

- Ata, Te (told by), & Moroney, L. (adapted by). (2003). *Baby Rattlesnake/ Viborita de Cascabel*. San Francisco: Children's Book Press.

  This bilingual retelling of a Native American tale is about a young rattlesnake who is impatient to get his rattle. The Spanish/English text, repetitive refrains, and compelling illustrations help make the book more accessible to newcomers. (Can be used in grades K–5.)

- Carle, Eric. (1969). *The Very Hungry Caterpillar*. London: Puffin Books.

The colorful pictures and text of this book have delighted youngsters for many decades. The illustrations and repetitive accompanying text make this a book that newcomers enjoy reading. Look for other books by the same author to use with young newcomers. (Can be used in grades K–2.)

- Christelow, Eileen. (1989). *Five Little Monkeys Jumping on the Bed.* New York: Clarion Books.

    This picture book recounts the familiar nursery rhyme of five silly monkeys who continue to jump on their bed, instead of going to sleep, despite their mother's and the doctor's admonitions. The repetitive and humorous text is engaging to young children and encourages them to join in. (Can be used in grades K–2.)

- Cisneros, Sandra. (1994). *Hairs/Pelitos.* New York: Dragonfly Books.

    In this picture book, a child describes the different kinds of hair people have in her family and how the smell of her mother's hair makes her feel safe. The story originally appeared in the book of short stories by Sandra Cisneros, *House on Mango Street.* (Can be used in grades K–6.)

- Crews, Donald. (1992). *Shortcut.* New York: Greenwillow Books.

    A picture book about some children who decide to take a shortcut on their way home. The shortcut they take is along a train track, where a train almost hits them. Some of the language can be difficult for newcomers, but the text is short, there is repetition, and the powerful illustrations all contribute to enhance meaning. (Can be used in grades K–4.)

- Cronin, Doreen. (2000). *Click, Clack, Moo: Cows that Type.* New York: Scholastic.

    A humorous picture book about activist animals on a farm who use letter writing to make their needs known. There are a lot of repeated phrases, literary fonts (e.g., bolded, enlarged fonts to illustrate urgency; wavy fonts to suggest typing), and intriguing illustrations, all of which help newcomers understand the storyline. (Can be used in grades K–5.)

- English, Karen. (1999). *Nadia's Hands.* Honesdale, PA: Boyds Mills Press.

    This picture book tells the story of a Pakistani American girl who is nervous about being a flower girl in her aunt's traditional Pakistani wedding because her hands will be decorated with intricate designs using *mehndi.* This makes her very nervous because she isn't sure how her classmates will respond when they see her hands. The text can be difficult for newcomers, but the illustrations help a lot in building understanding. (Can be used in grades 2–8.)

- Galdone, Paul. (1984). *The Teeny-Tiny Woman*. Boston: Houghton Mifflin Harcourt.

  This picture book recounts a classic folktale in which a teeny-tiny woman picks up a bone in a graveyard to make soup for her dinner and is haunted until she returns the bone to its rightful owner. The story is entertaining and includes a lot of repetition. (Can be used in grades K–5.)

- Kyuchukov, Hristo. (2004). *My Name Was Hussein*. Honesdale, PA: Boyds Mills Press.

  This picture book is set in Bulgaria and is about a Roma (Gypsy) boy, Hussein, who is a Muslim and is forced to change his name after soldiers occupy his village. The story is based on the author's life. (Can be used in grades 3–8.)

- Kurtz, Jane, & Kurtz, Christopher. (1997). *Only a Pigeon*. New York: Simon & Schuster.

  This is a beautifully written and illustrated picture book about a young boy who lives in Addis Ababa, Ethiopia. He spends half the day in school and the other half as a shoeshine boy, but his passion is raising racing pigeons. Although the language can be challenging for newcomers, having visuals handy to augment the illustrations can help a lot. The themes in the book often resonate with newcomers and the book often generates a lot of discussion. (Can be used in grades 2–8.)

- Luen Yang, G. (2007). *American Born Chinese*. New York: First Second.

  This graphic novel interweaves three stories that deal with themes of immigration, acceptance, and assimilation. The language is challenging for newcomers, but the illustrations help carry the narrative and support comprehension, and the book addresses themes that are compelling to adolescents. (Can be used in grades 7 and up.)

- Martin, Bill. (1970). *Brown Bear, Brown Bear, What Do You See?* New York: Holt, Rinehart and Winston.

  The title of this book is repeated throughout, making the book accessible for young readers. The colorful illustrations by Eric Carle accompany each page. Look for other predictable books by the same author to use with young newcomers. (Can be used in grades K–2.)

- Neitzel, Shirley. (1995). *The Bag I'm Taking to Grandma's*. New York: Greenwillow Books.

  A picture book about a child who is packing a bag to stay with Grandma, but Mother takes everything out. However, it ends well for the child, who has stashed the discarded objects in another bag. The story has a cumulative, predictable structure (*This is my mitt. . . . , Here is my pillow . . . , Here are my cars . . .*) and a circular story arc, which help make the story accessible to newcomers. (Can be used in grades K–2.)

- O'Brien, Anne Sibley. (2015). *I'm New Here.* Watertown, MA: Charlesbridge.

    This picture book describes the experiences of three newcomer students from different countries arriving at a new school. The language of the text is relatively simple, but the experiences and challenges are relevant to older newcomers. (Can be used in grades 2–8.)

- Polacco, Patricia. (1997). *In Enzo's Splendid Garden.* New York: Philomel Books.

    A humorous picture book about a series of events that start with a bee landing on a tree, which leads to a young boy dropping his book, which trips up the waiter . . . It is filled with rich vocabulary, which can be challenging for newcomers, but the illustrations and cumulative structure of the book help build understanding. (Can be used in grades 2–6.)

- Ransome, James E. (2019). *The Bell Rang.* New York: Antheneum Books for Young Readers.

    This picture book describes a week in the life of an enslaved African American family in the United States. While the text is relatively simple, the content and themes engage older students in considering the injustices and difficult decisions that confronted enslaved people. (Can be used in grades 3–8.)

- Slobodkina, Esphyr. (1987). *Caps for Sale.* New York: Harper & Row.

    This picture book recounts the folktale of a peddler who is selling caps and a group of mischievous monkeys who torment him. The storyline is simple and humorous, and the text uses a lot of repetitive language. (Can be used in grades K–5.)

- Telgemeier, Raina. (2016). *Ghosts.* New York: Graphix, an Imprint of Scholastic.

    This graphic novel tells the story of two sisters who have moved to a coastal town because the youngest sister has cystic fibrosis. They meet new friends, both living and ghosts, and learn about Día de los Muertos, a tradition that their Mexican American family had stopped practicing. The author has also written several other graphic novels (e.g., *Sisters, Drama),* which are engaging for middle grade readers and are also available in Spanish. (Can be used in grades 4 and up.)

- Van Allsburg, Chris. (1984). *The Mysteries of Harris Burdick*. New York: Houghton Mifflin
    _____. (1986). *The Stranger*. New York: Houghton Mifflin.
    _____. (1985). *The Polar Express*. New York: Houghton Mifflin.
    _____. (2011). *Just a Dream*. New York: Houghton Mifflin.
    _____. (1987). *The Z Was Zapped*. New York: Houghton Mifflin.

    In these books, the focus is on provocative and vivid illustrations that convey or suggest a story or a confusing set of events. In addition to inspiring discussion, newcomers enjoy examining the details of the images. (Can be used in grades 2 and up.)
- Woodson, Jacqueline. (2002). *Visiting Day*. New York: Scholastic.

    A beautifully written and moving picture book about a young girl and her grandmother who take a long bus trip to visit the girl's father, who is in prison. It is based on the author's own experiences. The vocabulary and sentence structure can be difficult for newcomers, but the stunning illustrations help build understanding. (Can be used in grades 2–6.)

TABLES AND FIGURES

REFERENCES

Abedi, J. (n.d.). *English Language Learners with Disabilities: Classification, Assessment, and Accommodation Issues.* Retrieved from https://www.testpublishers.org/assets/documents/Special%20issue%20article%202.pdf

ACLU. (2019). *Know Your Rights: Immigrants' Rights.* Retrieved from https://www.aclu.org/know-your-rights/immigrants-rights/

Ada, A. F., & Campoy, F. I. (2004). *Authors in the Classroom: A Transformative Education Process.* Boston: Pearson Education Inc.

Adames, H. Y., & Chavez-Dueñas, N. Y. (2017). *Cultural Foundations and Interventions in Latino/a Mental Health.* New York: Routledge.

Adelman, R., Reid, L.W., Markle, G., Weiss, S., & Jaret, C. (2017). Urban Crime Rates and the Changing Face of Immigration: Evidence Across Four Decades. *Journal of Ethnicity in Criminal Justice, 15*(1), 55-27.

Adoff, E. (Ed.). (1974, 1994). *My Black Me: A Beginning Book of Black Poetry.* New York: Dutton Children's Books.

Ahmed, R. (2015). *Five Essential Listening Skills for English Learners.* Retrieved from https://www.britishcouncil.org/voices-magazine/five-essential-listening-skills-english-learners

Alexander, R. (2019). A Mamá No la Vas a Llevar en la Maleta: Undocumented Mothers Crossing and Contesting Borders for Their Children's Education. *Anthropology and Education Quarterly, 49*(4), 347-473.

Allen, J. (2007). *Creating Welcoming Schools : A Practical Guide to Home-School Partnerships with Diverse Families.* New York: Teachers College Press.

Allen, R. V. (1976). *Language Experiences in Education.* Boston, MA: Houghton Mifflin.

Alvarez, L., Ananda, S., Walqui, A., Sato, E., & Rabinowitz, S. (2014). *Focusing Formative Assessment on the Needs of English Language Learners.* San Francisco: WestEd.

_____. American Immigration Lawyers Association. (2017). *Know Your Rights Handout: If ICE Visits a Home, Employer, or Public Space.* Retrieved from: https://www.aila.org/advo-media/tools/psas/know-your-rights-handouts-if-ice-visits

American Psychological Association. (2015). *Report of the Presidential Task Force on Immigration.* Retrieved from https://www.apa.org/topics/immigration/report

Amnesty International. (2019). *What's the Difference Between a Refuges and an Asylum Seeker?* Retrieved from https://www.amnesty.org.au/refugee-and-an-asylum-seeker-difference/

Anderson, C. (2005). *Assessing Writers.* Portsmouth, NH: Heinemann.

Anti-Defamation League. (2015). *Imagining a World Without Hate: Myths and Facts about Immigration*. Retrieved from https://www.adl.org/resources/fact-sheets/myths-and-facts-about-immigrants-and-immigration-en-espanol

Appy, C. G. (2018). *What Was the Vietnam War About?* Retrieved from https://www.nytimes.com/2018/03/26/opinion/what-was-the-vietnam-war-about.html

Asher, J. (1996). *Learning Another Language Through Actions* (5th ed.). Los Gatos, CA: Sky Oaks Productions.

Associated Press. (2018). *Honduran Exodus to the U.S., from Hunger and Violence*. Retrieved from https://www.telegraphindia.com/world/honduran-exodus-to-the-us-from-hunger-and-violence/cid/1672019

Atkins, L., & Yogi, S. (2017). *Fred Korematsu Speaks Up*. Berkeley, CA: Heyday.

Atwell, N. (1987). *In the Middle: Writing, Reading, and Learning with Adolescents*. Portsmouth, NH: Boynton/Cook. (Available from Heinemann).

Bacon, D. (January 4, 2012). How U.S. Policies Fueled Mexico's Great Migration. *The Nation*. Retrieved from https://www.thenation.com/article/how-us-policies-fueled-mexicos-great-migration/Bhana, Y. (2015). *The Meaning of a Smile in Different Cultures*. Retrieved from https://www.translatemedia.com/us/blog-us/the-meaning-of-a-smile-in-different-cultures/

Blau, F. & Mackie, C. (Eds.) (2017). *The Economic and Fiscal Consequences of Immigration*. Washington DC: National Academies Press. Retrieved from https://www.nap.edu/read/23550/chapter/1

Boal, A. (2002). *Games for Actors and Non-actors*. London: Routledge.

Bogado, A. (Nov. 5, 2018). *Investigation Finds Government Contractor Violated Policy While Transporting Immigrant Children*. Retrieved from https://www.pbs.org/newshour/show/investigation-finds-government-contractor-violated-policy-while-transporting-immigrant-children

Brabeck, K., & Xu, Q. (2010). The Impact of Detention and Deportation on Latino immigrant Children and Families: A Quantitative Exploration. *Hispanic Journal of Behavioral Sciences, 32*, 341-361.

Byers-Heinlein, K, & Lew-Williams, C. (2013). *Bilingualism in the Early Years: What the Science Says*. Retrieved from https://www.researchgate.net/publication/259822414_Bilingualism_in_the_Early_Years_What_the_Science_Says

Cassidy, J. (June 22, 2018). Why the United States Needs More Immigrants. *The New Yorker*.

California Department of Education. (n.d.). *English Language Proficiency Assessments for California (ELPAC)*. Retrieved from https://www.elpac.org

California Department of Education. (2019). *Facts about English Language Learners*. Retrieved from https://www.cde.ca.gov/ds/sd/cb/cefelfacts.asp

Calkins, L. M. (1986). *The Art of Teaching Writing*. Portsmouth, NH: Heinemann.

Chingos, M. M. (2012). *Strength in Numbers: State Spending on K-12 Assessment Systems*. Brookings Institute.

Clay, M. M. (1993, 2002, 2005, 2013). *An Observation Survey of Early Literacy Achievement*. Portsmouth, NH: Heinemann.

Clay, M. M. (2017). *Running Records for Classroom Teachers* (2nd Ed.). Portsmouth, NH: Heinemann.

Costello, M. (2016). *The Trump Effect: The Impact of the Presidential Campaign on our Nation's Schools.* Retrieved from https://www.splcenter.org/sites/default/files/splc_the_trump_effect.pdf

Delgado-Gaitan, C. (2004). *Involving Latino Families in Schooling: Raising Student Achievement through Home-School Partnerships.* Thousand Oaks, CA: Corwin Press.

Department of Homeland Security. (2016). *Table 39: Aliens Removed or Returned: Fiscal Years 1892 to 2016.* Retrieved from https://www.dhs.gov/immigration-statistics/yearbook/2016/table39

Derewianka, B. (1990). *Exploring How Texts Work.* Rozelle, New South Wales, Australia: Primary English Teaching Association.

Derman-Sparks, L. (2019). *Guide for Selecting Anti-Bias Children's Books.* Retrieved from https://socialjusticebooks.org/guide-for-selecting-anti-bias-childrens-books/

EAS. (2011). The Power of Networking: Teachers Advocating for Change. In C. Sleeter & C. Cornbleth, (Eds.), *Teaching with Vision: Culturally Responsive Teaching in Standards-Based Classrooms,* 144-152. New York: Teachers College Press.

Edelsky, C. (1986). *Writing in a Bilingual Program: Había Una Vez.* Norwood, NJ: Ablex.

Ernst-Slavit, E. & Mason, M. (n.d.). *Making Your First ELL Home Visit: A Guide for Classroom Teachers.* Retrieved from http://www.ldonline.org/article/59138/

Escamilla, K, Andrade, A. M., Basurto, A. G. M., & Ruiz, O.A., in collaboration with M. M. Clay. (1996). *Instrumento de Observación de Los Logros de La Lecto-Escritura Inicial.* Portsmouth, NH: Heinemann.

Ewing, W., Martinez, D. E., & Rambaut, R. G. (2015). *Special Report: The Criminalization of Immigration in the United States.* Retrieved from https://www.americanimmigrationcouncil.org/research/criminalization-immigration-united-states

Excel Math Placement Tests. (2015). AnsMar Publishers. Retrieved from http://excelmath.com/downloads/placement_test_spanish.pdf (Spanish version with directions in English)

FairTest. (June, 2018). *Just Say No to Standardized Tests: Why and How to Opt Out.* Retrieved from https://www.fairtest.org/get-involved/opting-out

Farlie, R.W. (August, 2012). *Open for Business; How Immigrants are Driving Small Business Creation in the United States.* Retrieved from http://research.newamericaneconomy.org/wp-content/uploads/2013/07/openforbusiness.pdf

Federal Educational Rights and Privacy Act (FERPA), (20 U.S.C. § 1232g; 34 CFR Part 99), 1974. Retrieved from https://www2.ed.gov/about/offices/list/oela/newcomers-toolkit/chap2.pdf

Fountas, I. C., & Pinnell, G. S. (2016). *Guided Reading: Responsive Teaching Across the Grades,* 2nd ed. Portsmouth, NH: Heinemann.

Fountas, I. C., & Pinnell, G. S. (2012). *Sistema de Evaluación de la Lectura.* Portsmouth, NH: Heinemann.

Freire, P. (1970). *Pedagogy of the Oppressed.* New York: Herder and Herder.

Gándara, P., Maxwell-Jolly, J., & Driscoll, A. (2006). *Listening to Teachers of English Learners*. Santa Cruz, CA: The Center for the Future of Teaching and Learning.

García, O. (2009). *Bilingual Education in the 21ˢᵗ Century: A Global Perspective*. Malden, MA and Oxford: Basil/Blackwell.

Gerstein, J., & Lin, J. C. F. (2018). *Why These 7 Countries Are Listed on Trump's Travel Ban*. Retrieved from https://www.politico.com/interactives/2018/trump-travel -ban-supreme-court-decision-countries-map/

Ginwright, S. A. (2016). *Hope and Healing in Urban Education: How Urban Activists and Teachers Are Reclaiming Matters of the Heart*. New York: Routledge.

Gjelten, T. (Jan. 16, 2019). *How the 1965 Immigration Act Made America a Nation of Immigrants*. Retrieved from https://www.npr.org/2019/01/16/685819397/how-the -1965-immigration-act-made-america-a-nation-of-immigrants

Gonzalez, N., Moll, L. C., & Amanti, C. (2005). *Funds of Knowledge: Theorizing Practices in Households, Communities, and Classrooms*. Mahwah, NJ : Lawrence Erlbaum Associates.

Gonzalez-Barrera, A. & Lopez, M. H. (December 16, 2016). U.S. Immigrant Deportations Fall to Lowest Level Since 2007. *FACTANK: News in the Numbers*. Pew Research Center. Retrieved from https://www.pewresearch.org/fact-tank/2016/12/16/u-s -immigrant-deportations-fall-to-lowest-level-since-2007/

Graham, C. (n.d.). *Teaching Jazz Chants to Young Learners*. Retrieved from https://www .youtube.com/watch?v=R_nPUuPryCs

Graves, D. H. (1975). An Examination of the Writing Processes of Seven Year Old Children. *Research in the Teaching of English, 9*(3): 227-241.

Graves, D. H. (1983). *Writing: Teachers and Children at Work*. Portsmouth, NH: Heinemann.

Graves, D. H. (1987). (Comments made during a workshop in San Mateo on teaching writing.)

Graves, M. F., & Watts-Taffe, S. (2008). For the Love of Words: Fostering Word Consciousness in Young Readers. *The Reading Teacher, 62*(3), *185-193.*

Gunderson, M. S. (2018). The Chicago Teachers Union's Rejection of The Common Core: A Case History of Teacher Resistance. In D. Santoro & L. Cain (Eds.) *Principled Resistance: How Teachers Resolve Ethical Dilemmas*, pp. 19-34. Cambridge, MA: Harvard Educational Press.

Hagan, J., Eschbach, K., & Rodriguez, N. (2008). U.S. Deportation Policy, Family Separation, and Circular Migration. *The International Migration Review, 42*(1), 64-88.

Hellman, L., Bear, D. R., Templeton, S., Invernizzi, M., & Johnston, F. (2012). *Words Their Way with English Learners: Word Study for Phonics, Vocabulary, and Spelling*, 2nd Ed. Boston: Pearson Education.

History.com. (2019). *U.S. Immigration Timeline*. Retrieved from https://www.history .com/topics/immigration/immigration-united-states-timeline

Hudelson, S. (1984). Kan You Ret an Rayt en Ingles: Children Becoming Literate in English as a Second Language. *TESOL Quarterly, 18*(2), 221-238.

Hudelson, S. (1989). *Write On: Children Writing in ESL.* Englewood Cliffs, NJ: Prentice Hall/Regents.

Horton, A. (2019). *ICE Deported Veterans While 'Unaware' It Was Required to Carefully Screen Them, Report Says.* Retrieved from https://www.washingtonpost.com/nation/2019/06/08/ice-deported-veterans-while-unaware-it-was-required-screen-them-with-care-report-says/?noredirect=on

King, S. H., & Goodwin, A. L. (2002). *Culturally Responsive Parental Involvement: Concrete Understandings and Basic Strategies.* New York: American Association of Colleges for Teacher Education.

Korducki, K. (2018). *Stop Saying 'Migrant Caravan': They're Asylum Seekers Escaping a Conflict That the U.S. Created.* Retrieved from https://www.yahoo.com/lifestyle/stop-saying-migrant-caravan-asylum-162246350.html

Langhout, R. U, Buckingham, S. L. Oberoi, A. K., Chavez, N. R., Rusch, D., Esposito, F., & Suarez-Balcazar, Y. (2018). Policy Statement: Statement on the Effects of Deportation and Forced Separation on Immigrants, Their Families, and Communities. *American Journal of Psychology, 62,* 3-12.

Lareau, A. (2011). *Unequal Childhoods: Race, Class, and Family Life. Second Edition. A Decade Later.* Berkeley, CA: University of California Press.

Lau v. Nichols, 414 U.S. 563, 94 S, Ct. 786, 39 L, Ed. 2d1 (1974).

Library of Congress. (n.d.). *Irish Catholic Immigration to America.* Retrieved from http://www.loc.gov/teachers/classroommaterials/presentationsandactivities/presentations/immigration/irish2.html

Markham, L. (2017). *The Far Away Brothers: Two Young Migrants and the Making of an American Life.* New York: Crown.

Mathewson, T. G. (2016). *Schools Are Under Federal Pressure to Translate for Immigrant Parents.* The Hechinger Report. Retrieved from https://hechingerreport.org/schools-federal-pressure-translate-immigrant-families

Miller, K. (2915). *From Humanitarian to Economic: The Changing Face of Vietnamese Migration.* Retrieved from https://www.migrationpolicy.org/article/humanitarian-economic-changing-face-vietnamese-migration

Moll, L. (1992). Bilingual Classroom Studies and Community Analysis: Some Recent Trends. *Educational Researcher, 21*(2), 20-24.

Moll, L., & Greenberg, J. (1990). Creating Zones of Possibilities: Combining Social Contexts for Instruction. In L. Moll (Ed.), *Vygotsky and Education* (pp. 319-348). Cambridge, MA: Cambridge University Press.

Nadler, R. (2008). *Immigration and the Wealth of States.* Overland Park, KS: America's Majority Foundation.

National Center for Education Statistics. (2019). *English Language Learners in Public Schools.* Retrieved from https://nces.ed.gov/programs/coe/indicator_cgf.asp

Niesz, T. (2018). Teacher Activist Groups: What Are Their Missions? How Influential Are They? *Phi Delta Kappan, 99* (8), 25-29.

O'Brien, A.S. (2015). *I'm New Here.* Watertown, MA: Charlesbridge.

O'Dea, C. *The List: 10 Most Common Languages of NJ's Polyglot Student Population.* Retrieved from https://www.njspotlight.com/stories/16/07/10/the-list-10-most-common-languages-of-nj-s-polyglot-student-population/

Orellana, M. (2009). *Translating Childhoods: Immigrant Youth, Language, and Culture.* New Jersey: Rutgers University Press.

Park, L.S. (2010). *A Long Walk to Water.* Boston: Houghton Mifflin Harcourt.

Pease-Alvarez, L. (2003). Transforming Perspectives on Bilingual Language Socialization. In R. Bayley & S. Schecter (Eds.), *Language Socialization in Bi- and Multilingual Societies* (pp. 9-24). Clevedon, England: Multilingual Matters.

Pease-Alvarez, L., & Samway, K. Davies. (2012). *Teachers of English Learners Negotiating Authoritarian Policies.* Dordrecht, The Netherlands and New York: Springer.

Pease-Alvarez, L., & Samway, K. Davies. (2014). *Elementary Teachers of English Learners Negotiating the Common Core State Standards.* Final Report to Oakland, CA Unified School District.

Ikielnik, R., & Krogstad, J. M. (2017). *Where Refugees to the US Come From.* Retrieved from https://www.pewresearch.org/fact-tank/2017/02/03/where-refugees-to-the-u-s-come-from/

Picower, B. (2012). *Practice What You Teach: Social Justice Education in the Classroom and the Streets.* New York: Routledge.

Portes, A., & Rambaut, R. G. (2014). *Immigrant America: A Portrait.* Oakland CA: University of California Press.

Peyton, J. K., & Reed, L. (1990). *Dialogue Journal Writing with Nonnative English Speakers: A Handbook for Teachers.* Alexandria, VA: Teachers of English to Speakers of Other Languages (TESOL).

Plyler v. Doe, 457 U.S. 202 (1982)

Radford, J. (2019). *Key Findings about U.S. Immigrants.* Pew Research Center. Retrieved from https://www.pewresearch.org/fact-tank/2019/06/17/key-findings-about-u-s-immigrants/

Ramirez, J. D, Yuen, S. D, Ramey, D. R., Pasta, D. J., & Billings, D. K. (1991). *Longitudinal Study of Structured English Immersion Strategy, Early-Exit and Late-Exit Transitional Bilingual Education Programs for Language Minority Children.* Washington, D.C.: U.S. Office of Policy and Planning.

Ray, K. W. (1999). *Wondrous Words: Writers and Writing in the Elementary Classroom.* Urbana, IL: National Council of Teachers of English.

Ray, K. W. (2001). *The Writing Workshop: Working Through the Hard Parts (and They're All Hard Parts).* Urbana, IL: National Council of Teachers of English.

Reese, L., Balzano, S., Gallimore, R., & Goldenberg, C. (1995). The Concept of Educación: Latino Family Values and American Schooling. *International Journal of Educational Research, 23*(1): 57-81.

Rigg, P. (1989). Language Experience Approach: Reading Naturally. In V. Allen & P. Rigg (Eds.), *When They Don't All Speak English.* Urbana, IL: National Council of Teachers of English.

Ritchhart, R., Church, M., & Morrison, K. (2011). *Making Thinking Visible: How to Pro-*

mote Engagement, Understanding, and Independence for All Learners. San Francisco: Jossey Bass.

Romero, S., & Dickerson, C. (2019). *'Desperation of Thousands' Pushes Migrants into Ever Remote Terrain.* Retrieved from https://www.nytimes.com/2019/01/29/us/border -wall-crossings.html

Ruiz, O. A., & Cuesta, V. M. (2000). *Evaluación del Desarrollo de la Lectura.* Bloomington, MN: Pearson. Retrieved from https://www.pearsonassessments.com/ store/usassessments/en/Store/Professional-Assessments/Academic-Learning/ Reading/Evaluación-del-Desarrollo-de-la-Lectura-2/p/100001842.html

Rush, N. (2018). *Refugee Resettlement Admissions in FY 2018.* Retrieved from https://cis .org/Rush/Refugee-Resettlement-Admissions-FY-2018

Samway, K. Davies. (1987). *The Writing Processes of Non-Native English Speaking Children in the Elementary Grades.* Unpublished doctoral dissertation, University of Rochester.

Samway, K. Davies. (1993). "This Is Hard, Isn't It?": Children Evaluating Writing. *TESOL Quarterly, 27*(2), 233-58.

Samway, K. Davies. (2006). *When English Language Learners Write: Connecting Research to Practice, K-8.* Portsmouth, NH: Heinemann.

Samway, K. Davies, & McKeon, D. (2007). *Myths and Realities: Best Practices for Language Minority Students* (2nd ed.). Portsmouth, NH: Heinemann.

Samway, K. Davies, & Taylor, D. (2008). *Teaching English Language Learners: Grades 6-12. Strategies That Work.* New York: Scholastic.

Samway, K. Davies, & Taylor, D. (October 2009). Worldly Possessions: Developing Word Consciousness in English Learners. *Language Magazine.* https:// languagemagazine.com/LangPages/WordlyPossession_LM_Oct09.pdf

Samway, K. Davies & Whang, G. (1996). *Literature Study Circles in a Multicultural Classroom.* York, ME: Stenhouse Publishers.

Samway, K. Davies, Whang, G., & Pippitt, M. (1995). *Buddy Reading: Cross-Age Tutoring in a Multicultural School.* Portsmouth, NH: Heinemann.

Santoro, D. A., & Cain, L. (Eds.) (2018). *Principled Resistance: How Teachers Resolve Ethical Dilemmas.* Cambridge, MA: Harvard Educational Press.

Schinke-Llano, L. (1983). Foreigner Talk in Content Classrooms. In H. Selinger & M. H. Long (Eds.), *Classroom Centered Research in Second Language* (pp. 146-65). Englewood Cliffs, NJ: Prentice Hall Regents.

Scott, J., & Nagy, W.E. (2004). Developing Word Consciousness. In J. Baumann & E. Kame'enui (Eds.), *Vocabulary Instruction: Research to Practice* (pp. 201-217). New York: Guilford Publications.

Silber, J. (2018). *An Honduran Priest Explains the Exodus of Migrants from His Country.* KAWL. Retrieved from https://www.kalw.org/post/honduran-priest-explains -exodus-migrants-his-country#stream/0

Southern Poverty Law Center. (2016). *After Election Day: The Trump Effect–The Impact of the 2016 Election on Our Nation's Schools.* Retrieved from https://www.splcenter .org/20161128/trump-effect-impact-2016-presidential-election-our-nations -schools

St. John, P., & Rubin, J. (2018). *ICE Held an American Man in Custody for 1,273 Days. He's Not the Only One Who Had to Prove His Citizenship. Los Angeles Times.* Retrieved from https://www.latimes.com/local/lanow/la-me-citizens-ice-20180427-htmlstory.html

Stauffer, R. (1970). *The Language Experience Approach to the Teaching of Reading.* New York: Harper & Row.

Storch, N., & Wigglesworth, G. (2003). Is There a Role for the Use of the L1 in an L2 Setting? *TESOL Quarterly, 37*(4), 760-770.

Sugarman, J. (2017). *Beyond Teaching English: Supporting High School Completion by Immigrant and Refugee Students.* Washington, D.C.: Migration Policy Institute. Retrieved from https://www.migrationpolicy.org/research/beyond-teaching-english-supporting-high-school-completion-immigrant-and-refugee-students

Swain, M., & Lapkin, S. (2000). Task-Based Second Language Learning: The Uses of the First Language. *Language Teaching Research, 4*(3), 251-74.

Taylor, D. M. (1990). Writing and Reading Literature in a Second Language. In N. Atwell (Ed.), *Workshop 2: Beyond the Basal* (pp. 105-107). Portsmouth, NH: Heinemann.

Teaching Tolerance. (2016). *The Impact of the Presidential Campaign on Our Nation's Schools.* Retrieved from https://www.tolerance.org/magazine/publications/the-trump-effect-spring-2016

The Washington Post. (2019). *Most Americans Oppose Key Parts of Trump Immigration Plans, Including Wall, Limits on Citizens Bringing Family to U.S., Poll Says.* Retrieved from http://apps.washingtonpost.com/g/page/national/washington-post-schar-school-poll-us-and-congressional-battlegrounds/2313/

Tierney, R. J., & Pearson, P. D. (1981). Learning to Learn from Text: A Framework for Improving Classroom Practice. In R. B. Ruddell, M. R. Ruddell, & H. Singer (Eds.), *Theoretical Models and Processes of Reading* (pp. 496-513). Newark: DE: International Reading Association.

U.S. Department of Education. (2015). *Our Nation's English Learners: What Are Their Characteristics?* Retrieved from https://www2.ed.gov/datastory/el-characteristics/index.html#one

U.S. Department of Education. (2016a). *Non-Regulatory Guidance: English Learners and Title III of the Elementary and Secondary Education Act (ESEA), as Amended by the Every Student Succeeds Act (ESSA).* Retrieved from https://www2.ed.gov/policy/elsec/leg/essa/essatitleiiiguidenglishlearners92016.pdf

U.S. Department of Education. (2016b). *Resources for Addressing English Learners with Disabilities.* Retrieved from https://www2.ed.gov/about/offices/list/oela/english-learner-toolkit/chap6.pdf

U.S. Department of Education. (2016, 2017). *Newcomer Toolkit.* Retrieved from https://www2.ed.gov/about/offices/list/oela/newcomers-toolkit/ncomertoolkit.pdf

U.S. Department of Education. (2017). *English Learner Tool Kit* (2nd rev. ed.). Washington, D.C.: U.S. Department of Education.

U.S. Department of Justice. (2014). *Fact Sheet: Information on the Rights of All Children to Enroll in School.* Retrieved from https://www.justice.gov/sites/default/files/crt/legacy/2014/05/08/plylerfact.pdf

U.S. Department of Justice, Civil Rights Division, & the U.S Department of Education, Office for Civil Rights. (2015). *Information for Limited English Proficient (LEP) Parents and Guardians and for Schools and School Districts that Communicate with Them.* Available at: https://www2.ed.gov/about/offices/list/ocr/docs/dcl-factsheet-lep -parents-201501.pdf.

Ulloa, J. (2016). *Bilingual Education Is Making a Comeback in California. But Some Educators Say the Fight Is Just Beginning.* Retrieved from https://www.latimes.com/politics/ la-pol-ca-bilingual-education-challenges-20161122-story.html

United Nations High Commissioner for Refugees (UNHCR). (2019). *Global Trends ; Forced Displacement 2018.* Retrieved from https://www.unhcr.org/en-us/statistics/ unhcrstats/5d08d7ee7/unhcr-global-trends-2018.html

United States Government Accountability Office. (2019). *Immigration Enforcement: Actions Needed to Better Handle, Identify, and Track Cases Involving Veterans.* Retrieved from https://www.gao.gov/assets/700/699549.pdf

Urzúa, C. (1987). "You Stopped Too Soon": Second Language Children Composing and Revising. *TESOL Quarterly, 21*(2), 297-304.

Valdés, G. (1996). *Con Respeto: Bridging the Distances Between Culturally Diverse Families and Schools.* New York: Teachers College Press.

Valdés, G. (2003). *Expanding Definitions of Giftedness: The Case of Young Interpreters from Immigrant Communities.* Mawah, NJ: Lawrence Erlbaum Associates.

Valdés, G., Capitelli, S., & Alvarez, L. (2011). *Latino Children Learning English: Steps in the Journey.* New York: Teachers College Press.

Valverde, M. (2017). *Trump Signs Executive Order to Increase ICE Deportation Officers.* Retrievedfromhttps://www.politifact.com/truth-o-meter/promises/trumpometer/ promise/1440/triple-ice-enforcement/

Vasquez, O., Pease-Alvarez, L., & Shannon, S. (1994). *Pushing Boundaries: Language and Culture in a Mexicano Community.* New York: Cambridge University Press.

Warren, R. (2019). *US Undocumented Population Continued to Fall from 2016 to 2017, and Visa Overstays Significantly Exceeded Illegal Crossings for the Seventh Consecutive Year.* Retrieved from https://cmsny.org/publications/essay-2017-undocumented-and -overstays/

WIDA. (n.d.). *ACCESS for ELLs.* Retrieved from https://wida.wisc.edu/assess/access

Wong Fillmore, L. (1976). *The Second Time Around: Cognitive and Social Strategies in Second Language Learning.* Ph.D. dissertation, Stanford University.

Wu, N. (Dec. 25, 2018). *The Trump Administration Is Closing the Door on Migrant Children.* Retrieved from https://www.theatlantic.com/politics/archive/2018/12/asylum -approvals-children-have-plummeted-under-trump/578614/

Zentella, A.C. (2005). *Building on Strength: Language and Literacy in Latino Families and Communities.* New York: Teachers College Press.

Zook, D. C. (2016). *In a Difficult Place: How Refugee Camps Corrode Our Humanity.* Retrieved from https://medium.com/@zookkini/in-a-difficult-place-how-refugee-camps -corrode-our-humanity-45a3aa2fe399

INDEX

Note: Italicized page locators refer to figures; tables are noted with a *t*.

ABOUT THE AUTHORS

Katharine Davies Samway is a professor emerita at San José State University (SJSU) in Northern California, where she taught literacy-related courses, all of which had a focus on learners from linguistically and culturally diverse backgrounds. There are two interrelated foci to her research: a) the literacy development of children from diverse backgrounds, especially English learners (ELs), and b) influences on teachers' beliefs and practices. She has published several books, including *Teaching English Language Learners, Grades K–5: Strategies that Work* (2007), *Myths and Realities: Best Practices for English Language Learners* (2007), and *When English Language Learners Write: Connecting Research and Practice* (2006). Although retired from SJSU, she continues to work with teachers and their students, do research, and write.

Lucinda Pease-Alvarez is a professor emerita at the University of California, Santa Cruz, where she was also Director of Teacher Education. She has worked with prospective and practicing teachers, parents, and teacher educators on projects devoted to enhancing the learning opportunities available to multilingual and immigrant children in schools and communities. Her scholarship focuses on topics related to the use and development of language, literacy, and content among this student population, as well as on the development of pedagogical perspectives that build on the resources that they and their families bring to schools and classrooms. In addition, she has investigated how teachers individually and collectively negotiate district, state, and federal language/literacy education policies and initiatives. She is the author of many articles and book chapters, and is co-author of the volumes entitled *Teachers of English Learners Negotiating Authoritarian Policies* (2012), *Learning, Teaching, and Community: Contributions of Situated and Participatory Approaches to Educational Innovation* (2005), and *Pushing Boundaries: Language and Culture in a Mexicano Community* (1994).

Laura Alvarez has spent 20 years as a teacher, researcher, and professional development provider focused on supporting bilingual and immigrant students. She currently teaches middle school newcomer students in Oakland, California, and has taught all subjects in grades 4–8, in transitional bilingual, dual language, and sheltered English programs. In addition to teaching, Laura facilitates inquiry-based professional development for teachers. She earned a Ph.D. in Educational Linguistics from Stanford University and conducts research focused on the language and literacy development of emergent bilingual students. Laura is the co-author (with Guadalupe Valdés and Sarah Capitelli) of *Latino Children Learning English: Steps in the Journey* (Teachers' College Press).